The Erotics of Corruption

The Erotics of Corruption

Law, Scandal, and Political Perversion

Ruth A. Miller

State University of New York Press

Published by
State University of New York Press, Albany

© 2008 State University of New York

All rights reserved

Printed in the United States of America

No part of this book may be used or reproduced in any manner whatsoever without written permission. No part of this book may be stored in a retrieval system or transmitted in any form or by any means including electronic, electrostatic, magnetic tape, mechanical, photocopying, recording, or otherwise without the prior permission in writing of the publisher.

For information, contact State University of New York Press, Albany, NY
www.sunypress.edu

Production by Ryan Morris
Marketing by Anne M. Valentine

Library of Congress Cataloging-in-Publication Data

Miller, Ruth Austin, 1975–
  The erotics of corruption : law, scandal, and political perversion / Ruth A. Miller
    p. cm.
  Includes bibliographical references and index.
  ISBN 978-0-7914-7453-2 (hardcover : alk. paper)
  1. Political corruption. 2. Sexual ethics. I. Title.

JF1081.M56 2008
364. 1'323—dc22
                                                                    2007035454

10 9 8 7 6 5 4 3 2 1

Contents

Introduction — vii
    Corruption, Democracy, and the Colony — ix
    A Vocabulary of Corruption — xii
    Theoretical Framework — xvii
    An Overview — xxii
    Conclusion — xxiv

1. Political Corruption as Sexual Deviance: A Literature Review — 1
    The Body Politic — 6
    The Developing State and Its Infantile Transgression — 9
    Striptease: Political Transparency and Self-Regarding Behavior — 20
    Incest, Cannibalism, and Corporate Responsibility — 25
    Conclusion — 35

2. Celebrating the Corrupt Leader — 37
    Pornography and Testimony — 40
    Getting to Know Abdul and Saddam — 43
    Developing State, Developing Star — 55
    Body Doubles and Doubled Bodies — 62

Confession	86
Conclusion	103
3. Condemning the Corrupt System	105
Biopolitical Space and Totalitarian Space	107
Salo: The 120 Days of Sodom	110
Bandits and Bureaucrats	113
The Portable Torture Nation	124
Bribery, Nepotism, and Decay	131
Dehumanizing Bureaucracies	141
Conclusion	152
Conclusion	155
Notes	159
Bibliography	195
Index	209

Introduction

This is a book about political corruption. I would like to begin, however, in a different place, with a discussion of late twentieth-century Internet pornography. Websites devoted to pornographic material became increasingly sophisticated throughout the 1990s and into the following decade, producing visual, audio, animated, and "live action" narratives, often "interactive," of bondage, fetishism, bestiality, schoolgirl intercourse, "virgin rape," and a variety of other situational sexual fantasies. Entering the words "sex" and "torture" into a search engine produces thousands of pornographic bondage sites. Among them are the following two: in the first, a young, unprotected woman is picked up on an urban street. She is drugged, thrown into the back of a van, and when she wakes up she is in a dark, cement cell. After remaining in isolation, she is taken to a torture chamber where she is threatened with a knife and told she must be obedient. When she resists, she is stripped naked, her hands are tied behind her back, and she is raped by three anonymous guards until she passes out. In the next scene, she wakes up in her cell, still naked and still tied up. The narrative continues without a great deal of variation for three further chapters.

In the second, a school-age, barely pubescent girl is sold into sexual slavery. She is first "displayed in [one of] row after row of zoo-like animal cages." When she resists having sex with her captors, she is

> dragged into a torture chamber in a dark alley used for breaking in new girls. She [is] locked in a narrow windowless room without food or water. On the fourth day, one of the madam's thugs wrestle[s] her to the floor and bang[s] her head against the concrete until she pass[es] out. When she awak[ens], she [is] naked; a rattan cane smeared with pureed red chili peppers shoved into her vagina.

One of the more obvious lessons to be learned from these two examples is that, as many sites as there are, Internet pornography is not replete with new and innovative narrative lines. But the point of pornography is of course not to innovate; it is instead to reinforce—to add slight or subtle variation to sexual fantasies that are on some level comforting to the consumer.[1]

A less obvious issue is the motivation behind producing these stories. Why would these narratives in particular be marketable, and who especially would buy them? Perhaps the best way to get at answers to these questions is to look at the self-presentation of the sites that sell them. The first is a site devoted to animated "celebrity porn."[2] The young woman at the center of the story is a pop singer, and interspersed with the comic-book images of her sexual humiliation are tabloid photographs of her in similarly embarrassing situations. The story that I have summarized is actually a "free preview" of the site, and for access to further chapters or other celebrity narratives, the subscriber has to pay $9.99 per month.

The second story comes from the website of a nonprofit human rights organization, and concerns the role that political corruption plays in the spread of AIDS and prostitution.[3] On the one hand, the images produced on the website are not as graphic as those on the celebrity porn site. But, on the other, the written narratives are far more detailed and the subscriber gets unlimited free access. An argument could be made that despite the similarity in presentation and storyline, the goals of the two sites are fundamentally different—the one to provoke a reaction and the other to provoke a reaction for a good cause. But the question of marketability remains: why would these unquestionably similar narratives serve such morally disparate aims?

Karen Halttunen has already convincingly demonstrated the link between humanitarianism and what she calls "the pornography of pain" in the post-Enlightenment period.[4] It is not my purpose to rehash her argument. Instead, I will attempt over the following pages to show that the "anti-corruption" narrative especially—an example of which we see in the second story—moves beyond even the usual spectacle of pain or humiliation that is so central to human rights activism. It is not just the eye-catching or spine-tingling anecdotes of innocence ground down by overwhelming (political) violence that we see in anticorruption narratives. The very vocabulary of the "anticorruption struggle" is itself pornographic—creating a space in which lawless chaos and sexual chaos are one and the same thing.

There is indeed a repeated return in this literature to tropes explored in eighteenth-, nineteenth-, twentieth-, and twenty-first-century pornography. A paper presented at the Tenth International Anti-Corruption Conference held in Prague in October 2001, for example, describes political corruption as a situation in which "the fangs of lawlessness and abuse of power bite dangerously on the vulnerable sector."[5] Equally evocative, a publication on the website of the anticorruption NGO, Transparency International, describes political corruption in the Czech Republic as a situation in which the police "would set their sights on a particular individual, and through artful blends of threat and seduction, of extortion and bribery, they would endeavour to get that person over to their side."[6] If nothing else, the strange frequency with which the word "incest" appears in descriptions of corrupt behavior or corrupt bureaucratic structures is telling.[7]

The following chapter will go into more detail about the vocabulary of corruption and its political ramifications. For now it suffices to say that this book is founded on the premise that the frequency with which words like "impotence" and "potency,"[8] "penetration" and "transparency,"[9] "seduction" and "resistance,"[10] "incest" and "unbridled passion"[11] appear in the anticorruption literature of aid agencies such as the World Bank, NGOs such as Transparency International, and academic gatherings such as the Anti-Corruption Conferences is not arbitrary. As corruption has been defined over the past decade as one of the most insidious "threats to democracy," the sexualized nature of this threat has become central to the rhetoric. Corruption narratives are not just pornographic, they are erotic—the very essence of corruption, its inherent disorder, has become sexual and sexually threatening.

Corruption, Democracy, and the Colony

In the 1990s, the menace that corruption apparently posed to "developing" democracies grew to such a degree that nearly every international aid organization devoted a department, an office, or at least a conference to combating it.[12] The academic literature on corruption likewise burgeoned over this period, leading scholars of the subject to designate the 1990s and their academic activity during this time as the "corruption eruption."[13] Although this mania for defining, analyzing, and combating corruption came to a peak in the 1990s, however, the turn of the twenty-first century was not the only moment in the modern period that such an obsession with the issue arose. Throughout the previous two centuries, the bureaucratic or financial deviance that is the hallmark of corruption literature was gradually becoming a subject of increasingly intense—even prurient—interest. The major British anticorruption bills came into force in 1889, 1906, and 1916, for example, and then again between 2001 and 2005—periods that also saw what one scholar has called, first, an "acceleration of mass cultural media,"[14] and, second, a fetishization of this culture, "hypersensitive to the sexuality of things."[15]

Although there is a great deal of talk about the domestic private, the bureaucratic public, and undesirable interaction between the two in the work of anticorruption specialists, therefore, I want to suggest in this book that they are operating in an analytical framework quite far removed from the universe of rational bureaucracy that they claim to be representing. Indeed, rather than, or in the process of, analyzing political structures for the sake of smooth bureaucratic function, they are also narrating stories of inappropriately intimate political, financial, and eventually sexual relationships.

Moreover, they are situating these stories squarely within colonial or postcolonial frameworks. It is true that most analysts are careful to avoid accusations of intolerance by arguing that corruption exists everywhere and that their goal is not to target solely colonized or postcolonial states. But the fact remains that whereas in Western Europe and North America we hear about scandal—anomalous, unnatural misbehavior that has been unmasked, that is cathartic and largely a reinforcement of the normality of self-described Western governance[16]—outside of these areas we hear about corruption—usually systemic, and always hidden, seductive, or monstrous. The corruption narrative in the African, Asian, or South American context is thus one in which the apparent failure of governments and functionaries to distinguish between the public and private takes on far more complex connotations.

I will indeed argue that the centering of corruption as a simultaneously legal and sexual threat to democracy writ large—a threat originating within and exploding out of colonized areas—occurs primarily when hegemonic structures are being challenged and when the response to this challenge is couched in a rhetoric of liberalism. The result, I will suggest, is a situation in which colonies or postcolonies become exceptional as theorists such as Giorgio Agamben and Achille Mbembe understand the term—areas that exist outside of the law while nonetheless constrained within legal discourse.[17] To the extent that law and liberalism are mobilized against corruption in the colonies, in other words, these colonies become sites of hyperbolic legal rhetoric while still remaining outside of the law. In the end, this spectacle of lawless violence turns colonies into settings in which the desires of those at the imperial center[18] can be played out safely removed from, but intriguingly still not quite outside of, familiar political structures.

The corruption narrative as a modern phenomenon is thus necessarily also a colonial one, developed within imperial structures and referencing unique, post-eighteenth-century imperial truths. Indeed, the basic defining characteristic of the "corrupt relationship"—the inappropriate overlap between public and private desires—could not have existed without the equally basic defining characteristic of modern imperial politics: the emphasis on separate public and private spheres. Literature on nineteenth- and twentieth-century imperialism in fact returns with frequency to this distinction, although most scholars who study sexuality and empire tend to emphasize the gendered nature of the dichotomy—critiquing in particular the rhetoric of the "feminine" private sphere and the "masculine" public one. What I will suggest in this book is an additional approach to the public/private paradigm, situated in what I see as the relationship between legal (or extralegal) space and pornographic space in narratives of corruption. I would indeed argue that the public/private distinction is not simply a gendered one, but also a sexualized one, with the public representing law or order and the private representing erotic disorder.

This leads us in turn back to the paradox of imperial knowledge and power. Although much literature on nineteenth- and twentieth-century imperialism begins with the imagined separation of the public and private spheres, this literature continues almost immediately with the further point that this separation is, again, *imagined*—the private anything but. As Michel Foucault has argued with respect to modern political structures in general, for example, it was precisely the (public) process of defining the intimate that produced and extended disciplinary power networks over the course of the nineteenth century.[19] As Laura Briggs has noted, this relationship between the private/intimate and the public/political became, if anything, more pronounced in colonial situations: the private or the intimate playing such a prominent role in British political expansion, for example, that the entire military was organized around it.[20] Ann Stoler has similarly seen the presence of European women and the ideology of domestic purity that surrounded them in Dutch colonies as fundamental to a "realignment in both racial and class politics."[21] It was, she notes, the very public politics (or biopolitics) of race and empire that served to create a private, domestic, "European" space within the colony, in which white women could exercise their civilizing, purifying influence.[22] The two spheres were thus both categorically separate—private from public as well as white from nonwhite—and also completely overlapped.

It therefore became both necessary *and* anathema to the colonial civilizing mission that the public/private distinction be broken down. The colony could not be reformed *without* an interpenetration of public and private—regulation reliant on the exposure and/or exhibition of domestic or sexual space—but it could not be protected from corruption *with* one. Thus, in the same way that the overlapping political and intimate, masculine and feminine, public and domestic indicated both the potential for, and the impossibility of, civilizing colonial space, so, too, did the overlapping legal and erotic. As the corruption narrative developed, it thus intersected repeatedly with the narratives of gender, sexuality, disease, and cleanliness that are at the heart of imperial identity formation.[23] Political corruption, like disease, dirtiness, and deviant sexuality (or often *as* disease, dirtiness, and deviant sexuality), likewise originated in colonial space, exploded out of it, infected those around it, and was fundamental to determining who could be defined legally and who could not.

A Vocabulary of Corruption

I would like to spend some time now examining a few specific examples of the broader trends that I previously noted—the placement of corruption into the colonies, the potential for corruption to infect those at the imperial center, and the key role played by the corruption narrative in imperial and neo-imperial identity formation. Again, first and foremost, the corruption narrative situates the corrupt relationship in the same space as so many other inappropriate or illicit desires: outside and in the colonies. By the twentieth century, indeed, corruption as deviant behavior was reported as growing, festering, and then bursting out of colonized, often tropical, and always unhealthy areas with startling frequency. Firmly situated in colonial political philosophy, a familiar fixture in a three-century-old rhetoric of civilization and savagery, it was both indigenous and unnatural, in need of exploration and unknowable.

Time also largely ceased to matter in discussions of the issue. Analysts in 1999 and 2000, for instance, could refer to "jungle[s] of nepotism and temptation,"[24] and could state with confidence that "corruption is a jungle and there is an urgent need for an authoritative guide to the flora and fauna."[25] Nearly half a century earlier, in 1957, a journalist for the *Economist* could argue in a remarkably similar vein that corruption occurred in areas where "the long arm of Victorian imperial reform failed to reach . . . [where] power has been given back to dependent peoples long before they have abandoned what is conveniently known as 'the custom of the country'"—a sentiment reproduced without apparent irony in a reprint of the article twenty years later.[26] In a less poetic vein, an analyst in 1997 could use as the starting point of his argument the simple fact that "in the Third World the extent of corruption was—it scarcely remains—a . . . well kept secret. Here corruption in the loosest sense is indigenous, much older than European contact or colonisation."[27] The question of whose secret it was and who was responsible for exposing that secret is an issue for the next chapter. It suffices to say for now that, throughout the twentieth century, the poetic and political geography of corruption placed it squarely, without much deliberation, and without any real change in tone, into the colonial and postcolonial world.[28]

Introduction   xiii

This is not to say that more recent corruption analysts—especially those writing in the 1990s—have not become conscious of the need to avoid neo-imperial rhetoric or, for that matter, outright racism, in identifying and describing corrupt practices and governments. There have been attempts to redefine corruption as a "global" rather than a "Third World" issue, for instance, and there have been similar attempts to produce more sophisticated definitions of corruption than those that motivated earlier writing.

One of the more interesting results of this repositioning is the growing work on scandal. Scandal is usually described in these studies as "corruption revealed,"[29] and, unlike corruption itself, it is usually seen as something healthy. Unsurprisingly, scandal has consequently come to be placed almost exclusively in Western Europe and North America, often in strange contradistinction to the corruption that plagues states outside of these areas.[30] Although analyzing scandal has been one means of retreating from the stark dichotomies of the earlier anticorruption literature, therefore, it largely reinforces the assumptions that inspired it.

A search for "scandal" in the ABC-Clio database of scholarly publications returns 496 results, of which 30 percent refer to areas outside of Western Europe and North American, while 70 percent are to states within these regions. In these articles, the uneasy relationship between scandal and corruption plays out in a variety of ways. Historically, for instance, one scholar notes that scandal "did not necessarily corrupt eighteenth century [British] politics with trivial issues; in fact, scandal opened up politics by revealing corruption and making political debate accessible to a wider audience,"[31] while another seemingly brings this point to its logical conclusion: "the importance in scandal is not the corruption itself, but the procedural corruption that follows in 'covering it up'.... [P]olitical scandal is only possible in liberal democracies . . . because of the belief in the 'rule of law.'"[32]

By maintaining that both scandal and corruption exist "everywhere," that "even" England has its Profumo affair,[33] that the United States has its Watergate,[34] that France has its Rainbow Warrior,[35] that the purpose of anticorruption literature and activism is not to target solely colonized or postcolonial states, academics and analysts manage to remove themselves from the vaguely embarrassing stance taken by midcentury writers. But by simultaneously invoking the rhetoric of liberalism, by insisting that scandal but not corruption has to do with public debate, with popular access to political power, with, above all, the "rule of law," by assuming that scandal is part and parcel of the normal functioning of healthy ("Western") democracies, these analysts are also reinforcing earlier imperial positions.

On the one hand, scandal and corruption are inextricably linked—the two cannot exist independently. On the other, what is important about scandal (in Western Europe and North America) is not "the corruption itself," but procedural perceptions. Similarly, although scandal helped to reveal corruption within, for example, eighteenth-century British politics, it did "not necessarily corrupt" the British political system. In other words, placing scandal in Western Europe and North America denies the importance or even the existence of any "pervasive" corruption alongside of it. Likewise, denying the possibility of scandal outside of these areas allows for the existence of a hidden, latent corruption in colonized or postcolonial countries that, given the absence of "organs of exposure," can never be sufficiently revealed. The rhetoric of the Western European or North American government especially as a liberal, democratic one thereby creates a situation in which it is the duty of the public to enjoy scandal, to seek out corruption, but in which real corruption still exists only in the colonized world.

The corruption that Western European and North American scandals reveal almost always has some connection to countries elsewhere. In a 1999 book on *The Criminalization of the State in Africa*, for instance, French President Jacques Chirac is portrayed as "brandishing a confidential report on the criminalization of politics in Africa . . . [stating that] the French government had to make a clean break with heads of state who were prevaricating in the face of change, and who were corrupt and autocratic."[36] Similarly, the French "Elf Scandals" were largely to do with rent seeking in former French colonies,[37] where, it seems, "clearly African oil money had a corrupting effect on the French and their European business partners. It also has an effect on the Africans involved, not so much corrupting them as providing large amounts of money to pre-existing power circles."[38]

In Italy, "corrupt" politicians were linked both to apparently neofascist Masonic groups and to the illegal flow of arms and toxic waste to Somalia, "reveal[ing] the [inappropriate political] influence wielded by the P2 Masonic lodge in Mogadishu, together with that of the Italian chemical industry, anxious to find a dumping ground for its toxic waste through the intermediation of members of the Honourable Society."[39]

Although it is something of an open secret that prisons in the United States are not bastions of rational punishment, the early twenty-first-century U.S. press was far more concerned with the scandal that was torture in Iraq than the scandal that was torture "at home."[40] Moreover, the most agonizing question surrounding this issue became the extent to which Iraq had "corrupted" U.S. soldiers.[41] Finally, even Christine Keeler, the personality at the center of the English Profumo affair, apparently "attracted police attention [only] when two West Indian (jilted) lovers assaulted her on separate occasions."[42]

In other words, the democratic organs of the liberal state that make scandal—the revelation of corruption—possible are not actually focused on the liberal state at all, but on the "outside." They are not interested in discussing corruption "inside," nor do they (as a result) aid in the fostering of public debate or popular political access. Instead they narrate stories of external corruption and pinpoint the various ways in which those "inside" are under threat, or already infected by, these practices. "The French and their European business partners" are capable of being corrupted by "African oil money." Africans are immune, presumably because corruption is part of their nature—hidden and incapable of scandalous revelation. Torture is antithetical to the liberal rhetoric of human rights. But the salient question in the Iraqi torture scandal was the extent to which young Americans were infected by inappropriate (Iraqi) attitudes toward power. The dichotomy between scandal and corruption produced in both activist and nonactivist literature thereby restates and reinforces the idea that corruption is solely a colonial or postcolonial affair.

A second means of seeming to move away from the intolerance of the earlier writing on corruption is to use perception indices rather than objective criteria in measuring it. Just as the scandal/corruption dichotomy further entrenched corruption within colonial space, however, this turn to perception likewise emphasizes the central role played by corruption rhetoric in imperial identity formation. Transparency International, for example, is most widely known for its annual Corruption Perceptions Index. Rather than engaging in the coercive and presumably culturally insensitive act of developing an external model of clean governance and then applying that model to various countries, Transparency International instead conducts polls. One of the most recent Corruption Perceptions Index, for example, is described by the NGO as "a poll of polls, reflecting the perceptions of business people, academics and risk analysts, both resident and non-resident. First launched in 1995, this year's CPI [Corruption Perceptions Index] draws on 17 surveys from 13 independent institutions."[43]

The CPI, in other words, is a *spectacle* of identity formation.[44] Its very tolerance is wed to the fact that identifying corruption, vilifying it, and combating it are purely discursive exercises. The question that is being asked is a question of perception and self-perception, of, in a basic way, identity. "Experts"—businesspeople, academics, and risk analysts—are invited to define the activities of various populations, designate them as corrupt or clean, according to their own rhetorical understanding of who these populations are. The result, unsurprisingly, is to reinforce the neo-imperial understanding of who "we" all are.

Despite the repeated insistence, for example, that "today's CPI demonstrates that it is not only poor countries where corruption thrives. . . .

[L]evels of corruption are worryingly high in European countries such as Greece and Italy,"[45] the numbers make the dichotomy clear. Of the top twenty-five perceived cleanest countries, only four—Singapore, Hong Kong, Chile, and Israel—are in Africa, Asia, or South America. Of the twenty-five most corrupt countries, not one is in the self-described West. So the "jungle of temptation" thrives even (and especially) when we approach these issues from an enlightened perspective.

Why should this be? In part, it is the obvious fact that perceptions are formed by power. The rhetoric of the imperial relationship—of what makes some places more prone to infection and infecting, of what areas are safe and what areas are not—is alive, well, and unquestioned. The linkage, for example, between "oil-rich" areas and their attendant corruption, of the extent to which oil as a resource rather than, say, natural gas or for that matter automobiles, produces inappropriate and often violent relationships is reinforced in the 2003 CPI.[46] Although oil-rich Norway ranks as the eighth "cleanest" country on the list, for example, a full paragraph and a half of the short introduction to the index are devoted to describing the unfortunate relationship between oil wealth and corruption.[47]

But Norway is rarely described or perceived as oil rich. "Oil rich" is something that African, Asian, and South American countries are—Nigeria, Angola, Iraq, Indonesia, and Kazakhstan, for example, numbers 132, 124, 113, 122, and 100 on the list, with 133 being the most corrupt. Oil wealth is something that does not go into open public bureaucratic institutions, but "instead disappears on expensive vanity projects or into the secret offshore bank accounts of politicians and public officials"[48] Oil wealth is not like the wealth that comes from exporting timber, operating systems, or pharmaceuticals, wealth that is used in a transparent manner. It is associated with both corruption and violence—it describes countries emphatically on the wrong end of the CPI.

Transparency International's Corruption Perceptions Index, much like the scandal/corruption dichotomy, thus merely reinforces the—in fact—perceptions accentuated by the earlier anticorruption literature. It makes possible, even, simple restatements of these mid-century positions. A scholar using the CPI to analyze corruption in the United States—ranked number eighteen—for example, argues that "Transparency International regularly ranks the United States somewhere in the middle of its scales. Intuitively, this ranking seems accurate, as the United States is the melting pot of most world cultures and would embody an average of the most and least corrupt."[49]

In other words, it is not just that corruption occurs in Africa, Asia, and South America. Those of African, Asian, and South American descent—even when they live in a clean country like the United States—

are predisposed to it. It is indigenous in every sense of the word. And if people of African, Asian, or South American descent had not "melted" into the United States, it would rank as high as homogenous, clean, number one Finland on the 2003 CPI.

In a similar manner, a 1990 book review of Robert Klitgaard's *Controlling Corruption* concludes as follows:

> Klitgaard returned from Equatorial Guinea in 1988, after having spent the better part of two years trying to administer a World Bank structural adjustment loan. It is also fair to say that he returned sadder but ruefully wise, having found that the best of intentions were no match for the wiles of those who deliberately or not stymied his (and others') attempts to reform the Equatorial Guinean system. He set down his experiences in an engaging but sobering book, *Tropical Gangsters*. Perhaps *Controlling Corruption* and *Tropical Gangsters* should be read consecutively, the former as analysis and prescription, the latter as self-critique.[50]

There are very few contexts in which a seemingly serious discussion of wily Africans frustrating the plans of well well-intentioned Western administrators out to improve their countries would fly in the contemporary context. Since the turn of the twentieth century, however, the corruption narrative has been unapologetically and explicitly colonial. It is not simply that corruption is situated outside of Europe and North America, or that discussions of it contain unquestionably racist overtones. The corruption narrative is and was about imperial power, knowledge, and identity formation. Klitgaard learned not just who the Equatorial Guineans were, but who he was. Transparency International is not just about identification, but about self-identification—about a seemingly voluntary self-positioning within a hierarchy of cleanliness. The scandal/corruption dichotomy does not just allow for discussions of political deviance on a supposedly global scale; it reinforces the imperial rhetoric of the liberal civilizing mission.

Theoretical Framework

I will be relying a great deal in this book on work that addresses law, colonialism, and the erotic or the pornographic. In particular, I will highlight the intersections between and among these three categories, and, even more so, the extent to which these areas of intersection have been defined as areas outside of the law—as spaces of legal exception or political indistinction.[51]

Although my primary interest is the rhetorical force of corruption, therefore—that half-legal, half-sexual threat to democracy and the rule of law—I will also be commenting more broadly on both the erotic nature of the state of exception and specific colonial or postcolonial manifestations of it. When I argue that analyses of corruption evoke erotic or pornographic tropes, and that these narrative devices in turn help to carve out exceptional spaces of lawless violence, I will thus be drawing on the work of a number of scholars who have already discussed similar themes in other contexts. What I would like to do now is take a few paragraphs to sketch in general outline some of these approaches to law, colonialism, and the erotic, and to address the ways in which they will serve as a framework for my argument over the following chapters.

One of the more fundamental points that will recur throughout this book is that narratives of corruption define and carve out exceptional space. To that extent, I will be engaging at some length with theorists such as Giorgio Agamben and Achille Mbembe, who have addressed the state of exception and—both explicitly and implicitly—its spatial manifestations. Agamben's analysis of biopolitics, for example—of the politicization of biological life—lends itself easily to a spatial reading. Indeed, a key aspect of his argument in both *Homo Sacer* and *State of Exception* is his assertion that the paradigmatic space of modern sovereignty is the Nazi camp—a legally defined lawless space in which the conclusion to biopolitical democracy is reached. The camp, he argues, is the most overt example of biopolitical or exceptional space—a space in which "every fiction of a nexus between violence and law disappears and there is nothing but a zone of anomie, in which violence without any juridical form acts."[52] It is likewise in this arena, he continues, that the biopolitical potential of a legal/not-legal focus on what he calls "bare life" is realized, and in which, every minute, biological detail of an inmate's existence is regulated, registered, ordered, and takes on increasingly powerful meaning.[53]

Achille Mbembe similarly focuses on the biopolitical—and eventually necropolitical—nature of exceptional space, and on the important role played by legal rhetoric in defining it; but he shifts his focus away from the camp and toward the colony. Drawing on the work of Frantz Fanon, Mbembe emphasizes the extent to which "space was . . . the raw material of sovereignty and the violence it carried with it."[54] Sovereignty, he continues, "meant occupation, and occupation relegated the colonized into a third zone between subjecthood and objecthood."[55] Mbembe likewise points out that this space has been defined by Europeans as, above all, lawless—that "in modern political thought and European political practice and imagining, the colony represents the site where sovereignty consists fundamentally of the exercise of a power outside the law (*ab legibus solutus*)."[56] This explicitly spatial understanding of the state of exception is in many ways reinforced by the work of scholars such as Veena Das and Arthur Kleinman when they note, for example, that

> a new political geography of the world has emerged in the last two decades, in which whole areas are marked off as "violence-prone areas," suggesting that the more traditional spatial divisions, comprising metropolitan centers and peripheral colonies, or superpowers and satellite states, are now linguistically obsolete.[57]

Although Das and Kleinman do not speak the specific language of colonialism or exceptionalism, what they are describing is not essentially different from Agamben's analysis of biopolitical space and Mbembe's analysis of its necropolitical variant.

For my purposes, what is key in the work of all four scholars is the way in which each situates these spaces of lawless violence *within* legal structures and the way in which each thus understands this violence as, in some way, a product of politics. In Agamben's analysis, these spaces are defined by the minute (intimate) regulation of biology or bare life—by a relentless biopolitical violence. In Mbembe's analysis, they are defined by a violence done to identity—by the relegation of the colonized to an indefinable position between subject and object. According to Das and Kleinman, they are spaces characterized by the violence of the everyday, by the hyperbolically political nature of daily life in the "violence-prone area." What I want to suggest in my own analysis is that they are likewise spaces determined by narratives of corruption—that "corruption-prone" is not in any obvious way different from "violence-prone," and that indeed one important function of the corruption literature is to define, delimit, and detach arenas of lawless or exceptional violence from spaces of supposed law and order.

An equally important aspect of my argument is that it is the erotic or pornographic nature of the corruption narrative that, first, makes these spatial designations possible, and, second, renders the violence that occurs within them emphatically biopolitical. What I would like to do now, therefore, is to look in more detail at three theories of pornography and the erotic in order to explain how I see them intersecting with the theories of exceptional space that I outlined earlier. Although the erotic and the pornographic are for the most part distinct—or even mutually contradictory—concepts, I want to suggest over the following pages that they do share some similarities that link them quite closely to the state of exception, and therefore to the corruption narrative.

The first of these characteristics is that each in a different way involves the simultaneous disordering and regulating of the bodily, the biological, or the intimate. The second is that each—although perhaps pornography more than the erotic—involves a process of segregating, enframing, and neutralizing as a means of producing desire. And the third is that each privileges bodily or biological narrative or testimony over verbal or linguistic narrative or testimony. To the extent, therefore, that exceptional space is by definition indistinct or disordered even while it is relentlessly regulated, to the extent that it is a space that segregates while defining and neutralizing, and to the extent that it is a space in which bare life is the only meaningful means of narration, it is likewise, by definition, erotic or pornographic space. As I will suggest over the next four chapters, it is thus exactly to the extent that the corruption narrative *is* erotic or pornographic that it *therefore* serves to carve out exceptional space.

I will look in more detail at theories of the erotic and the pornographic in later pages—especially in chapters two and three. For now, however, I would like to address in broad outline some of the scholars whose analyses will serve as a framework for my arguments in these sections. The first of these is Georges Bataille, the political force of whose work on death, embodiment, and sensuality has already been discussed in detail elsewhere.[58] I would thus like to highlight only one aspect of his argument on the erotic now—namely, the connection he forges among intimacy, eroticism and social disorder, between biological and political decay. "The business of eroticism," states Bataille,

> is to destroy the self-contained character of the participants as they are in their normal lives. Stripping naked is a decisive action. Nakedness offers a contrast to self-possession, to discontinuous existence, in other words. It is a state of communication revealing a quest for a possible continuance of being beyond the confines of the self. Bodies open out to a state of continuity through secret channels that give us a feeling of obscenity. Obscenity is our name for the uneasiness which upsets the physical state associated with self-possession, with the possession of a recognized individuality. . . . [E]roticism always entails the breaking down of established patterns, the patterns, I repeat, of the regulated social order basic to our discontinuous mode of existence.[59]

According to Bataille, in other words, one defining characteristic of the erotic is the way in which it disintegrates established boundaries, borders, and patterns—the way in which a state of bodily disarray reflects or highlights the potential for political or social disarray. The erotic therefore represents, quite basically, not just biological, not just political, but *biopolitical* disorder.

At the same time, however, as theorists of the pornographic such as Abigail Solomon-Godeau and Linda Williams have noted, this disorder has a regulatory quality about it that in many ways ties it explicitly and paradoxically back to these same established political and social structures.[60] Solomon-Godeau, for example, points out the importance of segregating, enframing, and debasing the body *parts* representative of "difference" even as the boundaries and borders of the body as a whole disappear. She writes that

> the enormous production of pornographic imagery attests to the impulse to master and possess the object of desire while debasing it and neutralizing its power and threat. . . . [P]ornography emphatically exhibits the physical sign of . . . difference, even to the extent of making the woman's genitals the subject of the image. But any potential threat is neutralized by the debased situation of the woman thus portrayed and the miniaturization and immobilization inherent in photographic representation.[61]

Williams meanwhile discusses the repetitive, highly ordered visual cues that signal, first, the creation of separate, violent spaces in sadomasochistic film pornography, and, second, the equally well-ordered, if "inarticulate," body language that indicates the "reality" of the sex or the death that is being portrayed within these spaces.

With regard to the former, for example, she notes that one common trope in violent pornography is the moment at which a girl (the "real girl") who is initially portrayed as a spectator of fictional sexual violence is suddenly trapped within this fictional narrative—the moment at which she is caught on film (or, more recently, the object of the webcam or cell phone) herself.[62] Williams argues that this transition from "fiction" to "reality" operates "to convince some viewers that if what they had seen before was fake violence belonging to the genre of horror, what they [a]re seeing now [i]s real (hard core) violence belonging to the genre of pornography."[63] It is, in other words, a well-worn narrative device in violent pornography for fictional space, where anything can happen, to entrap or to enclose "the real girl" or "real space" supposedly protected by rules or law—to suggest, that is, lawless violence operating within lawful structures. Moreover, as Williams argues in a second study of film excess in general, the narratives that occur in this space do so not via linguistic articulation or speech, but via body language or "uncontrollable convulsions."[64] "Aurally," she notes, "excess is marked by recourse not to the coded articulation of language, but to inarticulate cries of pleasure in porn, screams of fear in horror, sobs of anguish in melodrama."[65]

Both Solomon-Godeau and Williams, in other words, describe the same disintegration of bodily boundaries and attendant disintegration of social, political, or legal boundaries that Bataille does. All three suggest the chaotic, disordered, and indistinct nature of erotic or pornographic space. But Solomon-Godeau and Williams likewise note the paradoxically regulated nature of this space—the extent to which it could not exist and could not operate without the support of the systems that it apparently throws into turmoil. Like exceptional space, therefore, pornographic space is a zone of anomie, a space where anything can happen, but it is a space that is explicitly defined by law and legal structures. Like exceptional space, pornographic space is an arena in which every minute aspect of an individual's biological or bodily process is enframed, discussed, and segregated—in which power and dominance are not political but biopolitical. Finally, like exceptional space, pornographic space is populated by figures who can speak only via body language, whose verbal testimony is meaningless but whose bodily convulsions are translated into statements of the most crucial importance.

The only difference between the two is that pornographic space apparently produces desire, whereas exceptional space apparently does not. But it is here that I think my analysis of political corruption will prove useful. What I would like to suggest over the following pages, indeed, is not just that the rhetoric of corruption or corrupt intimacy has helped to carve out exceptional space; nor do I want to argue solely that this rhetoric invokes well-worn erotic and pornographic themes; rather, I hope to bring together the erotic and the exceptional—to pinpoint one arena in which erotic and pornographic narratives have served *directly* to produce a state of exception. To that extent, I will argue that exceptional space is as productive of desire as erotic space—that in fact the erotic nature of the corruption discourse is what has made it such a key component of recent neocolonial expansion. With that in mind, I will devote the following chapters of this book to addressing the ways in which corruption narratives have relied on these erotic and pornographic tropes, first, to carve out exceptional space, second, to displace this space onto colonies and postcolonies, third, to populate this space, and finally to condemn it.

An Overview

The first chapter of this book, "Political Corruption as Sexual Deviance," consists of an extensive literature review. Making use of political speeches, the websites of international organizations such as Transparency International and the World Bank, newspaper articles, academic analyses, and morality tales, it highlights the overlap between discussions of sexual deviance and discussions of political deviance from the nineteenth and twentieth centuries. In this section, I show that, with their emphasis on intimacy, infantile sexuality, illness, monstrosity, self-destructive abandon, and confession as cure, modern narratives of political corruption have left the realm of bureaucratic decay to enter the realm of erotic disorder. In the process, the tensions between conflicting liberal metaphors of family-as-state and body-as-state have both emphasized the legal and biological boundaries within which proper citizens must interact while at the same time breaking down these boundaries in a spectacular pornographic display.

The second chapter, "Celebrating the Corrupt Leader," begins with a discussion of the videotaped torture, death, and celebration of Liberian president Samuel Doe. Indebted particularly to Linda Williams's theoretical work on pornography[66] and Catherine Mills's work on nonverbal testimony in lawless space, this section analyzes the ways in which the corrupt leader is portrayed and presented as an object of consumption for global audiences. It focuses in particular on the Ottoman Sultan Abdülhamid II, who reigned from 1876 to 1908, and the Iraqi President Saddam Hussein, who ruled from 1979 to 2003. Although these two leaders were separated by more than a century, this section demonstrates that their narratives and the ways in which they have been marketed for a global audience have been identical. Just as Samuel Doe is remembered now almost exclusively as the star of one of the best-selling snuff films in history, Abdülhamid and Saddam Hussein were likewise transformed over their reigns from political leaders into "porn stars." Their fleshiness, sexuality, and in particular their inability to produce an articulate self-narrative that could compete with narratives of law and liberalism were all key components to their celebration. Their use of body doubles, for instance, was rearticulated as an assault on the legal right of habeas corpus, and their evasion of the gaze of the public as an attempt to circumvent the gaze of the law. Placed into the same exceptional space occupied by the "real girl" of sadomasochistic pornography, the corrupt leader both on the run and after his eventual capture came to be known almost exclusively via body language or inarticulate physical signs, rather than via the spoken or written legal word that distinguishes the legitimate political leader.

The third chapter, "Condemning the Corrupt System," examines corruption of the more "systemic" form. Rather than looking at the corrupt leader who is by definition a celebrated—and indeed hyperbolic—individual, the corrupt functionary is nameless, as are his or her victims. Framed within a discussion of the Pasolini film *Salo* and its indictment of "fascist corruption," this chapter attempts to account for the strange overlap between narratives of corruption and narratives of totalitarianism.

Looking in particular at the relationship between the appropriate, noncorrupt dehumanization idealized in the liberal bureaucracy and the inappropriate, corrupt dehumanization that occurs in the totalitarian bureaucracy, it suggests that the (only) difference between the two lies in the former's focus on abstract, legal norms and the latter's focus on concrete, biological norms. Whereas the collective manifested in the former has to do with citizenship or specialization—embodied, for instance, in the production of a passport photo—in the latter it has to do with blood and property, quite literally embodied in nepotism, bribery, or torture. At the same time, I argue, the line between the two systems is not as distinct as it might appear. The chapter thus concludes by arguing that the postcolonial (corrupt) "torture nation" is, for example, very much a part of (noncorrupt) rational legal structures, while the momentarily famous (corrupt) photographs taken in Iraq's Abu Ghraib prison are inextricably linked to the likewise momentarily famous (noncorrupt) Iraqi constitution.

Conclusion

I would like to conclude this introductory section by addressing one contradiction that is at the heart of my discussion of political corruption and that will reassert itself with some frequency throughout the next four chapters: there is a vast divide between the empirical, social-scientific methodologies favored by almost every scholar writing in the corruption field, and my own methodology reliant primarily on political philosophy and literary analysis. In many ways, it would seem that these two approaches are completely irrelevant to one another, and that this book is therefore destined from the beginning to fail. Analysts attached to anticorruption NGOs are unlikely to be interested in a discussion of rhetoric or narrative, and political theorists usually engage with ideas or issues that transcend the daily crises linked to empirical data and its verification. At the same time, however, as the literature review in the next chapter should make clear, I think that these two approaches are not as unrelated as they might at first appear. Anticorruption literature lends itself easily to literary analysis—so easily that it raises questions about the self-imposed roles taken on by anticorruption advocates. Indeed, when data collection occurs in aid of a broader philosophy of state formation, it is necessarily entering the realm of both rhetoric and narrative—and to the extent, therefore, that anticorruption advocates see themselves as humanitarians *or* internationalists, they are in fact already in a conversation with political philosophers and literary theorists.

As for the question of the relevance of this issue to scholarship produced in the humanities, I would like to emphasize that I intend this book not as a history of a region or of a place, not as a history of a period, but as a history of an idea. I am thus situating it quite squarely within a long tradition of histories of ideas, and in dialogue with the scholarship that grapples with this tradition. It may at first glance seem that corruption is not as fundamental as, say, sovereignty, secularism, or sexuality to this tradition. I would like to make the case, however, that its frequent, and indeed insistent, appearance in texts that address these and other similarly vital theoretical issues suggests otherwise—that it can and should play a role in analyses of power, politics, and narrative writ large. Although this book is not, therefore, a book about legal exceptionalism, about postcolonial theory, or about sexuality studies per se, my hope is that its subject can nonetheless add to ongoing conversations in these fields—that a focus on narratives of corruption can indeed help to highlight the legal or political nature of the erotic, the erotic nature of the state of exception, and various colonial or postcolonial manifestations of each.

1

Political Corruption as Sexual Deviance

A Literature Review

The purpose of this chapter is to situate the corruption narrative within a broader rhetoric of modern statehood and to link this rhetoric to discussions of the erotic. In particular, I want to examine the moments at which nineteenth- and twentieth-century anticorruption literature has appropriated, reimagined, and often rendered peculiarly concrete two major early modern metaphors of political belonging: the state as nuclear family and the state as biological body.[1] Each of these metaphors has been central to contemporary notions of effective state–citizen interaction, and—by linking state, family, and physical body—each has also produced a set of political, legal, sexual, and biological boundaries within which the contemporary citizen or institution is expected to act. Each has thus in turn reinforced the idea that operating beyond these boundaries is not only politically and legally, but also sexually and biologically, inappropriate, or—in a word—corrupt. The basic premise of this chapter's literature review is therefore that corruption involves, in one form or another, acting outside of these overlapping legal, sexual, and biological spaces.

More important, I would also like to suggest in this chapter that these political metaphors have produced a rhetoric of corruption that is explicitly erotic or pornographic—a rhetoric that erases and obliterates any line that may have existed between political or bureaucratic misbehavior on the one hand and sexual or biological misbehavior on the other. The linkage between state and family or state and body, in other words, has set the foundation for a narrative of political corruption that has gradually come to ignore the diseased, disordered, dying, or deviant state and come to focus instead on the diseased, disordered, dying, or deviant family or body that originally served only as the state's poetic substitute.

Before entering into this argument in detail, I would like to turn to a few anecdotal eighteenth-century examples of each of these metaphors in action. The first is the 1793 trial of the French queen Marie Antoinette. In more traditional literature, this trial is seen as the moment at which modern, liberal, protodemocratic ideologies triumphed over early modern, patrimonial, personal state structures—at which the, granted somewhat radical or extreme, notion of egalitarian citizenship displaced the newly "corrupt" despotic relationship. More recent scholarship has also noted the strangely pornographic nature of the case brought against Marie Antoinette. Nymphomania, pedophilia, and incest became flashpoints in the revolutionary narrative of illegitimate political rule produced in the trial, leading one historian to argue that it in fact demonstrated widespread "anxiety over the menace of 'feminization' of the new republic."[2]

I would also suggest that the trial—with its conflation of inappropriate governance and inappropriate familial or sexual behavior—likewise indicates the extent to which the state-as-family metaphor had already become concrete, the extent to which political corruption was not just *like* sexual deviance, but actually *was* so. Indeed, at one point in the trial, the public prosecutor of the Paris Commune noted that the imprisoned dauphin's guard had "often caught the child in the most indecent acts [masturbation] which the child says he learned from his mother and aunt, who often put him to bed between them; it appears, from this child's statements, that he was frequently both witness to and actor within the most scandalous, the most libertine of scenes."[3]

With the freedom of a show trial, the duty to produce a political spectacle, and complete narrative power in his hands, in other words, the public prosecutor chose deliberately to frame the corruption and illegitimacy of prerevolutionary French governance within a vocabulary of incest, masturbation, and infantile sexuality. By 1793 already, that is, the rational, progressive, liberal state was demanding an irrational, disordered, and erotic narrative of corruption to support it.

It will be one function of this chapter's literature review to demonstrate that nineteenth- and twentieth-century versions of this narrative were a direct legacy of the revolutionary moment previously described. By the end of the nineteenth century, and then into the twentieth, I will argue, echoes of Marie Antoinette as corrupt "bad mother"[4] repeatedly recurred in the discourse of the corrupt state, evoking an eroticized, rather than bureaucratized, disorder and decay. Descriptions of the corrupt state or corrupt space likewise became overtly sexual—the infantile sexuality of the long dead royal heir to French political power infiltrating in unexpected ways analyses of weak and tainted "developing" systems. Moreover, this coming together of corrupt governance and corrupt sexual or familial relationships had a direct bearing on liberal and neoliberal colonial expansion. Indeed, it set a foundation for discussions of the sort analyzed by Inderpal Grewal, in which the immediate "solution to despotism" was "a transparent society of representative government and its counterpart in home and marriage," and in which "colonization be[came] a way to render transparent that which [wa]s [both politically and domestically] threatening."[5]

The second key metaphor of modern political belonging—the state-as-body, the healthy state as healthy body, and the unhealthy state as diseased body—picks up on similar themes. In this case, however, rather than discussing the various means by which sexual or biological vocabulary infiltrated political rhetoric, I would like to look instead at the almost immediate transformation of eighteenth-century sexual and biological narratives into nineteenth- and twentieth-century political realities. I will begin once again with the Enlightenment—but this time I will focus on the ways in which it manifested itself in medicine rather than the ways in which it played out in revolution.

Samuel-August Tissot, author of the famous 1760 medical treatise, *L'Onanisme, ou Dissertation physique sur les maladies produites par la masturbation*, was born in Switzerland in 1728.[6] Although he was already a celebrated physician when *L'Onanisme* appeared, it was this work that catapulted him into the realm of the renowned thinkers of his day, leading the tutor of one aristocrat, for example, "to prepare himself for his pedagogical task [by] studying 'physics, morals, and teaching,'" and by drawing "'from the reading of Tissot, Rousseau, and Locke.'"[7] Leaving aside Tissot's status alongside such prominent political philosophers for the moment, I want to look more closely at the nature of his medical writing, in particular his 1757 description of "death by masturbation":

> I learned of his state, I went to his home; what I found was less a living being than a cadaver lying on straw, thin, pale, exuding a loathsome stench, almost incapable of movement. A pale and watery blood often dripped from his nose, he drooled continually; subject to attacks of diarrhea, he defecated in his bed without noticing it; there was a constant flow of semen; his eyes, sticky, blurry, dull, had lost all power of movement; his pulse was extremely weak and racing. . . . [t]hus sunk below the level of the beast, a spectacle of unimaginable horror, it was difficult to believe that he had once belonged to the human race.[8]

This passage is a purely medical one, with no overt connection to the rhetoric of liberalism and citizenship that was being produced simultaneously by Enlightenment-era ideologues. At the same time, however, the ease with which Tissot moves from the medical, sexual, and biological to the civilizational, to questions about who does or does not belong to the human race, also leaves open the possibility, at least, for a political reinterpretation of this vocabulary—a reinterpretation, indeed, that Rousseau effects a few decades later. In his *Confessions*, published in 1770, Rousseau notes that he was taught to masturbate by "a Moorish bandit he met in Turin," a "dangerous supplement" that has "deprived men of their health, their vigor, and sometimes even their lives,"[9] He thus takes Tissot's medical analysis to its logical conclusion, directly and explicitly reinforcing the dichotomy between uncivilized, non-European, criminal onanists and civilized Europeans who keep their bodies pure—between healthy bodies/healthy citizens on the one hand and the diseased bodies/diseased citizens on the other. He helps to transform Tissot, that is, from a physician into a philosopher—and the diseased, corrupt, sexually deviant body into a diseased, corrupt, sexually deviant body politic.

In this way, he and Tissot together set one foundation for the late twentieth-century work of corruption analysts—of scholars like Robert Payne, who in 1975, for example, argued that the individual investigating a corrupt state

> will find himself in the position of a doctor dissecting a plague ridden corpse. . . . [T]he dead body remains active, but it is in a state of passive activity. Things are happening within it, but they are not things over which the body has any control. It suffers these things to happen to it, it has become finally a creature of necessity, at the mercy of forces incomparably stronger than itself. . . . [L]eft alone to rot, the physical body assumes savage colors, purple, red, and green, with strange yellows and liquescent blacks. Just as ugly, and ultimately just as incomprehensible are the corruptions of the mind and the corruptions of society . . . like a decaying corpse, a corrupt society festers and poisons the atmosphere.[10]

This passage is a purely political one. At the same time, however, the rhetorical debt that it owes to Tissot's writing from two hundred years before is obvious. In both passages, the doctor or analyst plays the role of the interrogator, while the confessant—the diseased body or body politic—offers up, physically, violently, biologically, the secrets of its interiority. In both passages the illness, sexual or biological in the first case and political in the second, cannot be hidden, and indeed, the doctor's role in each scenario is not so much to heal as to watch and to record—to look on in horror. In the same way that the corrupt physical body has no choice but to confess to Tissot, the corrupt body politic likewise cannot hide its secrets from Payne. Willingly or not, the sexual or political disease—the existence of the private—will manifest itself and will out.

At the same time, the act of confession in both passages is an erotic and pornographic one. To the extent that the attraction of pornography lies in its ability to create a spectacle of difference, to debase that difference, to cut it into tiny pieces even, all in the service of a dominant discourse,[11] these passages fall squarely into the genre. Simultaneously titillating and consumable, each first of all produces a spectacle of difference within the familiar—death, the plague ridden corpse, not even "part of the human race" anymore (although it once, intriguingly, was)—and second, debases this difference and regulates it, highlighting its exposure, its inability to move, its lack of agency and control, and, most important, its complete degradation in the face of the doctor/analyst.[12] Moreover, the process occurs in the service of an ideology, reinforcing in the end the implied consent to the rule of, on the one hand, bourgeois sexual morality, and on the other liberal political structures. By giving up their secrets, by exposing their obvious, physical shame, by (implicitly) regretting the activities that led them to this debased state, the corrupt body and the corrupt body politic are quite basically admitting and confessing that those already in control—the doctor and the analyst—ought to remain so.

Both the metaphor of the state-as-family and the metaphor of the state-as-body thus create a context in which modern narratives of political corruption are able to become erotic and eventually pornographic. To a certain extent, anticorruption rhetoric can in fact be seen as one bridge between the discourses of deviant politics and the discourses of deviant sexuality that have been addressed by so many scholars of the modern period. By rendering the legal and political boundaries within which proper citizens must act simultaneously sexual and biological, these eighteenth-, nineteenth-, and twentieth-century notions of political belonging indeed set a rhetorical foundation for understanding corrupt political behavior as nothing more nor less than corrupt biological and above all sexual behavior.

The rest of this chapter will examine the ways in which this relationship among the political, the legal, the sexual, and the biological plays out in nineteenth- and twentieth-century anticorruption literature. In the first section I will discuss in more detail the development of the body politic as a political metaphor. In the next, I will make use of this metaphor to suggest a connection between the fear of infantile sexuality and the fear of the "developing state." The third section will analyze the behavior of nineteenth- and twentieth-century consumers of the striptease and pornographic confession on the one hand, and nineteenth- and twentieth-century advocates for political transparency and political confession on the other. Finally, I will examine the overlapping tropes of the monstrous and the diseased in modern pornography and modern anticorruption literature, with a particular emphasis on the role of the political and/or biological "constitution" in warding off the threat posed by each.

The Body Politic

Although his work is removed chronologically and to some extent geographically from my own, I would like to contextualize this literature review within a discussion of Ernst Kantorowicz's *The King's Two Bodies: A Study in Medieval Political Theology*. Kantorowicz's intention in this study is to trace the doctrine of the of the physical (rather than spiritual) duality of the monarch throughout the medieval period and into the Renaissance, especially in England,[13] and especially vis-à-vis Christian politics and ideology.[14] At the same time, as Agamben has pointed out, the book has been of enormous value to historians of modern political theory as well[15]—in particular to the extent that it addresses questions of sovereignty and power more broadly. For my purposes, therefore, Kantorowicz's work will serve as an excellent starting point for examining the metaphor of the body politic in the nineteenth-, twentieth-, and twenty-first centuries—and thus for addressing the various concrete manifestations of this metaphor that we see in the corruption narrative.

Whereas it is true, in other words, that Kantorowicz situates the "secular" body politic squarely within a religious context,[16] and whereas it is true that he cautions against associating the king or the Crown of medieval England too closely with the "state" of continental Europe,[17] I think that a number of the points that he raises as he examines the gradual articulation of this body politic are relevant to my discussion now. What I would like to do over the next few pages is first to highlight a few major themes that emerge in Kantorowicz's work, second, to discuss the relationship between these themes and similar issues that arise in Agamben's and Carl Schmitt's analyses of the state of exception (and its biopolitical potential), and, third, to explain how these themes will influence the direction of this literature review.

With that in mind, I should begin by noting that whereas I highlighted both the state-as-body *and* the state-as-family in the introduction to this chapter, I am focusing solely on the former in this subsection. I do this not because the metaphor of the state-as-family is of less importance than, or secondary to, the metaphor of the body politic, but rather, as we will see, because the two are not as distinct as they might at first appear.

As Kantorowicz argues, "especially when discussing the inalienability of fiscal property"—that issue fundamental to contemporary anticorruption advocates—jurists "fell to the metaphor of the ruler's marriage to his realm.... [U]nder the impact of juristic analogies and corporational doctrines, the image of the Prince's marriage to his *corpus mysticum*—that is, to the *corpus mysticum* of his state—appeared constitutionally meaningful."[18] In late medieval and early modern France in particular, he continues, "both the *corpus mysticum* analogy and the metaphor of the king's marriage to his realm were linked with the fundamental laws of the Kingdom."[19] According to Kantorowicz, in other words, one of the most basic implications of the body politic metaphor is that it assumes an eventual nuclear family metaphor—as soon as sovereign power becomes embodied, it takes on the characteristics of every other body.

At the same time, however, as Kantorowicz is at pains to emphasize, the body politic, or sovereignty embodied, remains a contradictory and ambiguous thing. On the one hand, for example, it is "'more ample and large' than the body natural," and contains within it "mysterious forces which reduce, or even remove, the imperfections of the fragile human nature."[20] It is something that "never dies, is never under age, never senile, never sick, and is without sex."[21] On the other hand, the Crown "as a composite body," possessing a "corporate character," is explicitly understood to be "a perpetual minor [i.e., underage] ... with the King as its guardian."[22] Moreover, the relationship between the king—as both guardian/husband and representative of this body politic—and "the Law" writ large is also inconsistent. The king is first of all "above the Law"—a situation "perfectly 'legal' and guaranteed by Law"[23]—but also simultaneously "below the Law." Nonetheless, as Kantorowicz concludes, whereas "the seemingly self-contradictory concept of a kingship at once above and below the Law has been criticized as 'scholastic and unworkable'.... [t]o the political thinkers and legal philosophers of the late Middle Ages, these contradictions did not appear unworkable at all."[24]

In general, therefore, Kantorowicz presents the body politic as a chaotic, but nonetheless highly regulated, metaphor. It is physically and biologically perfect—unblemished, sexually pure—if nonetheless subject to a certain gigantism. It is simultaneously displaced onto the sovereign, married to the sovereign, and under the guardianship of the sovereign—both never underage and a perpetual minor. Finally, it is at the same time too great for the law and too despicable for the law to touch—legally defined as legally indefinable. The body politic, in other words, has the explicit potential to live up to Tissot's, Rousseau's, and Payne's wildest fantasies of the healthy, pure, untouched, clean organism and the equally explicit potential to live up to the Paris prosecutor's fantasy of a sexually inert, open, hygienic family. At precisely the same time, however, the body politic is just as capable of fulfilling the unmentionable aspects of these fantasies—of becoming the precociously sexual minor, the incestuous child/spouse, or the monstrous, absorbing organism too contemptible for the law to consider. It is this second aspect of the body politic that will interest me in this literature review—the body politic given up to its monstrous, erotic, despicable, and, above all, corrupt, potential.

Indeed, I am particularly interested in two specific aspects of this body politic out of control. The first is suggested by Agamben in *Homo Sacer*, when he notes that one logical conclusion to Kantorowicz's study is that the "political body of the king seem[s] to approximate—and even to become indistinguishable from—the body of *homo sacer*, which can be killed but not sacrificed."[25] Agamben continues by arguing that what matters in this situation is not that in the case of the king, homicide is more than homicide, whereas in the case of *homo sacer*, homicide is less than homicide. Rather, what is important is that in the case of neither is killing actually homicide.[26] Kantorowicz's work, in other words, suggests and even insists on the pervasively, rather than narrowly, biopolitical nature of the body politic. It is not just the king whose body is simultaneously constrained and expelled by the law; it is each and every future citizen and future *homo sacer*. It is not just the king who occupies indistinct, biopolitical space; it is the body politic as a whole that exists in this indistinct space. What Kantorowicz is describing, therefore, is both a particular metaphor of sovereignty *and* the reality of the exceptional space assumed by this metaphor.

A second scholar whose work is intimately linked to Kantorowicz's, in fact, is Carl Schmitt—perhaps one of the most influential theorists of the state of exception. Whereas it is true, as Agamben notes, that Kantorowicz's study of "medieval political theology" is a "demystification" of the concept, whereas Schmitt's work on "political theology" in the modern period is emphatically not,[27] the fact remains that Kantorowicz and Schmitt were working within the same intellectual tradition and—more important for my purposes—were in many ways describing similar phenomena (i.e., states of exception). I would therefore like to highlight one point of intersection between the work of Schmitt and the work of Kantorowicz that will be useful for contextualizing this literature review.

In his *Political Theology*, Schmitt outlines a number of corollaries that follow from assuming that juridical systems are less about objective, rational, abstract norms than they are about sovereignty and sovereign decision—that follow, to use Kantorowicz's terminology, from the sovereign existing both above and below the law. One of the most basic of these is that, as he argues, "the exception in jurisprudence [becomes] analogous to the miracle in theology."[28] The exception, in other words—the sovereign violation of the sovereign's law—performs the same nonlegal but nonetheless legitimizing role in jurisprudence that the miracle, the divine violation of the (divine) laws of nature, does in theology. Each shatters a system of norms and each blurs the boundaries between the rational and the irrational; but each in doing so demonstrates the foundational power of law/politics or law/divinity. It is, in other words, not just that the exception, the construction of a lawfully lawless space, lends meaning to contemporary sovereign relations. It is that it lends a particularly *miraculous* meaning to contemporary sovereign relations, predicated on an irrational, nonverbal acceptance of political power. Sovereign legitimacy, that is, rests on a miraculous absence of legality.[29]

Like Agamben and Kantorowicz, therefore, Schmitt likewise implies a body politic that insists on exceptional or biopolitical space. In his work, too, there is the same blurring of borders and boundaries, the same reliance on the nonverbal aspects of sovereignty, and the same consequent if paradoxical reinforcement of sovereign power. All three describe the effective functioning of the body politic as something that leads inevitably to an aggressively disordered, if nonetheless well-regulated, conclusion. All three identify the potential for exceptionalism that occurs when the political is simultaneously and emphatically displaced onto, first, territory, second, space, third, the sovereign, fourth, the subject, and finally the body.

When I discuss the erotic themes that occur and recur in the corruption literature, therefore, I am not interested solely in their sexual meaning. Rather, I am situating them precisely and explicitly within these theories of law, politics, biopolitics, and exceptionalism that I addressed earlier. It is not just that narratives of the "developing state" messily collide with narratives of infantile sexuality, in other words—in turn suggesting the perpetually minor and perpetually precocious "Crown" of Kantorowicz's study. Nor is it simply that the rhetoric of incest and monstrous gigantism on which the corruption literature relies likewise invokes the body politic's unavoidable multiplicity and self-obsession. Rather, again, it is that these themes work together to create exceptional space and biopolitical sovereign/subjects; they work together to delimit this miraculous space of legitimacy characterized by the absence of legality.

The Developing State and Its Infantile Transgression

In his *History of Sexuality*, Michel Foucault discusses a transition in modern political and legal rhetoric from a focus on what he calls "a symbolics of blood" to a focus on "an analytics of sexuality."[30] Over the course of this argument, he draws upon a number of examples and case studies, emphasizing in particular the extension of surveillance networks into the supposedly private realm of children's sexual behavior. It is not my intent in this section to revisit Foucault's theses of sexuality or biopolitics in detail. Instead, I would like to highlight two aspects of his discussion of infantile sexuality that become relevant when the literature of the corrupt developing state begins to intersect with the literature of the sexually active child.

First, Foucault notes that the nineteenth-century efforts to eradicate infantile sexuality—especially masturbation—were not about eradication per se, but instead about a never-ending process of producing and then monitoring the "secret" that was children's sexual behavior. Even as it was uncovered, evidence of infantile sexuality suggested the existence of more that was hidden, more that cried out for additional discovery, and more that demanded the further extension of surveillance networks.[31] Second, Foucault examines the role of the modern expert in extracting confessions from misbehaving children or deviants. The production, policing, and exposing of the secret, he argues, created a context in which the expert would help to provide the child/deviant with an appropriate self-narrative, and in which the child/deviant might thus take on a recognizable social, sexual, and political role.[32] The modern obsession with infantile sexuality therefore, first, allowed for an ongoing process of discovery and exposure, and, second, created a context for an equally continuous process of subject formation.

I would like to turn now to a second discussion of the relationship between children's sexual behavior and modern political identity, this time, however, focusing on the twentieth-century United States. In his analysis of Vladimir Nabokov's *Lolita*, Frederick Whiting argues the following:

> Humbert the pedophile threatened the home, innermost bastion of privacy and the last redoubt guarding liberal democratic freedoms. His victim, children, were the very embodiment of that privacy, incarnations of innocence possessing no public existence whatsoever save their cameo appearances in the protective statutes designed to reinscribe them, even more safely, in the domestic sphere.

He continues that,

> on the one hand, the discussions [of *Lolita*] depended on what Donald Peese has described as the distinction, traditional to liberal democracies, of the private and public realms; on the other, they are informed by what Richard Rorty has identified as a liberal democratic desire—the legacy of the Greek Philosophers and Christian theology—to fuse the public and the private.[33]

Discussions of *Lolita* in the twentieth-century United States were, in other words, one arena in which the fear of infantile sexuality collided with fantasies of the public/private distinction as a foundation for the functional liberal state. Whereas Foucault described a process in which the invention of children's (deviant) sexual behavior led to the extension of power networks into supposedly private space, Whiting is describing a process in which it is precisely the overlap of public and private that is responsible for the deviance. It is the inappropriate intermingling of the two spheres that allows for sexual abuse, that turns Lolita from a protected innocent into a victim and perpetrator of deviant behavior. In both the nineteenth and twentieth centuries, that is, discussions of infantile sexuality evoked both the horror of and desire for "corruption"—for the irrational and obscene intersection of the public and the private.

The final aspect of infantile sexuality that I would like to discuss in this overview is its role in the colonial relationship. As a number of scholars have noted, the conflation of the child with the savage, and the infantilization of colonized populations, is an integral element of imperial and neo-imperial power structures. In her *Race and the Education of Desire*, Ann Stoler draws on Foucault and takes this point to its logical conclusion, bringing together the savage, the child, and the sexuality of both—arguing indeed that children

> enter on *both* sides of that equation, for theirs is both an endangered and dangerous sexuality. They must be protected against exposure to the dangerous sexuality of the racial and class Other, not because their sexuality is so different, but because it is "savage," unrestrained, and very much the same. This discursive connection between the "savage as child" and "child as savage" is not one that Foucault makes, but it will be crucial to us. Both representations were constructs of a civilizing, custodial mission and a theory of degeneracy whose bourgeois prescriptions would turn on the contrast and equation between the two.[34]

Here, in other words, we have a final variation on the theme of the threat of infantile sexuality. In the colonial context, what was only suggested before becomes overt: infantile sexuality is both attractive and repellent, worthy of protection and itself a danger, representative of the need for a civilizing mission and also indicative of the degeneracy to which all civilization might eventually succumb. The trope of childlike innocence, bound up as it is with the trope of childlike deviance,[35] thus *explicitly* develops in the imperial context alongside nineteenth-century notions of political progress and duty. By the late twentieth century, it had become an ineradicable metaphor for the hope and despair embodied in the continuing liberal civilizing project.

Over the remainder of this section, I will situate the corruption narrative within this rhetorical framework. In particular I will argue that discussions of both the corrupt "developing" state and its corrupted citizens were and are firmly anchored in nineteenth- and twentieth-century notions of the innocently savage and savagely innocent infant victim/perpetrator of unmentionable acts. This is something of a departure from more anthropological approaches to the relationship, which focus primarily on the construction of cultural or civilizational others. Indeed, although it is related, my interest here will be emphatically political and legal. I want to address in particular the *institutionally* corrupt state–citizen relationship—a relationship, I will argue, in which the corrupt state takes on the double role of both abusive father and deviant, malformed child, while the corrupted citizen acts as the simultaneously savage and innocent victim/perpetrator of the state's obscene desire.

One of the most striking aspects of the victims of political corruption in both the nineteenth and twentieth centuries, for example, is the extent to which they were without exception always innocent and always childlike in their inability to protect themselves from improper behavior. Whether the protagonists of these narratives were infants and infantilized woman suffering at the hands of the "neo-patrimonial," "paternalistic" state or the confused, underdeveloped state itself, it was the threat to their innocent and unaware condition that became the centerpiece of the spectacles surrounding them. Likewise, it was the slippage between inappropriate political desire and inappropriate biological or sexual desire that made these stories harrowing, and that demanded the extension of networks of surveillance.

Three late nineteenth-century examples of the American corruption narrative—the first two focusing on the threat posed by idiot/foreign-child-savages to the purity of political processes "at home," and the last addressing the source of such deviant behavior in the colonized "abroad" (in this case, China)—indeed set an excellent foundation for a further exploration of this overlap. Each begins with an invocation—the first spatially, the second economically, and the third politically—of the public/private divide that Whiting argued was so central to liberal rhetoric. Each also, however, quickly moves from this starting point to a conclusion resonant more of *Lolita* than Locke. In the first, for instance, an 1894 article in *The Arena* entitled "Political Corruption: How Best Oppose," there is a discussion of vote buying in the United States, and of the people victimized by the practice. In one anecdotal story cited in the article, "a man kept a half-idiot who was working for him shut up in his cellar for some days before an election to prevent the opposing party from capturing and voting him. Then, on election morning, with a man on each side to guard him, he was marched to the polls with a prepared ticket in his hands, and voted."[36]

The second article, from 1892, and entitled "Responsibility for Political Corruption," makes the connection between the political and the infantile, between the inappropriate state–citizen relationship and the inappropriate adult–child relationship more apparent. In an attempt to absolve the infantilized "foreigner" of sole responsibility for the corrupt state of U.S. politics, the anonymous author plays with the trope of the simultaneously victimized and criminal "foreign" child/savage. The author writes,

> instead of being the source of our political corruption, the ignorant voter is the victim of it. If he be foreign-born, almost the first lesson he receives in American politics is that elections are controlled by corrupt men for corrupt purposes, and that the rich and respectable members of American society supply money for this work of debauchery. Instead of educating him to a high and just conception of his duties and privileges as a citizen, we are teaching him the lowest one possible. The dangerous consequences of such teaching need not be pointed out.[37]

The message in both of these anecdotal pieces is clear: the victims of political corruption are, first and foremost, the marginalized, the weak, the innocent, and the childlike. Whether it is the half-idiot worker incapable of deviance on his own or the half-educated foreigner who, like the curious child, might be tempted into such behavior, it is the neglected duty of the functional state to civilize both of them via compassion or correction. But when the state itself becomes corrupt, loses sight of its fatherly mission, the result is a slide into "debauchery," of which the "dangerous consequences . . . need not be pointed out." The defining characteristic of the corrupt political situation in these two passages is thus one in which the childlike citizen is abused by the patrimonial state, leaving the citizen with no choice but to take on a debauched identity himself.

Again, however, like so many other aspects of modern, Euro-American political rhetoric, the logical conclusion to the corruption narrative is reached only in the colonial context.[38] It is only in colonized space that the politically corrupt, the infantile, and the sexual all come together to produce the story in its full form. I would like to turn now, therefore, to one case study "abroad," in China, rather than "at home," in the United States. One of a number of articles published during the 1900 Boxer Rebellion,[39] this piece, written by John Foord, Secretary of the American Asiatic Society, discusses the movement's possible motivations and attempts to assign to the disturbance a palatable meaning. Like that of most of his colleagues, Foord's solution to the dilemma is above all to associate what was seen as patently illegitimate political violence with patently illegitimate politics in general—it involved, that is, forging the first of a number of indissoluble links between anticolonial activity in China on the one hand and Chinese political corruption on the other. Anticolonial activity in turn became something not just frightening politically, but frightening sexually—child-savages involving themselves in adult political behavior as repellant as children involving themselves in adult sexual behavior. As Foord noted, "like tigers who have tasted human blood, these men will not return to peaceful callings. They have become trained in the school of crime. The lawless life of the past will cause them to long for a life in which money can be gained without the sweat and toil of months at the spade or wheelbarrow." He continues, however:

> These companies of bandits were children of the government's own raising, and it became evident that, in the absence of any honest desire to suppress them, a reign of terror was imminent. . . . [T]he Chinese terror has been raised not by missionaries, merchants or railroad builders, but by the ignorance, incapacity and corruption, and chiefly the corruption, of the rulers of China.[40]

These rebels, then, these infant/savages—simultaneously "tigers who have tasted human blood" and "children of the government's own raising"—were both victimized by and perpetrators of Chinese political corruption. The illegitimate Chinese government created them, raised them, neglected them, and in the process it victimized them—leading them away from an honest path. At the same time, however, the rebels were also guilty themselves, lost by virtue of being tempted, irredeemable because they could not respect the value of money gained through honest (non-corrupt, politically neutral) toil.

But the Chinese state itself also played both infant victim and infant perpetrator within this narrative. Foord concludes:

> The appetite of the palace for tribute has been that of the two daughters of the horse-leech continually crying, "give, give" and government has been one vast system of bribes, "squeezes," and wholesale robbery. Offices, great and small, have been a matter of purchase, and the purchaser has been mainly intent on making the most of his bargain. Official peculation is the curse of China, and the root of all the evils from which it is suffering. Let that be cured or abated, and the people who starve while the Palace favorites grow rich can be made to see that the foreigner may be the instrument of their well being—"the advance agent of prosperity." Of all the punishments that Western civilization can contrive, as a penalty for the misdeeds of the Empress Dowager and her clique of obscurantist advisers, none would be so exquisitely painful or so productive of results in the highest degree beneficial to the world, as to deliver the Government of China into the hands of honest Chinamen.[41]

The state, that is, embodied and feminized in the person of the Empress Dowager, is first and foremost a selfish and irrational infant, compared to the "daughters of the horse-leech" who cry for more and more without regard for anything beyond immediate, physical desire. Official functionaries also, however, both give and take, bribe and are bribed, coerce and are coerced themselves. The solution to the situation, therefore—a situation both threatening and pitiable—is a combination of the medical, the sexual, and the punitive. The Chinese state and in particular the Empress Dowager has to undergo a punishment above all "exquisitely painful." But this punishment must also be productive of results, "beneficial" to the world and implicitly (but, interestingly, not explicitly) to "honest Chinamen." In this narrative—and in particular in the fantasy of pain and reform with which it concludes—the infantilized Chinese population and state are thus both innocent and criminal, in need, like their sexually deviant child counterparts, of both compassion and coercive control.

These three examples of the corruption narrative are all anchored squarely in place and time—produced in the late nineteenth-century United States and discussing issues both politically inside and politically outside. It is worth noting as well, however, that one characteristic of later, twentieth- and twenty-first-century anticorruption literature is that more often than not it operates in virtual or postmodern space. By the 1990s in particular, anticorruption agencies and scholarly communities existed for the most part on the internet, and their messages were necessarily divorced from both the concrete "reality" of the nation-state and any sort of linear, modern timeframe. The narratives that these agencies produced were situated in the abstract universe of "development" and addressed to and from unnamed "developing states," or at best continent-wide constructions like "Africa." The rhetoric in turn became broad and diffuse, with corruption itself taking on a personality more than a definition, and the corrupt state/citizen relationship acquiring a poetic meaning more than a political one. The incestuous, patrimonial corrupt political relationship, the growth that was inhibited by corruption, and the savagely innocent nature of the corrupt state and corrupted citizen were therefore all transformed as corruption became a late twentieth-century issue of global, and then virtual, concern.

It is perhaps unfortunate, for instance, that these twentieth-century discussions of corruption rely so heavily on the nineteenth-century dichotomy between "rational" states and "patrimonial" ones.[42] By evoking images of fatherhood and, given the implicit moral connotations of patrimonialism, inappropriate or ineffective fatherhood, the temptation to designate the equally abstract citizens of such states as victimized children seems to have been too much for many to stand. As Elizabeth Barnes has noted with regard to the family–state metaphor broadly defined, "the liberal construction of familial sympathy as the foundation for social and political unity" creates a situation such that "the conflation of familial and social ties results in an eroticization of familial feeling in which incest is the 'natural' result. What this suggests is the cultural cost of setting up the family as a model for politics."[43] When the family becomes the model for *dysfunctional* politics, the downward spiral is inevitable.[44] In the corruption narratives of the twentieth century, therefore, the fragility, powerlessness, innocence, confusion, and hence desirability of the victimized child are applied with great enthusiasm to the corrupt(ed) individual, the corrupt(ed) state institution, and the corrupt(ed) state itself.

Over and over again, "world leaders" like Mary Robinson and "global analysts" like John Githongo tell "us," the international community, that "at the end of the day it is the poor and the weak who face the true brunt of corruption,"[45] that "the losers are likely to be exceptionally poor, female, and marginalized, whilst the winners are already wealthy and part of an inefficient, swollen state,"[46] that corruption "affects women[47] in particular. . . . [T]hey are the primary victims, including through prostitution and pornography. Corruption . . . exposes them to pollution and dangerous environments."[48] Those threatened by corruption, in the abstract, outside of a national or chronological framework, are thus the weak and the innocent, people in danger of subjugation to an inappropriate sexuality—people likely to be polluted. It is not entirely clear, for example, what the exact link between political corruption and pornography is—although the story of the child-woman sold into sexual slavery or prostitution is a recurrent trope in the literature.[49] But the emotional connection is obvious. It is endangered, helpless, and therefore attractive innocence, women and children at risk of taking on unnatural sexual roles, that are at the center of the virtual twentieth- and twenty-first-century anticorruption movement.

At the same time, however, again, this innocence is not without its underside. Just as the victims of infantile sexuality are also perpetrators, are also threats to abstract notions of social and political probity, the victims of political corruption are likewise irrevocably tainted by it. Robinson continues her speech, for example, by noting that bribery requires both a "giver" and a "taker," with all that this sort of relationship implies.[50] The question thus becomes to what extent force, desire, and vulnerability play a role. Indeed, the twin responses of the victimized citizen to a corrupt and corrupting patrimonial state are, familiarly, first, a descent into inappropriate sexualized behavior, and, second, a growing mistrust of the security and capability of state structures. Like the victim of infantile sexuality, the victim of political corruption sinks into promiscuity, pursues unhealthy relationships, and thus ceases to be the trusting child, secure in a blissful familial bond. As Robinson notes, "corruption destroys a crucial social good, trust, in society and in government. This ... inhibits growth. It also ... may foster the belief that democracy is not capable of providing needed security."[51]

The lack of trust that corruption fosters thus not only prevents healthy political development, it also undermines the ideal of the secure, healthy (innocent) state–citizen relationship, a relationship indeed explicitly tied back to an idealized, fetishized domesticity a bit later in the speech. After invoking Eleanor Roosevelt and her focus on "small places, close to home," Robinson concludes with the horrific story of Juma Ali, Fatma Ali, and their daughter—a family that undergoes so much oppression in one day (they are unable to pay for water, heat, or their daughter's school bus, their daughter cannot enroll in school, Juma must bribe his employer to continue working, the whole family is evicted from their house, the house is then demolished, and finally the family cannot pay for transportation to a new development)[52] that less sensitive listeners might find themselves inadvertently entertained by the story's heart-wrenching melodrama. Whatever the case, however, the lesson to be learned from the narrative is summed up in one question: "how is Juna (sic) and Fatma's sense of self worth affected by the bribes they have to pay ... how do they see themselves in the eyes of their daughter, Amina?"[53] At issue therefore is not necessarily any notion of civic function, but the "self-worth," and by extension the moral authority of the "small," "close to home," little nuclear family. The narrative of corruption in this speech concentrates above all on the weak, powerless, infantilized innocents' progressive disordering and lack of self worth—a disordering that in its spectacularization, immediately becomes the possession of the public at large.

But the weak, infantilized citizen was not the only victim of political corruption. In the "developmental" context, the abusive patrimonial state was also at risk of both losing its innocence, disordering its identity, and endangering its future health. It, too, was "vulnerable";[54] it too was subject to "debilitation";[55] and, above all, it, too, was "young and fragile."[56] The judicial system in particular became a subject of scrutiny—necessary to protecting society, but "unreliable because the rule of law is often fragile, and therefore can be captured by corrupt interests."[57] Indeed, as one corruption analyst, Peter Langseth, noted in the 1990s,

> emerging democracies in particular brave considerable political risks if corruption is not contained, as the corrupt can greatly weaken the authority and capacity of the fledgling state ... [it has been argued that] "cowboy capitalism" is just a transition state that must be endured on the way to a more mature market economy. The danger, however, is that corruption can become so widespread that it can undermine and destroy the transition stage itself.[58]

As Herbert Welsh, Langseth's counterpart in the 1890s, noted:

> the political diseases [corruption] which afflict our young and vigorous Nation are sufficiently serious; but in view of the youth and vitality of the patient they furnish no ground for despair of a complete recovery. On the other hand, let us beware lest we fall into a fatuous neglect of them and a failure to seek with promptitude sound medical advice, to apply obvious remedies, and to secure good hygienic conditions for their removal.[59]

In both scenarios, that is, the capacity of the young, fragile (or vigorous) state was under threat, in need of both surveillance and properly hygienic (read as "clean" in the twentieth century) conditions. Even while potentially dangerous or abusive, the young state was first and foremost cast in the role of child patient. Development, in other words—in the basic, pediatric sense of the word—was both at risk and necessary for the future health of the infant nation. The disease might have been difficult to detect and difficult to define, but its damaging effects were many and varied, and the first line of defense was proper surveillance combined with compassion and control.

Again, though, once infantilized, both the corrupt state and the corrupt citizen were also subject to a certain demonization. Like the children whose sexuality—by virtue of being infantile—marked them as simultaneously victim and perpetrator, ill and vicious, the underdeveloped nature of politics in the corrupt state—by virtue of being underdeveloped—marked it and its citizens as similarly so. In both late twentieth- and late nineteenth-century anticorruption literature, there was a constant invocation, for example, of the child perpetrator as the child victim. Githongo, writing of corruption in twentieth-century "Africa," for instance, notes:

> a falling regard for the profession of teaching among the youth. . . . [T]oday because it is the corrupt who seem to succeed most in terms of acquiring material wealth, the product a teacher sells—education—simply does not seem to have as high a value as it once did. Short cuts to wealth seem more effective. Many youths opt to wait for that single big deal that can bring sudden wealth by virtue of what are euphemistically described as "connections."[60]

Although it was the youth in particular who were victimized by corruption, in other words, they were also responsible for its growing hold on society. Rather than respecting appropriate authority, they were seduced by the lure of corrupt wealth. Via "connections"—relationships made illicit by the quotation marks around them—they became perpetrators of the system, both victimized in their inability to distinguish genuine success from the deviant version, and threatening in their emulation of "the corrupt who seem to succeed."

But it was, again, not just individuals within the corrupt state who embodied the victim/perpetrator role, it was also the state itself and its institutions. Since corruption was above all about an inappropriate, often sexualized relationship, at issue in discussions of it were notions of coercive and voluntary intimacy. The victims of corruption were without a doubt victims—the intimacy of the corrupt relationship was unhealthy, damaging, and inappropriate for them. But to the extent that they engaged in this relationship willingly, or without an overt fight, they were also tainted by it. Robinson follows Githongo, for instance, arguing that "in relation to education: Corruption is demanded and given during registration,"[61] that "business is often as much the perpetrator of corrupt practices, as it is the victim," but that "many firms bribe under duress."[62] All of which creates in the end what Githongo refers to as "an incestuous relationship between business, politics and the bureaucracy."[63]

The relationship among the state, its institutions, and its citizens, then, became a relationship in which both the threat and the draw of an innocently deviant intimacy were foregrounded. It is not obvious what exactly is meant by "corruption demanded and given," but the rhetorical value is clear. Corruption is something evil, it is something that—without being demanded—would not be given. But on being demanded, it creates a simultaneously coercive and voluntary intimacy between the taker and the giver, a relationship both appealing and repulsive. Similarly, businesses were both victims and perpetrators of corruption—explicitly so in this instance.[64] At the same time, however, many became so "under duress"—resisting, disliking, not wanting the relationship, but unable to withstand it nonetheless. In both situations, therefore, the victim/perpetrators of corruption writ large reenacted the roles of the victim/perpetrators of infantile sexuality: unwilling innocents who were nonetheless drawn into, and eventually became responsible for, an unhealthy and immoral intimacy.

They thus tread a fine moral line in the popular and political imagination. Infantile and manipulative, attractive in their repulsiveness, they embodied all of the fascinating aspects of the deviant relationship. The only way to deal properly with them was via a combination of medicine and punishment, reform through pain. More important, however, this process of reform had to involve the destruction (and spectacularization) of the inappropriate relationship and its replacement with an appropriate one. Indeed, as Michael Wiehen, a corruption specialist of the late twentieth century, suggested: "developing countries should be able to offer limited preferences to their infant industries, provided these incentives and preferences are fully transparent, strictly regulated and are announced openly."[65] Provided the relationship between the patrimonial state and its infant industry was a healthy and appropriate one, emphatically not "incestuous," and one that conformed to the narrative of proper development, everything would be fine. If not, however, the punishment and correction implied in "strict regulation" would presumably be employed.

Striptease: Political Transparency and Self-Regarding Behavior

I would like to spend some time now recontextualizing the corruption narrative within a second major erotic trope of the modern period—the pornographic confession. In his work on sexuality and subjectivity, Jeremy Tambling suggests a direct connection between the circulation of pornographic tales sold as confessions and the creation of the bourgeois subject in the nineteenth century.[66] Post-eighteenth-century sex, he argues, could not "be thought of outside a discourse of secrecy," and thus sexual behavior became a matter for confession, and confession in turn an erotic act.[67] I will argue throughout this section that post-eighteenth-century narratives (or confessions) of political corruption occupied the same rhetorical space. My particular interest will be the relationship between the late nineteenth-century invention of the striptease and the simultaneous invention of the caught, contrite, and exhibited corrupt state or citizen. After first discussing two theoretical approaches to the striptease, I will move on to a twentieth-century case study of corruption-as-burlesque in Italy, and then finally an analysis of more abstract anti-corruption rhetoric, especially as it is embodied on websites advocating "transparency" and decrying "self-regarding behavior."

Between 1890 and 1920, the striptease became a culturally significant phenomenon in Europe and North America.[68] Over this period, the spectacle of a fully or partially clothed woman gradually exposing herself—often impersonating a "belly dancer" or "harem girl"—became something worth watching and something worth paying for. The erotic juxtaposition of the attainable and the inaccessible, the exotic and the familiar, reached a new intensity with the striptease, and the burlesque show that surrounded it became one of the most marketable products available to a newly consumerist public. As Jon Stratton notes, two questions follow from this phenomenon: "first, why [did men] want to look at the naked female body? And second, why d[id] they want to see its gradual revelation?"[69]

Stratton argues that the popularity of the striptease at the turn of the twentieth century was the result of "the eroticization of the world," which "couple[d] the sight of the female body—in this case as a commodity—and manufactured commodities in a fetishistic structure of desire expressed through the male gaze."[70] This does get at the importance of the woman's nudity in the striptease—there is no doubt that women's naked bodies became fetishized commodities over the modern period. But it addresses the "gradual revelation" of her body only obliquely. The male gaze *is* important, but more so is the interaction between the gaze and the "tease"—it is the relationship that is the key to the act. It was not just women's bodies that were spectacularized and eroticized over these years, in other words, it was the act of revelation, and participation in that revelation, itself.

Katherine Liepe-Levinson addresses this second issue—the relationship between the viewer and the performer, between those "with control" and those "out of control"—more explicitly. With regard to the striptease in the late twentieth century, for example, she argues that

> the issue of "control" for many striptease aficionados may have far less to do with discrete and gendered positions of dominating and being dominated than is usually theorized, and much more to do with the spectators' wish to play at being sexually overwhelmed or to play at jeopardizing *self-control* through performance scenarios.[71]

The interaction among control, self-control, and lack of control is, in other words, the key to the erotic nature of the act, and the exposure of the stripper as it related to the *possibility* of exposure on the part of the watcher was central. The stripper's uncovering did occur outside the realm of the viewer's universe, but it was also contained, simultaneously and provocatively, within it. It was, therefore, the *relationship* between one party who reveals or confesses and a second, usually invisible, party who watches or interrogates—but who might always slip into the dominated position—that became one of the most erotically charged relationships of the late nineteenth and late twentieth centuries.

Once again, the ease with which the literature on political corruption appropriated and mobilized these seemingly unrelated themes for its own purposes indicates more than anything else the staying power of eighteenth-century notions of appropriate and inappropriate political behavior. Exposure and surveillance, confession and interrogation, as well as an eventual financial reward when the coverings have all been discarded are central to both descriptive and proscriptive analyses of the corrupt state. The corrupt state is, after all, a state with something to hide—and it is therefore also a state with something to be discovered. Indeed, by the late twentieth century, the "donor community" was both expected and encouraged to withhold its gifts until the corrupt state had revealed itself (to be clean). The reward could not and would not appear until the moment of exposure and interrogation—the relationship among all of these players one in which the tension gradually built up among those with control, those with self-control, and those (provocatively) in danger of losing both.

With that in mind, I would like to turn to a relevant case study of political corruption "exposed" in late twentieth-century Italy. Sergio Cusani, an industrial financier attached to the Italian political establishment, was one of the most famous victims of Italy's "clean hands" campaign. The "clean hands" investigation began in 1992, when a prominent member of the Italian Socialist Party, Mario Chiesa, was arrested for corruption. Bettino Craxi, the leader of the party, immediately distanced himself from Chiesa, but he, too, was soon under investigation, under arrest, and then in 1995 convicted of bribe taking and influence peddling. Throughout 1993 and 1994, the extent of the corruption—the extent of the inappropriately intimate relationships among politicians, the national energy council, and private industrialists—was revealed. And it was revealed in particular to a fascinated audience of millions of television viewers. The Cusani trial, the centerpiece of the campaign, became necessary viewing for months, until it ended in April 1994, with Cusani sentenced to eight years of prison for violating laws on political financing.

Roberta Sassatelli's analysis of the Cusani trial focuses on the symbolic relationship between the trial and political degradation, as well as on how this relationship came to be codified for a popular audience. Although it is therefore not part of the "corruption literature" genre per se, her article does invoke a number of themes that have become common at this point. She begins, for instance, with the fact that Italy is a country on the margins of the "modern West"—"a Mediterranean and Catholic country where the lack of a bourgeois revolution, the persistence and transformation of family allegiances and patron–client loyalties have informed both the political and the economic transition to modernity."[72] It is, in other words, only within the self-consciously dichotomous framework of the liberal, bourgeois, (noncorrupt) West on the one hand and nonliberal (corrupt) not-West on the other that the Cusani trial—with its spectacular interplay among the media, public opinion, celebrity prosecutors, seductive defendants, and law productive and reproductive of the confessional relationship—can be properly understood.

Moreover, after first situating the trial within this framework, Sassatelli continues with a vocabulary—although, it is true, a vocabulary conscious of its implications—full of "stripping" corrupt politicians of the "marks of their authority,"[73] and insistent that "politicians . . . now appear 'naked.'"[74] Unlike the earlier "years of terrorism when the media supported the state,"[75] and the public did not especially care whether politicians were "clean" or not, by the 1990s, Sassatelli argues, the exhibition of politicians, their "nakedness," and their exposure in political corruption trials drew millions of television viewers. Most important, however, she notes that in the Cusani trial itself,

> the seductive relationship between Di Pietro [the public prosecutor] and Craxi was instrumental . . . in reinforcing the symbolic value of the occasion. Thanks to this, as well as to the temporary tactical alliance between prosecution and defense which made them seemingly part of the same moralizing enterprise, the trial acquired symbolic value from within. Confronting the legal sphere with a political stance, Craxi was preparing the ground for the trial to become something different from a mere legal matter, changing the meanings attributed to the roles played within it.[76]

Again, Sassatelli's argument is more about the symbolic value of the corruption trial in delegitimizing Italy's political class. The central position of the confessional relationship, its erotic nature, and its value to large numbers of spectators, however, is obvious. The public prosecutor acted as the interrogator/surrogate audience, extracting information from a simultaneously willing and unwilling, deviant and attractive, corrupt politician. Like the relationship between the stripper and patron, a narrative stylized and uniform in presentation, the Craxi case relied on role playing rather than spontaneous interaction. Indeed, according to Sassatelli, the specific ways in which Craxi had been corrupt, the role of the judge in reinforcing the rule of law, even the importance of the adversarial prosecution/defense relationship in a trial situation, were of almost no interest. Instead, prosecutor and defendant, prosecution and defense, interrogator and confessant all worked together to create a consumable narrative of political corruption that—like the striptease—entertained the population for hours at a time.

With this case study in mind and operating as a framework, I would like to turn now to the more abstract corruption narrative—detached from time and place and existing in the academic, and then the virtual, world of the online NGO or international aid agency. In this world, the three key aspects of pornographic confession—the eroticized exposure and uncovering of a dirty interiority, the not quite voluntary admission of deviance on the part of the exhibitionist, and the tense interplay among those with control and those without—all continue to operate with ease, lending their rhetorical strength to the anticorruption campaigns. In his foundational 1975 discussion of political corruption in the abstract, for instance, Robert Payne makes an explicit, if unintentional, linkage between the stripper and the corrupt state, between the healthy, asexual vigor of the "clean" society and the effete if euphoric degradation of the (now naked) corrupt one:

> corruption takes hidden forms and wears brilliant coverings; we can strip it naked and see the horror for what it is. We learn how societies sometimes become aware of the corruption inside them, struggle against it and even conquer it, and we learn what disposes them to surrender meekly to a comforting euphoria and a lingering death.[77]

The metaphorical value of this passage is quite clear—as is its basic message: if the corrupt state refuses to strip off its brilliant coverings voluntarily, it is our duty as audience to expose it forcibly. If not, all that awaits is euphoria on the one hand and a lingering *petit mort* on the other—horrifying but at the same time strangely comforting. The realm of the pornographic confession and the realm of the political confession become, in other words, one—an effective setting or framework for similar trends in the later corruption literature. There is the emphasis on the dirty and unknowable interior, the equally resolute emphasis on the external gaze, the insistence on extracting a confession, and the erotic pleasure attendant upon both the success *and* the failure of these endeavors.

Indeed, a key aspect of Payne's striptease-like description of the corrupt state is the central role played by control, self-control, and lack of control in it. Just as in narratives surrounding the stripper, what is fundamental to the efficacy as well as the enjoyment of the spectacle described by Payne is the (in)voluntary *self*-exposure undergone by the exhibitionist. Yes, an outside observer or an expert can define and identify the dirty secret—indeed, that is his or her job. But for the therapeutic process to develop and the spectacle to gel, the deviant has to participate as well. It is all well and good for the stripper or state to give up its secrets involuntarily, that is, but far more effective is an ongoing, mutually satisfactory, voluntarily involuntary relationship between interrogating analyst and revealing subject.

Whereas it is true, therefore, that one means of combating governments that are "enemies of transparency" and keep their corruption "under wraps" is to publish information on their political process and on procurement, more important is the idea that "LDCs [less developed countries] . . . be convinced that in most cases it is in their own interest to open up procurement to international competition, and to make the process fully transparent."[78] The interchangeable, uniform, and stylized "LDC," in other words, has to participate voluntarily in the confessional process. It has to remove its wraps on its own, become transparent, and open *itself* up. It has to "operate transparently" and be "subject . . . to public scrutiny"[79] because the willing/unwilling participation of the confessant is necessary *both* to maintaining the dominance of the interrogator *and* to producing a meaningful relationship. There is thus a constant tension between the therapeutic value of a government getting over its "denial" and admitting its need for recovery, and the spectacular value of the subjection, submission, and degradation of this same government—each in a different way highlighting the *possibility* of the spectator's loss of control via its own "unbridled excesses."[80]

Like the stripper, therefore, the corrupt state is identifiable both in its infinite, degraded depth and in its ability to engage successfully in the eroticized relationship between confessor and confessant, exhibitionist and audience. Again, the analyst who wrote that "to many, corruption is like pornography; they know it when they see it"[81] was not making a point about its erotic nature. But the idea that one knows pornography when one sees it is based on a number of unstated assumptions. The most obvious of these is that, since pornography is not rationally definable, the way that we identify it is via an irrational, visceral reaction. It exists in a space separate from the realm of law and reason. Presumably the same is true, in this formulation, of corruption. Corruption is simultaneously repellent and attractive, comforting and disturbing, secret and, by definition, exposed. The fact that confession plays such a key role in both pornographic narratives and narratives of corruption thus makes a great deal of sense. Indeed, the corruption narrative situates the corrupt state precisely within pornographic space—rendering it indefinable except through our biological, irrational, and sexual responses to it.

Incest, Cannibalism, and Corporate Responsibility

One final trope that pervades the corruption field, and that I would like to discuss in this literature review is the trope of the sexualized "monster." I am particularly interested in this section in four aspects of this theme, namely, the monster as a product and/or perpetrator of incestuous relationships, the monster as a victim and/or source of disease, the unnaturally monstrous appetite—especially as it is manifested in cannibalistic desire—and finally the aesthetic and political linkage that we see in a number of fields between the monstrous and marginalized populations. I am going to start, therefore, in perhaps an unexpected place, with a brief discussion of the 1965 Moynihan report on the "poor black family" in the United States and its "tendencies" toward inappropriate sexual behavior. After situating the Moynihan report within a larger rhetoric of the monstrous, I will suggest that it is equally relevant to discussions of political corruption, especially to the extent that the corrupt "African leader" bears a striking rhetorical resemblance to the report's "poor black father," and the corrupt Chinese citizen a similar resemblance to his incestuous, self-hating children in the U.S. rhetoric of corruption.

With that in mind, I would like to turn immediately to Daniel Patrick Moynihan's report on *The Negro Family: The Case for National Action*, which appeared in 1965 and which has served as a template for discussions of the African American family (and what to "do" about it) for the past half-century. Indeed, as Patricia Hill Collins notes, the report is in most ways indistinguishable from a CBS Bill Moyers special, *The Crisis in Black America*, produced twenty years later in 1986.[82] Both link the "deteriorated condition" of the black family to an apparent inability on the part of African American youth to become socialized within "mainstream" American culture, and both present to their audiences an "inside-out world," where "men refuse to support their children, women feel they can get along without husbands, and the husband–wife family unit no longer is desired."[83]

The Moynihan report, in other words, plays with well-worn themes common to nineteenth- and twentieth-century Anglo-American sexual and political rhetoric—the incestuous nonwhite or working-class anticitizen is in trouble, in need of regulation, and crying out for correction.[84] The report is likewise securely anchored in a U.S. literary trend that by the twentieth century associated incest almost exclusively with poor black or poor southern (read as miscegenated) families.[85] Taking up this literary trend and turning it into a science, it situates "the poor black family at the 'center of a tangle of pathology,' with 'a weak family structure [a female-headed family]' now the principal source of 'most of the aberrant, inadequate or antisocial behavior.'" It incorporates "the idea that poor black families are 'doing it to themselves,' so to speak . . . into the metaphor of the incestuous black family, an inbred breeding ground of deviant black men, too strong yet easily preyed-upon women, and illegitimate children."[86]

With, once again, only a very slight shift, corruption narratives made use of nearly identical themes. Like incest (or *as* incest) corruption was also something that the marginal did. It was both damaging and compelling. It was "inside out." And the self-destructive nature of the states, bureaucracies, citizens, and leaders who practiced it marked them as both diseased and rightly so. Like the twentieth-century African American family or the nineteenth-century working-class child or domestic servant, in other words—defined by their susceptibility to incestuous relationships—the colonized or neocolonial state came to be known first and foremost by its propensity for corrupt relationships. Corruption was thus something that others did, something that they did to themselves, a self-destructive behavior, and something that—against all normal expectations—they enjoyed. The corrupt state and corrupt citizen were by definition self-hating. They could not be otherwise given the way that they reveled in the very activity that made them inferior and powerless.

I would like to turn now to three case studies that bring together these sexual and political themes. The first is a brief discussion of Sani Abacha, the former ruler of Nigeria, and a popular and recurring figure in twentieth- and twenty-first century anticorruption literature. Abacha came to power in 1993 after having served in prominent positions in the Nigerian army, and after having been instrumental in a number of political coups. As Abdul-Karim Mustapha notes, "the ascendancy of the military regime in Nigeria did not begin with General Sani Abacha," it was instead the product of decades of colonial rule, anticolonial protests, and postcolonial revolts and riots.[87] Abacha the individual, however, portrayed as *personally* rapacious and merciless has become one of the most widely used accessories in discussions of a self-destructive, uniquely violent, continent-wide "African" governance, as well as in discussions of corruption writ large. In his speech, "Closing the Corruption Casino," for example, Peter Eigen begins with the following invocation of Abacha before moving on to make more transnational points:

> Abacha, who ruled Nigeria until his death in June 1998, stripped Nigeria of at least US $7 billion, a sum vast enough to begin to turn the tide of the HIV AIDS epidemic, a tragedy that is threatening the lives of a new generation in sub Saharan Africa from the moment each child emerges from a mother's womb.[88]

Abacha, that is, is not just a bad leader, he is a hypermasculine one, abusive of his patrimonial position, and a threat not only to the "stripped" Nigerian nation,[89] but to all of sub-Saharan Africa. He is a looming menace to unborn African children, as well as to the wombs of a generation of mothers. He is, in other words, *the* representative of the antisocial, incestuous-patrimonial African political structure. Abacha was the reason for African deviance and inferiority; he made any discussion of more distant issues like colonialism or postcolonial legacies completely unnecessary.

This slippage between the corrupt, patrimonial African leader and the abusive, rapacious African father figure becomes even more overt in discussions of political corruption in 1990s Somalia. Here, in fact, the inappropriately intimate relationship between the corrupt state and the corrupt citizen produced explicitly monstrous results, brutalizing, feeding, draining, sapping, and spreading throughout political space. The disordered lack of control evidenced by the incestuous, corrupt political relationship directly linked perversity on the political level to perversity on the individual level—playing up once again a very basic eroticism inherent in the metaphors of state-as-family and state-as-body.

To contextualize these stories, in January 1991, the Somali government, lead by Mohamed Siyad Barre, disintegrated, leading to a political crisis that by mid-1992 was being broadcast by most of the world's television news agencies.[90] Between 1993 and 1995, the United Nations maintained "humanitarian" troops in Somalia, but eventually withdrew them when it became clear that Somalia as a functional state had effectively given way to autonomous, self-governing units. The crisis continued throughout the 1990s, its primary cause, as one scholar has noted, being "the ferocious fighting between the heavily armed clan-based forces of the so-called 'warlords,' all dubious relics from the Siyad era."[91] Another culprit in the continuing decentralization of Somali power was, however, political corruption.

In October 2002, for example, the U4 anticorruption agency uploaded a press release from the Somali Peace Rally that linked the perpetuation of the civil war in Somalia to, in particular, the corrupt behavior of the "warlords" in power there. The article argued that

> the main motives of Somali warlords for the perpetuation of civil war and for the breakdown of any peace process strongly stem from the fact that they do not want to see their unbridled passion (sic) of assets and power to be constrained by a Somali state with the capability to make rules, collect revenue and enforce the rule of law. . . . [T]he SPR believes that all necessary milestones along the road to a sustainable peace can not be laid out by corrupt leaders and warlords who have willfully tainted and smashed all the machinery of the Somali state for the promotion of their individual interests. Therefore, the SPR strongly urges the international community to hold back the warlords.[92]

The warlord trope in narratives of political violence in Somalia is one that has appeared in a variety of other contexts. The appropriation of the warlord by anticorruption activists, however, leads to a number of very specific and meaningful rhetorical outcomes. Patently illegitimate, the warlord's military activity occurs outside the bounds of the civilized "rules of war," while his designation, "lord," likewise places his goverment outside the realm of liberal political process.[93] A warlord is not even a "leader" of the Abacha sort—he represents instead basic, physical, and indeed "unbridled" force. Quite literally a monster rather than a human being, his "unbridled possession of assets and power" slips with extraordinary rhetorical ease into the less meaningful, but far more evocative "unbridled passion of assets and power." The corrupt warlord defies rational constraint. In his selfishness, ignorance, and passion, he taints and smashes appropriate bureaucratic machinery; the only way to deal with him is to find some stronger force to hold him back. Like the neo-patrimonial African dictator and the aberrant, inadequate, antisocial African American father, the warlord is simultaneously violent or passionate and self-defeating or self-destructive. His inappropriate relationship to those metaphorically (or actually) related to him is both far too close and far too distant.

At the same time, although I have been discussing Abacha and the Somali warlords as specific case studies, anchored in time and space, I would also like to emphasize that "Africa" occupies a slippery space in the larger corruption discourse. Nigeria, Somalia, and the like are discrete, politically definable states. With remarkable frequency, however, discussions of one or another African nation-state give way to a discussions of "Africa" as a whole, which in turn lead to discussions of "corruption" as a theoretical concept. "Africa" thus operates both at the level of the concrete case study and at the virtual level, an idea rather than a place linked inextricably to corruption as an idea rather than a behavior. I would, therefore, like o move on to my final case study—of the corrupt citizens of China—via a rhetorical move based in "Africa" as simultaneously place and analytical framework:

> in many societies, corruption has become so entrenched that it is beyond effective remedy. China, Indonesia, Nigeria, Thailand and the Philippines, among others, readily come to mind as examples of countries governed for decades by regimes that are not only utterly corrupt, but also bankrupt of moral, social, and ethical values. . . . [The corporate sector] is totally opportunistic and considers it its duty to manipulate the often inadequately enforced laws and regulations in order to create an environment that encourages and promotes practices that would have made Tiny Rowland, even in the heyday of his African adventurism, blush. . . . [S]elf-imposed sanctions, quite simply, have not worked in the past.[94]

What we have here, then, is, first, the invocation of yet another patriarchal, patrimonial, rapacious African leader who, second, places China et al. into the same perversely pathological place occupied by African states. Tiny Rowland and African adventurism are not being analyzed themselves—they are instead the rhetorical backdrop against which we are expected to understand the corruption that exists in other, more concrete state structures. That the African adventurer himself would have "blushed" at the unnamed "practices" of these corrupt states, and that this pathology was inherent, entrenched, and "beyond effective remedy," indeed sets up a relationship between African corruption as an abstract, theoretical notion, and China et al. as specific concrete cases to be understood only within this larger theoretical framework.

With that in mind, I would like to look now at what it is about Chinese governance that led corruption analysts to examine "China" through this theoretical lens of "Africa." First of all, a 1981 discussion of corruption in Hong Kong notes that

> there was little public discussion and debate on corruption among the Chinese people, and consequently little public pressure on the government to make reforms. . . . [C]ertain practices that are defined by law as corrupt may be regarded by the people as a normal way of life. . . . [T]he emphasis on personal relations is strengthened by a long standing characteristic of Chinese society—i.e. the dominance of social and moral norms (the particularist) over legal norms (the universal).[95]

Citizens of China, that is, are in a very basic way incapable of understanding the value of universal, abstract political standards. For them, flesh, blood, and biology override law—and the result, as we will see in a moment, is an incestuous mess. But I want to emphasize here that this mess was a mess more than a century in the making. One hundred years before, for example, a discussion of corruption in the abstract turns to the Chinese as a case study, and comes to nearly identical conclusions, noting that they "are yellow, Mongolians, Monarchists and Pagans; but we do not see that, except in their want of patriotism, they are any worse than certain classes in New York, who are white, Anglo-Saxons, Republicans, and, in theory at least, believers in Christianity."[96]

The Chinese are foreign, in other words, because they are racially and religiously different. But they are *really* foreign because of their "want of patriotism"—because of their inability to operate on a universal, rather than on a particularist level. Indeed, a final discussion from 1889 brings all of these notions together, arguing that it is "the Chinese rule" to place "love of clan . . . before love of country," despite the obvious fact that "nepotism is political incest and . . . will breed the progeny of incest."[97] In all three of these analyses, in other words, the Chinese state and Chinese citizens are engaged in a patently violent and inappropriate relationship—their foreignness derived first and foremost from the weird enjoyment they seem to derive from a strange, and blatantly destructive form of sympathy. Corruption residing in Nigeria and Somalia, abstracted via its connection to "Africa," is thus resituated and rendered concrete in the inability of the Chinese citizen to get over his or her proclivity for incest.

With this slippage between the concrete and the abstract as a starting point, therefore, I want to turn now to the virtual twentieth-century corruption narrative as it has operated on behalf of online NGOs and aid agencies. Again, the basic message of most of the rhetoric produced by these organizations is that corruption is something that marginalized groups do, and it is something that they do to and with themselves. Deliberately or not, there is a distinct and familiar dichotomy set up in the literature between white, middle-class vigor[98] and nonwhite, marginalized lassitude or—stranger—degraded satisfaction, which turns the victims into their own victimizers. Indeed, it becomes clear that it is in the nature of the corrupt state to be self-destructive and its inherent pathology to be self-hating. The bizarre pleasure that corrupt leaders, states, bureaucracies, governments, and even citizens take in their self-destructive behavior in fact underlines their natural deviance just as much as it underlines their natural inferiority. As one late twentieth-century analyst noted,

> a message that comes through in this book is not so much that people do not know what to do about corruption as that they tend to lack sufficient will, fortitude, stamina, resolution, and persistence to do anything about it. . . . [P]erhaps things are not as bad in some parts of Asia [as they are in Africa] although some countries on this continent rank among the lowest in governance simply because corruption has always been a way of life. An overwhelming sense of fatalism pervades.[99]

The fact that the word "vigor" was not added to will, fortitude, stamina, resolution, and persistence is likely purely accidental. But what we do have here is, again, a basic dichotomy set up between the fortitude of those who are willing to "do something" about corruption and the overwhelmed fatalism of those who are not. At the same time, however, those who are unwilling are naturally, inherently so, because for them "corruption has always been a way of life." Not much more needs to be said. And indeed, this particular take on the pathologically weak, victimized, but also victimizing Asian or African state was reproduced in a variety of contexts, including, for example, a 2004 report also on "global corruption" that stated "unfortunately many governments lack the political will to give teeth to supervisory agencies lest it work to their disadvantage once out of control."[100] Lacking both "teeth" and "will," these governments simply produce and reproduce pathological cycles of violence.[101]

But these states remained nonetheless weak and diseased—their "infection" constantly spreading, a constant cause of inadequacy, impotence, weakness, degradation, sterility, and leakages of various unpleasant kinds.

That "corruption is contagious," for example, appears with repetitive frequency in a variety of contexts,[102] and that corruption predisposes the body politic to a number of unspecified, but nonetheless frightening consumptive afflictions is a given in most anticorruption literature.[103] In the space of one paragraph of a UN report entitled "Why a Global Programme Against Corruption," for instance, the government, institutions, and judiciary of an abstract corrupt state are described variously as "faulty," "failing," "inadequate," "weak," "crippled," and "undeveloped."[104] Issues of "flow," "leakage," "drainage," and a lack of "productivity" (i.e., "sterility") also appear repeatedly in the corruption literature, where, for example, various analysts for Transparency International tell us that corruption "leads to lower capital inflows and lower productivity," causes "leakage in educational funding,"[105] distorts "smooth predictable and free flows [of trade],"[106] and can result in a "brain drain."[107] The most common weakness associated with corruption, however, is "impotence." This is either explicitly so, when analysts argue that "corruption thrives when public institutions have been rendered impotent,"[108] or slightly less so, as when they ask, with reference to the malady, "how far does a 'soft' or 'hollow' state exist,"[109] and to what extent, "if unchecked, [will] official corruption eventually result in a 'softness of state?'"[110]

The vocabulary of the consumptive, self-destructive object of disease is thus alive and well, placing the corrupt state into a realm redolent simultaneously of infection and sexual abnormality. The state is hollow, unproductive, and therefore sterile. It is soft. It drains and leaks, but is incapable of normal smooth flows. And although this sort of vocabulary continues ad infinitum, there is never any detailed causal relationship posited between corruption and its horrific results. Corruption thus represents and is symbolic of Disease broadly defined. Any specificity of symptom would undermine this representation. It is an arena in which modern political and social threats are understood, and a rhetorical context in which they are fought. Discussions of it therefore rely on "medical" detail only as much as this detail helps in conflating a sexual/biological vocabulary with a political vocabulary.

As evocative as the narrative of "corruption as disease" was, however, it could not exist without the support of the equally evocative trope of "corruption as a monstrosity." Indeed, it is not just variations on the theme of "fangs of lawlessness" biting "vulnerable sectors"[111] that reinforce the idea that corruption is something that monsters do and that produces monsters. Wide-ranging discussions of feeding, gluttony, savagery, deformity, and lack of control are scattered throughout the anticorruption literature. Corruption thereby becomes something frightening not just in its subversion of (imperial) order, but also in its sexually charged lack of humanity or purity. These discussions also, however, reassure. The monstrosity that is the corrupt state may be horrifying, but in its very deformity it is self-defeating, incapable of reproduction and doomed to an abnormal, sterile existence.

The idea that corruption produces grotesque parodies of appropriate political function or that despite the weakness, leakage, and impotence, there is a certain passionate gigantism associated with it appears in a number of contexts. One analyst notes, for example, that the "contempt [of corrupt officials] harbors within it the seeds of megalomania that, if allowed to flourish, eventually blossoms into grosser and grosser acts that may lead to monstrous crimes against humanity."[112] Corruption flourishes and blossoms, in other words, but it also becomes gross and monstrous. Left alone, the thing that seems normal will grow into a thing deformed, repulsive, and criminal.

Often, however, the monstrous nature of corruption is not even remotely related to anything human. As Githongo states, "even though one cannot sometimes tell from the outside," corrupt power structures have "tentacles in all economic, political and social sectors."[113] In this scenario, corruption hides itself from the "external" observer, but, like some nineteenth-century sea creature that we all know is "down there," it wraps its tentacles around the life force of the state. It is, in other words, either something human that has gone in a horribly wrong direction, or something animal that hides, "runs rampant,"[114] and then bites or strangles the unsuspecting.

The sexual connotations of these various invocations of the monstrous are relatively clear, but they become more so when the "insatiable appetite"[115] of the corrupt state, leader, or bureaucracy takes center stage. The same analyst who warned us, for example, of the megalomania and monstrous crime that result from a corrupt environment continues later on,

> this planet still contains many unpleasant features—cannibalism, slavery, abject misery and poverty, persecution, violence, crime and so on. It is the democratic spirit . . . that abhors such nasty features, that tries to work at ways and means of ridding humanity of them . . . [corruption] embodies the antidemocratic ethos.[116]

This is a very nice sentiment, and one with which few people would likely disagree. At the same time, however, if a random assortment of people were asked at the end of the twentieth century what exactly was wrong with the world, arguably very few would have come up with cannibalism. And yet it is with cannibalism that the list starts—cannibalism, that most inappropriate of inappropriate feeding habits,[117] *the* metaphor for deviant sexuality (homosexuality and incest especially) in the late nineteenth century,[118] that serves simultaneously as one of the most pervasive analogies to political corruption in the twentieth. It was not just that corruption consumes as a disease from within, in other words, it also consumes in a monstrous, cannibalistic way, "addicted" to eating without regard for similarity or for difference, for appropriate or inappropriate sympathy or lack thereof.[119]

Feeding, cannibalism especially, and distorted sexuality thus all come together in the narrative of the corrupt state, producing a distinct dichotomy between the eroticized "nasty features" described earlier and the "democratic spirit" that presumably prevents them.[120] It is corruption that comes to represent desire, inappropriate desire, and indeed diseased and monstrous desire. In this way, the corrupt state becomes both threatening and despicable. Again, however, it also reassures, and as one late nineteenth-century writer bemoaning the corrupt condition of American politics asked, "Shall we wait for some barbarian horde to discover and apply the more perfect form and prove its superior fitness over us by surviving while we pass away?"[121] The barbarian horde, the subhuman monsters may have been on the verge of proving their "superior fitness," even their humanity. But it was still implicitly within the power of the civilized world to correct its course. The *threat* of the monstrous was there, like the stripper's manifest lack of control, but it existed most emphatically to underline the *actuality* of civilizational superiority.

Anticorruption literature thus produces a rhetorical arena in which issues of (collective) sexuality and issues of (collective) politics can be brought together, and in which the threat and the draw of both can be performed. Confusing the individual with the collective, attributing collective meaning to individual deviance and individual motivations to collective bodies, the corruption narrative can tell us simultaneously, for example, first, that "the challenges facing corporate governance in Southeast Asia stem from the somewhat relaxed cultural, social, and political attitudes to stewardship, a concept that does not seem to have taken root in either the individual or national consciousness," and, second, that governments there "secretly" dip their "sticky fingers into the national pension fund."[122] Individual and national consciousness in this way become one and the same thing. The collectivity that is the government demonstrates with its "sticky fingers" a completely inappropriate personal desire, while personal attitudes are displaced onto a continent-wide collective.[123] The political and the sexual thus collapse into each other, becoming one in the threat that they pose, one in their dangerous collectivity, and one in their despicable individuality.

Conclusion

The pornographic show trial constructed around Marie Antoinette produced a French nation-state very much aware of its political, legal, and biological boundaries. It was a rational, democratic, law-based state in which the inherent disorder and the inherent eroticism of political collectivity and political violence could be displaced onto the corrupt body of the outlaw queen. It was within these boundaries, therefore, that the narratives of the healthy, functional collective and its unhealthy, dysfunctional counterpart developed. Likewise, it was simultaneously within and without—in the carnivalesque space of democratic spectacle, turned hyperbolic in the late nineteenth and the late twentieth centuries—that these narratives were performed. Indeed, liberal audiences expected pleasure from the spectacle, from their right and duty to know; they responded to aesthetic skill, and they demanded recognizable narrative tropes. As the corrupt state, corrupt leader, and disintegrating, lawless corrupt collective were created, analyzed, defined, and narrated, they thus took on the stylized repetitive force of the pornographic confession. The lawless, corrupt space was made equivalent to Marie Antoinette's body, and what happened there necessarily belonged to the world of flesh rather than to the world of law.

It was not, that is, just that the infantile sexuality associated with corrupt relationships helped to reinforce imperial notions of the child as savage and the savage as child. Infantile sexuality was erotic. It placed the savage into bed with the French queen and her violated son. And just as the late twentieth-century story of, say, the child-performer JonBenet Ramsey's precocious sexuality and snuff-film-like end kept U.S. audiences hooked for months, the policy community's appropriation of the vocabulary that surrounded it placed political corruption exactly where it belonged. Indeed, the idea of the twisted innocent who victimizes and is victimized became fundamental to the development world's evocation of the corrupt, undeveloped state as an autoerotic child or naïve victim/perpetrator.

Likewise, it was not just that the relationship between the exhibitionist deviant and the hidden interrogator, the interaction between the confessing corrupt state and the healing international community, supported existing imperial power structures. It was also that confession, exhibitionism, and exposure were erotic and produced an arena in which political corruption could be understood. The stripper, the putrefying body, and the corrupt state or leader all played recognizable and comforting roles in the same way that the burlesque show audience, the doctor, and the transparency advocate did. Audiences both participated and watched. There was a constant tension between power and subjugation, among the interrogator's coercive force, the confessant's manipulative response, and the relationship between the two. It was a relationship that brought people together—a relationship that was, in fact, democratic. The invocation of democracy as the thing that stops corruption was indeed directly linked to this same tension, linked to the problematic relationship between inappropriate sexual or biological collectives and appropriate legal and political ones.

Finally, the conflation of the incestuous black family with the incestuous, neo-patrimonial/self-regarding state was fundamental to the development of the corruption narrative. Sani Abacha and what he "did" to Nigeria was as much a part of defining appropriate and inappropriate political violence as the deformity, impotence, uncontrolled passion, and inappropriate appetite of the Somali warlords. Like infantile sexuality, exhibitionist tendencies, and racial deviance, both were simultaneously consumable and politically indispensable. As such, both also played obvious and central roles in the narratives of corruption that developed within and helped to define the boundaries of the noncorrupt liberal nation-state.

The corruption eruption of the 1990s and the century and a half of writing that preceded it were therefore not random phenomena. They were the result of intersecting trends in cultural production that had *already* posited intimacy—infantilized, racialized, or set in exotic locales—as the thing that was wrong with the modern world. In the same way that masturbation and incest, for example, were not about sex alone, corruption, with its public and its private, its passion and its regulation, its secrecy and the horrific way in which it manifested itself, was not just about politics. Each borrowed freely of the vocabulary of the others, and each created a rhetorical space in which political, biological, and sexual norms could reinforce one another. It was with this eroticized rhetoric that corruption was understood in the late nineteenth and late twentieth centuries. And it was with this sexual vocabulary that stories of corruption were told.

2

Celebrating the Corrupt Leader

Pop singers are not the only celebrities who make frequent appearances on Internet pornography sites. Another sought-after figure—with perhaps more of a cult following than that of those in the music industry—is the former president of Liberia, Samuel Doe. The September 1990 video of Doe's torture and death at the hands of "rebel leader" Prince Johnson has become a snuff film with global appeal—on sale two decades after its production not just in Liberia, but on international websites such as "SlutSnacks Free."[1] Interestingly, such websites are one of the only places from which one can access the video. Amazon.com does not carry it. Nor do most university libraries. Despite the fact that it went on "general sale in cities throughout West Africa," that "Johnson took pleasure in showing [it] to visitors to his headquarters," and that "extracts were even broadcast on British television news,"[2] the video is now pornography and nothing more. Doe, once a charismatic political leader, has been recast as an—arguably equally charismatic—porn star. What used to belong to the realm of political commentary has descended to the realm of the cheap thrill—celebrated but not openly so.

That in 1990 the video was shown "even" on British television deserves some further attention. Although Doe's torture was and is a subject of fascination for an international audience, it was immediately cast as the product of the uniquely "savage" Liberian context.[3] Whereas in Liberia, the video went on "general sale," British television showed only "extracts"—the whole presumably being too violent for sensitive audiences. Newspapers such as *The Guardian* likewise always mediated the narrative through the personal reactions of their reporters—this despite the suspicious frequency with which stories related to the torture were run. An article of October 1990 entitled "Liberian Rebels Replay the Last Hours of President Doe: Mark Huband in Monrovia Sees a Gruesome Video of the Former Leader's Torture and Death," for example, deliberately sets up a distance between *Guardian* readers as spectators and Liberians as spectators, in which the reporter watches both the video and its Liberian audience:

> "Do you want to see my film?" Prince Johnson asked. He was sitting at his desk in the glare of his camera crew's television lights. . . . [P]rince's wife said that she would fast forward the video so we did not have to watch the ordinary shots of rebel troops. The large colour television was wheeled across the verandah. Behind it the rain fell across the meadow. The band played on. We were given chairs in the front row. Somebody brought beer. Behind us, the young army gathered to watch, again, the torture of Samuel Doe. The man in the next seat kept talking. The screen burst into life. A group of children played in the meadow beyond the verandah. They yelled to their friends gathered behind us watching the film.

Huband casts himself as completely external in this scenario. He is playing the good guest to Johnson's host, not for his own pleasure, but to bring objective news to his readers. The "gruesomeness" of the situation is undoubtedly its "normality"—the bourgeois verandah, the beer, the children playing—which emphasizes the inhuman lack of empathy among the Liberian audience. Nonetheless, Huband has no qualms in recounting key aspects of the film to his readers—even as he continues to turn his attention to the reactions of the audience:

> Doe, his face bruised, flabby and naked except for his underpants, his hands tied behind his back, looked up from the television screen, from the floor of the room next to ours. The music inside grew more passionate. The film rolled on. Doe watches his death approaching as his captors yell orders at each other, and his underpants soak-up more blood from the gun-shot wounds received in his legs when he was captured three weeks ago. "I want to say something, if you will listen to me," he says, half-smiling, half sneering, totally terrified, watching the ritual of his own death as it is acted out in front of him. Prince sits at his desk. Behind him Christ is caught in the bright television lights. Prince's wife watched the film of her

wiping the rebel leader's brow: "Cut off his ears," Prince tells his men, his hands held in semi-prayer. He doesn't say it loud. The camera swings to the victim. The rebels stand on his body, lying him flat. A knife flashes in the bright lights. The camera gets close. The knife saws through the screaming President's ear and the ritual has begun. Doe shakes his head to prevent them cutting off the other one. But somebody grabs his head hard. The scream pierced the air. For a second the audience around the screen was silent, then they clapped. Beyond the meadow, on the creek, a small fishing boat sent ripples across the still water.[4]

Again, the primary and relatively obvious purpose of the journalistic distance here—despite the detailed discussion of the actual torture—is to absolve Huband and his readers of the guilt of enjoying the video. This is African violence. It is news, the public has the right to know, but it is also patently abnormal—the result of a Liberian political dysfunction that has nothing to do with Britain or with the self-described West writ large.

There is, however, a second, less obvious consequence of this *Guardian*-style reporting that I would like to explore in this chapter. Playing on common themes of celebrity narrative, Huband and his reportage are also instrumental in turning Doe into a "star." Using framing devices that, as Solomon-Godeau has noted, on the one hand distance and degrade, and on the other produce an uncomfortable, if titillating intimacy, Huband, I want to suggest, works *together* with Johnson to replace Doe's political persona with a pornographic one. It is as a result of both Johnson's story and the media representations of it that Doe ceased to be a leader and instead became a celebrity. And his celebrity indeed was such that the video became an object of consumer desire all over West Africa. *The Guardian*, *The Times*, and the various television stations that showed bits of the video were integral to this process. By turning what was once a single text—the video—into extracts, still photos, commentaries, mediated reportage, gossip, and editorials, the international press made Doe's torture a media event. They completed Johnson's work of constructing Doe as a star.

The rest of this chapter will play up the normality of Doe's transition from political leader to porn star. After first contextualizing my argument within an extended discussion of pornography and (legal) testimony, I will examine the ways in which the themes that I explored earlier in the literature review play out more specifically in narratives of the corrupt leader. I will in this way situate Doe's story within the broader corruption discourse and will suggest that that his role was mapped out from the beginning. Given the uniformity of these narratives, indeed, the repeated display of Doe's decaying dead body for both local and global audiences was not in any obvious way different from the repeated display of, say, Saddam Hussein's decaying live body, his dying body, and then his recently dead body for the same consumers. Both exhibitions were key stages in the construction and narration of the corrupt leader as corrupt body and corrupt body politic—of the corrupt leader as a being existing and operating in exceptional space. Samuel Doe, Saddam Hussein, and, in the late nineteenth century, the Ottoman Sultan Abdülhamid II, in other words, each represented corruption personified. The battle over narrative power that all of these leaders waged—and eventually lost— with media and human rights organizations was essentially a battle over whether each would be represented politically or biologically. And in the end, each was transformed from a leader into a celebrity or celebrated *homo sacer*—from the (legal/political) nation personified into a (bodily/biological) star.

Pornography and Testimony

My purpose in this chapter, therefore, is to address the ways in which the political identities of these corrupt leaders were gradually replaced with biological and then biopolitical identities—the ways, in other words, in which the corruption narrative has situated and then imprisoned corrupt leaders within exceptional space. I would like to focus in this introductory section, however, not just on exceptional space itself but also on its pornographic counterpart—not just, that is, on the purely political aspects of the corrupt leader's story, but also on its erotic aspects. Indeed, what I want to suggest is that the legal rhetoric surrounding the corrupt leader is such that pornographic space eventually replicates or displaces exceptional space as the narrative unfolds, leading to a situation in which pornographic testimony trumps legal or political testimony.

With that in mind, I will begin with Agamben's zone of indistinction. As I noted in the first chapter, one of the most obvious examples of this area, and an example that has been discussed in detail by a number of theorists, is the Nazi camp. The camp is a space, as Agamben argues, where "every fiction of a nexus between violence and law disappears and there is nothing but a zone of anomie, in which violence without any juridical form acts"[5]—a space in which every tiny, biological detail of an inmate's existence is regulated, registered, ordered, and takes on increasingly powerful (political) meaning.[6] A second and related characteristic of this space, implied but not developed earlier, is that it likewise produces a new form of testimony, confession, or witnessing—a form of witnessing in which the individual incapable of speech is also, counterintuitively, the individual most capable of testifying. As Catherine Mills has noted in analyzing this contradiction, Agamben's

> privileged figure of the new horizon of ethics is the *Muselmann* [i.e., the Muslim] of the Nazi concentration camps, who, he argues, put into question the very "humanity of the human" and thus the ethical material of testimony. In taking the *Muselmann* as the limit figure of the human and hence of ethics, Agamben argues that testimony arises on the disjuncture of the human and the inhuman—the speaking and the living being respectively. . . . [L]ocating the figure of the *Muselmann* at the zone of indistinction between the human and the inhuman, Agamben elaborates on [Primo] Levi's paradox that the *Muselmann*, the one who cannot speak, is the true witness of the camps.[7]

The exceptional space of the Nazi camp is thus a space in which two connected biopolitical processes occur: there is first the relentless, untiring regulation of bodily and biological function, and, second, the gradual construction of "witnesses" whose ability to testify is proportional only to their inability to speak.

I would like to suggest at the same time, however, that this space is not far removed from the spaces defined and carved out by pornographic narrative. To the extent, for example, that a common trope of pornographic narrative is, as Williams argues, the entrapment of the "real girl"—her sudden objectification as she becomes the focus of the camera[8]—and to the extent that the purpose of the real girl's inarticulate convulsions and cries is to provide "documentary evidence of involuntary pleasure in female bodies that do not give as ready evidence of this pleasure as male bodies,"[9] she is quite identical to the inhabitants of that other zone of anomie. In such films, the real girl leaves a space where something might happen, and enters a space where anything can and does happen. She moves from a realm of the rational and the articulate to a realm of the senseless and physically violent—from the arena of law and verbal testimony to a lawless space in which testimony is predicated precisely upon an inability to speak. Indeed, like the inarticulate witness or confessant in the camp, who is paradoxically the most capable of testifying or confessing, the real girl in pornographic space bears witness to this space only and especially to the extent that she does not or cannot speak.[10] In this way, therefore, pornographic space is identical to exceptional space. In both, every physical or biological movement is monitored, dissected, and invested with meaning. In both, violence without juridical form is simultaneously the norm and the exception. In both, testimony and confessions can happen only in the absence of speech—via spasms or convulsions of the body. In fact, the only obvious difference between the two is that the arena inhabited by the "real girl" is not actually "real," whereas the indistinct space of the legal exception, apparently, is.

What I would like to suggest over the following pages is that the corruption narrative—especially in its portrayal of the corrupt leader—bridges this gap between fiction and reality. The corrupt leader as simultaneously porn star and *homo sacer* realizes both the political potential of the pornographic narrative and the pornographic potential of the political one. As both subject and sovereign, body and body politic, reality and fantasy, he without question inspires the "the macabre and grotesque rite," discussed by Agamben, "in which an image was first treated as a living person and then solemnly burned," and "in which the political body of the king seemed to approximate—and even to become indistinguishable from—the body of *homo sacer*."[11] But he just as definitely inspires the euphoric aspects of the rite as it was originally described by Kantorowicz, where "the juxtaposition of the lugubrious and the triumphal, the mourning for the dead king and the exaltation of the effigy . . . responded to some very general and deep feeling in the late Middle Ages."[12]

Again, however, this general and deep feeling was clearly not unique to medieval Europe. As the corruption narrative writ large has been mobilized on behalf of the corrupt leader, it has been precisely these grotesque, "dark," macabre, exalted, and triumphal feelings that have come repeatedly to the fore. Indeed, as I will suggest over the following pages, "getting to know" the corrupt leader in essence has meant knowing him physically and biologically—investing his clothing, his psyche, and the nature of his crevices and orifices with political and charismatic meaning. Similarly, to the extent that the corrupt leader as precociously sexual child has been situated within the rhetoric of the "developing" state, he has gradually turned into a child star, positioned within the half-fictional, half-real realm of the exception. The monstrous nature of the corrupt leader—his sexual impurity, his unquenchable appetites, and the grotesque doubling and tripling of his body—has likewise been a trope that renders him both porn star and *homo sacer*. It is not just that the corrupt leader's body is almost comically sexual in its monstrosity; it is also that this monstrosity is a direct assault on the rule of law—something that by its very nature *must* exist in lawless space. Finally, as I will suggest in the last section of this chapter, these narratives of the corrupt leader all serve in turn to produce an emphatically biopolitical and pornographic testimony on his part—a confession in which there is a hyperbolic importance attached to "body language," physical convulsions, and a snuff-film-like end, but in which speech and verbal exchange code as inarticulate nonsense.

Getting to Know Abdul and Saddam

Abdülhamid II became the sultan of the Ottoman Empire in 1876 when his elder brother, Murad V, stepped down after three months of rule. Murad V had been declared insane and unfit for monarchical responsibility, but at the time of his removal and throughout Abdülhamid's reign, various theories appeared ascribing political rather than medical motivations for the change. Whatever the case, Abdülhamid's "progressive" bureaucrats were delighted at the new sultan's accession, and expected him to usher in a dawning period of Ottoman liberalism—optimistically promulgating a new Constitution as soon as he took power. Abdülhamid's bureaucrats were mistaken in their expectations. The sultan suspended the Constitution less than two years after it took effect, and over three decades of rule he turned the Ottoman Empire into a modern authoritarian state, far more concerned with responsibilities and security than with rights or liberty. In 1908, however, Abdülhamid himself was deposed by the Young Turks, who reinstated the Constitution and exiled the former sultan to Salonika, where he and his household remained until his death.

Abdülhamid II thus ruled the Ottoman Empire over precisely the fin-de-siècle period that saw a growing global fascination with political corruption. As a result, in addition to "Oriental despot"—a role that Abdülhamid would have played in the European and North American imagination in any case simply by virtue of being a political leader in Asia—the sultan also became the epitome of the corrupt modern leader. There is without question much discussion of harems, veils, poison, daggers, jewels, coffee, couches, carpets, and various feminized sexual predilections in media representations of Abdülhamid. But these discussions dovetail with an equally prominent narrative of Abdülhamid as corrupt leader. The institutions and events that signify the sultan's illegitimacy in these narratives—his spy network, the disappearance of political opponents, the massacres of minority populations—are depicted as the result of his being not only an Oriental leader but, almost more so, a corrupt one.

Abdülhamid thus came to embody both collective cultural difference *and* "prevailing notions of what it means to be an individual." He was both a civilizational signifier and a celebrated private individual. He was presented, that is, not just as an Oriental who could not represent himself,[13] but as a corrupt celebrity leader who overrepresented. As such,

Abdülhamid was understood to be on intimate personal terms with his audience—his emotional ups and downs, his fashion sensibilities, his reading preferences, his medical and grooming procedures, his general fleshiness, both physical and mental, all became tropes as common to his narrative as his imprisoned odalisques, his "refined and subtle" cruelty, and his fascination with "scientifically Chinese" torture.[14]

Saddam Hussein al-Majid became the president of Iraq in 1979, after having spent the previous decade climbing the ranks of the ruling Ba'th party. Both the original 1968 Ba'thist coup and Saddam Hussein's 1979 purge of political opponents led his detractors to label his rule patently illegitimate. Whatever the case, Saddam Hussein spent his two decades as president consolidating his political power and turning Iraq into a radically modern authoritarian state. In 1990, after a decade-long war with Iran, he ordered the invasion of Iraq's neighbor, Kuwait, and in 1991 the "international community," led by the United States, imposed sanctions on Saddam Hussein's government. Between 1991 and 2003, Saddam Hussein ruled Iraq under the constant surveillance of both military and media organizations, until eventually, in December 2003, he was captured by the U.S. military and removed from power. His death by hanging in 2006 was "accidentally" broadcast to millions of viewers in much the same way—and over much the same networks—as Samuel Doe's.

Saddam Hussein, in other words, ruled Iraq over precisely the fin-de-siècle period that witnessed the second "corruption eruption." In addition to representing a simple form of big-bad Third World gangster rule, therefore—with a healthy dose of Oriental despotism thrown in via the "belly dancers . . . shaking like bowls of crème brulée"[15] across his administration—Saddam Hussein, like Abdülhamid, also became the epitome of the corrupt political leader. Between 1991 and 2006 especially, the global media, politicians, academics, biographers, and native informants of vast and varied pedigrees all worked to turn Saddam Hussein into flesh—to make him into a celebrity and a star. He, too, was portrayed as an individual who simultaneously failed to represent and overrepresented himself. And he, too, became the intimate friend of the global population.

The intimacy that was the hallmark of the world's relationship with both Abdülhamid and Saddam Hussein took basic as well as more sophisticated forms. One of the most straightforward of these and one of the most effective means of bringing these leaders into the sitting rooms of an international audience was to endow them with "first" names. Like other stars, Abdülhamid II and Saddam Hussein al-Majid quickly came to be known simply as "Abdul" and "Saddam." In the space of a single month in 1909, for instance, the *New York Times* ran articles ranging from "Abdul Described as Abject," to "Abdul Reported Dead," to "Abdul Not to be Tried," to "Abdul Shed Tears as He Lost Throne."[16]

Saddam Hussein as "Saddam" has become notorious for its narrative power, producing such headlines as "Saddam Redux?" "Saddam Does Vegas," and, intriguingly, "If Saddam Were Only Brazilian."[17] Again, this is not a particularly sophisticated move—the brand recognition of the "first" name sells. It is worth emphasizing, however, that whereas most stars are in the business of selling their celebrity, Abdülhamid and Saddam Hussein were—ostensibly—not. They were political leaders. Their name recognition, such as it was, was intended to play up the notion of political collectivity and not personal intimacy. Newspaper headlines of this sort, however, forced them into the flesh—made them known in a far different way to the readers of the papers than the leaders themselves could have ever intended.

Indeed, it is worth pointing out that these headlines—whether they use just the "first" name or not—rarely read along the lines of "Abdul Institutes New Tax Plan," or "Saddam Appoints Cabinet Ministers." Instead, they highlight the presumed (and inarticulate) emotional or physical state of the leader—portraying him as an individual with feelings and reactions just like our own. Abdülhamid is abject, shedding tears, or, for that matter, dead. Saddam Hussein does Vegas. Similar headlines from the *New York Times*, the *London Daily Telegraph*, and the *London Times* tell us on a number of different occasions that Abdülhamid is "drinking heavily," "angry," "retaliating," "infatuated," "on his good behavior," "apprehensive," and "in a panic." He often "wants revenge," and yet, as one headline makes clear, this rarely works out well: "Appeals of Abdul Hamid: He Implores Lord Salisbury to Have Confidence in Him: Promises to Execute Reforms: Gives his Word of Honor."[18] Saddam Hussein likewise often shows "defiance" and makes "appeals." He "blasts Bush" and tries to bluff his way out of situations by "acting tough." But the results of Saddam Hussein's behavior and emotional state—both the rewards and the punishments—are also made clear with headlines such as "Cuddling Saddam," "Keeping Saddam Hussein in a Box," and "Slapping Saddam's Wrist."[19]

The purpose of these headlines, however, is not just to turn these corrupt leaders into individuals for us. It is not just to make us empathize or identify with their faulty private personalities. It is also, with the talk of tears, anger, infatuation, dominance, slapping, and cuddling, to humiliate them in the way that only celebrities—and especially porn stars—can be humiliated. Again, as Williams argues in her discussion of snuff films, one of the primary purposes of sadomasochistic pornography is to provide "documentary evidence of involuntary pleasure in female bodies that do not give as ready evidence of this pleasure as male bodies."[20]

As we will see, both Abdülhamid II and Saddam Hussein gradually came to tell their stories solely through body language of this sort. If they did try to articulate, to act the part of the leader, or to represent that essentially language-based form, "the law," they were emphatically *not* heard. Instead, audiences were prepared to react to Abdul and to Saddam as porn stars—having far more to say with their bodily excretions and their inarticulate cries than with any voluntary statement. Whereas the one weeps, the other acts tough, and both are constrained or constricted, be it "in a box" or "in a panic." It was therefore a (feminized) involuntary form of self-expression that these newspaper headlines were attributing to the two corrupt leaders. Abdülhamid may have been the "most talked about man in the world today,"[21] he may have appeared on the society pages as a "most conspicuous gentleman in Europe just now,"[22] but it was as a celebrity, and emphatically so, that he was talked about and made conspicuous. Saddam Hussein's face may have become recognizable to millions of people around the world, but, again, it was solely his face, the fleshiness of it, the way in which it was coded for consumption, that was recognizable. With neither leader was there ever any obvious political attribution to his identity, be this attribution a "good" one or even a "bad."

And all aspects of Abdülhamid's and Saddam Hussein's fleshiness, body language, and physicality were presented for this audience. Both their fashion sense and their physiognomy told us more about who they were and what they really meant than any political speeches they might make or laws that they might enact. As celebrities, their daily grooming habits and sartorial choices were dissected for popular entertainment—indeed, even when they outfitted themselves like "gentlemen," it was the minutiae of their clothing and grooming that drew attention. One very common theme in the literature, for example, is the extent to which both Abdülhamid and Saddam Hussein overdo their military uniforms. Unlike noncorrupt leaders, who wear a suit of some sort, corrupt leaders and their bureaucrats are colorful. Whereas Abdülhamid "dresses like an ordinary European gentleman, always wearing a frock coat," nonetheless "the breast of [this coat], on great occasions, is richly embroidered and blazing with decorations."[23] Saddam Hussein similarly can only give a political speech after "pinning several pounds of medals and hanging multiple sashes and honorary swords from the 'mother of battles' on his top lieutenants and political cronies."[24]

But if the colorful surface produced by their sartorial choices is interesting, the interior secrets and frailties that the corrupt leader's clothing hides are far more so. It is not *just*, for example, that Saddam Hussein was "a 66 year old bottled brunette,"[25] or that Abdülhamid sported "a short beard, now quite gray, and which he himself dyes very clumsily various shades of brown and brownish red with a mixture of coffee and gall nut, the recipe for which was given him by a sheikh."[26] It was that these attributes eventually replaced any political attributes that the leaders might have had. The gray hair, stooped shoulders, short stature, and bad skin[27] that would apparently be revealed when the dress was stripped away thus came to be of far more importance than the political horrors of corrupt rule that would apparently be revealed when the leader articulated his confession. With reference to the early Saddam Hussein, for example,

> his oiled black hair, brush mustache and rheumy-looking eyes had not yet earned the instant, global recognition they would after he sent his armies into Kuwait. . . . [W]ith his gold Rolex watch, French cuffs and entourage trailing behind him, he evoked nothing less than an expertly tailored, well-barbered gangster.[28]

And,

> though a virulent anti-communist, Saddam obviously grew to admire the Soviet leader for more than the thick Stalin-like moustache he sports. Stalin's totalitarian state has strong echoes in Iraq where Saddam has also adopted Stalin's cult of leadership and penchant for building monuments to himself.[29]

Saddam Hussein, that is, invaded Kuwait, engaged in "gangster rule," and adopted a totalitarian style of leadership—the straightforward activities of a corrupt, "rogue" leader. Upon invading Kuwait, however, what "gained global recognition" was not any obvious military or political exploit, but his hair style, mustache, and bloodshot eyes. His gangster rule was manifested not in street violence, but in his flashy watch and inappropriately tailored shirt. Likewise, although Saddam Hussein constructed Iraq's political structure in accordance with a totalitarian, "Stalinist" model, what he admired first and foremost about Stalin—and what is mentioned prior to anything else in this passage—is, it seems, his facial hair.

In the case of Abdülhamid as well, we see discussions of the sultan's fashion choices and grooming habits quickly replacing or informing analyses of his political ideology or his legislative activities. We see, in other words, the sultan moving inexorably from corrupt leader to celebrated star. One passage on "the imperial pockets" is particularly telling:

> we must not leave this subject without adding a word about the Imperial pockets. Abdul Hamid has many, all deep and queerly arranged according to his own directions to his tailor. . . . [with regard to the pockets of others] the discreet folds and mysteriously obscure slits, secret entrances to impenetrable hidden places, cause him visible uneasiness, and he would gladly forbid

his subjects their use dare he decree so tyrannical a law. However, if Turks are allowed to have pockets, it is a crime to put one's hand in them or unbutton one of one's garments in the presence of the Padishah.[30]

Again, the "discreet folds," "obscure slits," and "impenetrable hidden places" that make the sultan so uncomfortable are *coat pockets*. Obviously, however, there is more going on here than tailoring. And indeed the question of orifices, who has them, and who gets to inspect them is a running theme throughout the narrative of the corrupt leader as well as the narrative of his sartorial preferences. The leader's as well as his subjects' clothing, what it covers, what it reveals, and who may remove or open it become key components of analyses of corrupt political systems writ large and the leader's role in managing these systems more specifically.

Although the previous passage ostensibly focuses on Abdülhamid's desire to decree "tyrannical laws," for example, the political and the legal are immediately replaced in it by the personal, sexual, and psychological. If he could, Abdülhamid would maintain his own "queerly arranged" slits and folds, their placement known only to himself and to his tailor, while forbidding via *legislation* any sort of unplumbed interiority to his subjects. As it is, however, all he can do is regulate such openings, "criminalizing" the unauthorized searching of their depths within his presence.

By conflating the legal, the sexual, and the strangely sartorial in this way, this passage is setting itself up as narrative foreshadowing. It is a given that the corrupt system and leader will eventually be brought down, that the tyrannical laws will be replaced with rational and humane ones. But by tying together the leader's clothing and his legislation, his fashion sense or his grooming habits and his inappropriate political ideology, the hypothetical future moment is one at which not just the political and the legal situation, but also the personal, the sexual, and the sartorial will be reversed. Both Abdülhamid and Saddam Hussein will be subject not just to legal punishment, in other words, but to sexual and sartorial versions of the same. Indeed, just as in the porn narrative, Saddam Hussein's flashy, fleshy, well-tailored arrogance and the sultan's deep, secretive, and queerly arranged orifices are presented as provocations—and provocations especially to a rational, masculine authority. The "attitude" of both leaders is "tyrannical," and in need of disciplinary action broadly defined.

This question of intimacy eventually becoming interiority—the notion that the fleshiness of the corrupt leader can tell us more about him, bring him closer to us, and help us discipline him more effectively than his or our words or deeds—becomes far more overt in discussions of hygiene, health, and physiognomy. Physiognomy as a science that would reveal an individual's interior secrets was far more respectable in the late nineteenth century than in the late twentieth. This does not mean, however, that the vocabulary of physiognomy was not mobilized in celebrating Saddam Hussein almost as much as it was in celebrating Abdülhamid. Whereas Abdülhamid was compared unfavorably to his "disinherited brother," for example, "whose sympathetic physiognomy contrasts absolutely with that of the usurper,"[31] and whereas we can really get to know the aging sultan based on the fact that

> his jaws have grown broader, giving his face a brutality it did not have before; the cheek-bones, formerly unnoticeable, protrude prominently on hollow cheeks . . . his forehead bulges out slightly. . . . [H]is nose has become more hooked. A strange moustache . . . which his delicate and thin hand often caresses with a mechanical gesture, now conceals almost entirely the upper lip, which is thin and cruel. The lower lip has become still thicker and has accentuated his sensual expression,[32]

we can know Saddam Hussein equally well from the eyewitness accounts of reporters, who remind us that "that morning when he came in the palace for the interview that Richard Blystone and I did, every strand in his head was in place, manicured fingernails. And the one lasting physical impression I have of Saddam Hussein, this man has very, very soft hands."[33]

Again, it is not just that the repeated return to physicality brings us closer to these leaders, it is that the physicality can tell us things that their words cannot. With the nineteenth-century science of physiognomy, this is overt. In the late twentieth and early twenty-first century, however, it is almost more strongly implied. Bernard Shaw was conducting an interview— an exchange of words—with Saddam Hussein. But it is his "lasting physical impression" that he chooses to describe later on to Wolf Blitzer. It is Saddam Hussein's strangely soft hands that become the object of his reminiscence, not anything that Saddam Hussein may actually have said.

And indeed, the physicality of these corrupt leaders is what is repeatedly reinvoked as they are presented and represented for the global audience. Both of them are described as obsessively clean, often to the point of paranoia. Both of them expect similar cleanliness in their subjects and those who surround them—often insisting on "humiliating" searches of much more than coat pockets prior to granting audiences. Abdülhamid, for example, is described as

> naturally a very clean man, washing himself every five minutes —there are lavabos in every corner of his apartments—and

exceedingly particular, the Sultan pays the greatest attention to everything related to health and antiseptics, and follows the programs of bacteriology with passionate interest. One cannot imagine what ridiculous precautions his microbiophobia prompts him to take. . . . [A]ll the papers, reports and documents intended for his Majesty must first pass through a disinfecting stove.[34]

Saddam Hussein, meanwhile, "had a terrible fear, perhaps paranoia, about germs. . . . [e]ven the eyes, ears, and mouths of his closest aides were examined for signs of disease."[35] And, as Ahmad Chalabi noted to Charles Gibson in 2002, "people are forced to strip and their orifices are examined with surgical gloves, looking for all kinds of hidden weapons or, or poisons."[36]

In both scenarios, once again, we have a bringing together of, first, the physicality of the leader and, second, the leader's political office. It is not just that Abdülhamid cleans himself constantly, is passionate about bacteriology, and terrified of microbes. It is also that the official reports and documents that he reads—symbolic of his office—must be disinfected before he handles them. Likewise, it is not just that Saddam Hussein is "obsessed" with hygiene and disease. It is also that the orifices of his bureaucrats must be examined prior to any meeting with him. We have simultaneous references, that is, to the leader's flesh or skin—and, given that he is constantly washing it, his naked flesh or skin—and the legal/physical/sexual corruption or abuse that results from the simple existence of this flesh. Audiences may be fascinated with the flesh of the corrupt leader but, like that of the celebrity, this fascination is nothing compared to the self-obsession of the leader himself. The process of celebration is thus one in which, again, there can be no means of communication except the most intimate, in which reality of the corrupt leader's body means far more than the representation of his political identity.

This being the case, it makes a great deal of sense that the corrupt leader's doctors and dentists get invoked or interviewed nearly as frequently as disgruntled bureaucrats or political opponents on the run from the tyrannical regime. Informants who know the ins and outs of the decaying political system are certainly not discounted. But an informant who can tell us more about the ins and outs of the corrupt leader's celebrated body is a gold mine. At the same time, since it is the flesh rather than the words or the political deeds of the leader that can reveal his secrets, the relationship between him and his doctor or dentist is often the most complex and fraught.

Abdülhamid, for example, came to power only on the word of the doctors who declared his brother insane. As a result, his fear of, and gratitude toward, doctors as well as questions about the skill or even the authenticity of the doctors who surround him became of great public interest. Moreover, given that prior to the moment of confession, at least, it is only doctors who have access to the "slits" and "folds" of the corrupt leader's body, their translations and transmissions to the waiting audience are particularly valued. Their role, however, is also a dangerous one, as indicated by the experiences of Abdülhamid's dentist, who was a bit too energetic in plumbing the sultan's depths: "only a short time ago a dispatch stated that the Sultan, while having his teeth attended to, drew a revolver on the luckless dentist, who had happened to give him accidentally a little extra wrench."[37]

The relationship between Saddam Hussein's doctors, whom he "didn't like," and the leader, as well as what the doctors can tell us all about Saddam as Celebrity are more overt. In 2003, for example, *The New Yorker* ran an article entitled "Saddam's Ear: An Iraqi Doctor Had a Unique Role in Saddam Hussein's Life." The ear pun is relatively straightforward—the doctor is portrayed as a confessor to Saddam Hussein while also examining his body. Upon reading the article, however, the way in which Saddam Hussein's political identity is demolished by his physical identity, the extent to which his words are meaningless whereas his flesh is absolutely articulate, and the role of the doctor in reading this flesh "for us" become glaringly obvious. We learn from the doctor at one point, for instance, that

> on February 1, 1991, during the Gulf War, Saddam Hussein had some kind of accident, and I used to see him every other day. He never said precisely what had happened, but it looked to me like a car accident. He had a sharp, deep cut on the left side of his chin, right down to the bone, and the small finger of his right hand was almost hanging off.[38]

In this first scenario, Saddam Hussein refuses to speak, "he never said precisely what had happened," and it is the role of the doctor to read the signs left on the leader's body to find out what happened. But as a medical expert, he does not need the leader to articulate—he can tell the audience exactly what happened (a car accident), simply by noting the sharp deep cut and the nearly severed right-hand finger. A bit later, however, we learn that even if Saddam Hussein does speak, it makes no real difference:

> I remember as he was speaking I was looking at his ear. The sun was coming right through it, and it looked like wax. Because of this, I wasn't really listening to him, or concentrating

on what he was saying. But he was talking about being an Arab, about Islam, and he seemed to be trying to come up with a reason for their uprising against him.[39]

Here, it seems, Saddam Hussein is completely forthcoming. He is articulate, he is apparently trying to make a political or ideological point—"something about being an Arab, about Islam"—but the doctor sees no purpose in listening. He thinks *only* about the leader's body, and indeed we never learn what exactly Saddam Hussein's political point was. We learn only that the sun came through the leader's ear and that his ear looked like wax. In this construction, again, it emphatically does not matter what the corrupt leader might say—we know him, we understand him, and we appreciate him *only* via his flesh. The role of the doctor is indeed to tell us what is important and what is not in this context—to read the flesh for us while filtering out any babbling, any attempt at articulate speech that Saddam Hussein might produce in an attempt to draw our attention away from the meaningful.

It is not, however, just physical intimacy that these discussions invoke in turning corrupt leaders into stars. In the same way that the use of the "first" name brings us psychologically closer to them, and that the focus on fashion helps us to empathize with them in matters of taste, running discussions of Abdülhamid's and Saddam Hussein's (vulgar) literary preferences help us to identify with them emotionally as well. Even these discussions, however, follow a narrative taken straight from pornography or horror. Almost without fail, we learn, first, that the leader has a taste for violent, sexual, and implicitly or explicitly "working-class" literature. Second, we learn—more disturbing—that the leader himself often takes a hand at writing such literature, attempting to create his own narrative and to bring his subjects into his own twisted world. And then finally—disturbing, but also a relief—the leader gets taken in by his own trap. Again, like the "real girl" of the pornographic narrative, who signifies a slippage between reality (hard-core porn) and fiction (horror), the corrupt leader trapped in his own story produces a confused relationship between the reality and the representation of corrupt politics. As he becomes the fictional, often sexualized, object of his own narrative fantasies, he ceases to be a leader and becomes a media event. In the case of Abdülhamid, for example,

> before going to sleep he has his foster-brother, Ismet Bey, Grand Chief of the Wardrobe, read to him. . . . [T]he Sultan, from the beginning of his reign, has shown a marked preference for shop-girl literature. Books which deal with rape,

assassination, the abduction of children, substitution of wills, incendiarism, and deeds of violence excite his interest.[40]

On the one hand, that is, the sultan is feminized and infantilized—his preferences are those of a "shop-girl," and he must be read to sleep at night. On the other, however, his favorite stories involve political, sexual, and legal violence—strangely reminiscent of the violence attributed to his corrupt regime. And indeed, when rumors circulated that Abdülhamid was writing his own autobiography a year after this character sketch appeared, the great question was whether the "Sultan has the gift of self-revelation, which he has not hitherto permitted the world to suspect."[41] If he did, the book would likely be "wonderfully important," but according to the article "Abdul as Author," no one was holding his or her breath: "Perhaps it would be well not to build very strong hopes of literary entertainment on the announcement that the Sultan of Turkey is writing his memoirs to be published after his death."[42]

Again, the point to be made here is that there is a distinct slippage between the world of fantasy—be it the sultan's or the public's—and the world of political "reality." Abdülhamid is fascinated by violent literature, the violent literature mirrors his own regime, but when it comes out that he is attempting to create his own narrative of the regime, it is doubted that he "has the gift of self-revelation" or the ability to produce "literary entertainment." The fact that the two are synonymous—the former a product of the "real" and the latter a product of the "fictional"—indicates the extent to which the sultan had become the object of someone else's fantasy rather than the creator of his own.

In the case of Saddam Hussein, this transition is more obvious. Over and over again, his unstatesmanlike taste in books and films is held up for fascinated viewing. Oprah Winfrey tells her audience, for instance, that "Saddam is thought to love American movies. His favorite is *The Godfather*,"[43] while the *Daily Telegraph* noted a week later that he "watches Western films. *The Day of the Jackal* and *The Godfather* trilogy are said to be his favourites."[44] As with Abdülhamid, however, this taste in gangster films and westerns has a far more sinister meaning. As the *Observer* reported,

> His world view . . . is coloured by the films he watches and the novels he reads again and again: *The Day of the Jackal*, *The Conversation*, *Enemy of the State*—all books which paint the outside world in terms of conspiracy theories and violence. Or perhaps it is the other way around. These are books and films that simply confirm the peculiar world view

of a violent, clever and manipulative dictator who has cast his country in the model of his own notorious clan—as a gangster bureaucracy.[45]

First of all, the fact that he reads them "again and again" indicates a certain obsessiveness—that these books and films mean a great deal not just to us watching him, trying to read him, but to Saddam Hussein himself. More to the point, we see here the beginning of the overlap between fiction and reality—is it that his worldview is influenced by fiction or that fiction confirms his already twisted worldview? It does not really matter in the end—Saddam Hussein's "gangster bureaucracy" mirrors *both* the fiction and his "own notorious clan."[46]

Even while he is creating these part real, part fantasy political and legal narratives, however, he is also himself slipping into the traps that he has set. Whereas Abdülhamid had a taste for "shop-girl literature," for instance, Saddam Hussein actually produced it. But it is not just, as Oprah notes, that he has written "several romance novels." It is also that these novels somehow mirror—or become—Saddam Hussein's "real life," that he is trapped as an object in the fictional world that he created:

> he became a novelist and dictated books to his secretaries. One of them, *Zabibah and the King*, is about a beautiful village girl, married to an evil and brutal husband, who falls in love with her king. The latter is quite clearly Saddam himself. Saddam's name does not appear on the title page but it was obvious to Iraqis from the ecstatic way the book was reviewed that he had written it. Saddam's own home life was even more dramatic than his novels. In 1995 the world woke up to the extraordinary news that two of Saddam's nearest relatives and trusted supporters had fled to Jordan. Lt Gen. Hussein Kamel was married to Saddam's daughter Raghad and his brother to her sister-in-law Rina.[47]

In this case, again, the novel is, if not autobiographical, apparently an articulation of one of Saddam Hussein's fantasies. More than this, however, "Saddam's own home life was even more dramatic than his novels." When "the world" as audience "woke up" to the new plot twist, therefore, Saddam Hussein immediately took on the role of the pornographic "real girl."[48] He had thought that he was creating the narrative and that indeed he was outside of it. But the "reality" was that he was and always had been trapped within it—the object of the global audience's gaze. Editorialists like Thomas Friedman in fact made repeated use of this narrative trope when producing editorials of the "Saddam's Page Turner" and "Pulp Fiction" sort.[49] The point of these editorials may be the prosaic notion that fact is stranger than fiction. They rely, however, on the already confused relationship between Saddam Hussein as "real" political leader and Saddam Hussein as "fictional" celebrity—between the horrific and the pornographic. Like the celebrity, the corrupt leader exists on a narrow continuum between "reality" and "fantasy"—his own, our own, and "the world's."

The intimacy that these portrayals of Abdülhamid and Saddam Hussein create—intimacy between world audience and corrupt leader, between corrupt leader and corrupted subject, among corrupt and corrupting bureaucrats—is not simply a means of undermining their rule. Nor is it simply a means of selling newspapers, films, books, or interviews—the creation of celebrity for purely commercial purposes. By turning these leaders into celebrities and stars, by forging a relationship of flesh, fashion, taste, physiognomy, and fantasy between them and "us," these narratives are also making a statement about law, who gets to embody it, and what stories it may appropriately tell. In a noncorrupt state, ruled by a noncorrupt leader, the law, it is implied, is transparent, rational, articulate, (and masculine). The noncorrupt leader embodies the law precisely because we are not in an intimate relationship with him—because we know him only via what he tells us in speech and writing.

The corrupt leader's words, contrarily, are discounted in favor of the emphatically *not* transparent secrets that these other (feminine) texts—his body, his clothing, his health, his taste in literature—may reveal. His intimacy with us indeed renders him an entirely inappropriate conduit for law, while simultaneously reminding us of what law ought to be. The creation of this intimacy is in fact the first step in the telling of a larger story about the relationship among law, legitimate state power, and illegitimate state power. Again, these portrayals of both Abdülhamid and Saddam Hussein explicitly set the groundwork for an eventual climax in which the two illegitimate leaders will be stripped of their power sartorially and physically as well as politically and legally. These portrayals require a "money shot" of the sort described by Williams, a point at which their body language will provide the confession that their failed attempts at speech and lawmaking managed to obscure.

Developing State, Developing Star

The recurring references to infantile sexuality that appear in the corruption discourse writ large become far more blatant when the focus moves to the corrupt leaders themselves. The child/savage–savage/child theme, the simultaneously attractive and repellent nature of children's sexuality, and indeed the extent to which the corrupt leader can be known via recourse to his prepubescent antics and attitudes are all key elements of the larger narrative. In the case of Abdülhamid and Saddam Hussein, for example, we see constant references back to their—usually disturbed—childhoods as a means not only of explaining, but of situating, their present violent behavior. It is not just that a spate of difficult early years made them what they are today. It is that these early years are still being lived: both leaders are simultaneously naïve and capricious, innocent and destructive in ways that only a child can be. Both of them are likewise simultaneously victims and perpetrators of the difficulties in which they find themselves. The reaction elicited from the watching audience is thus not horror—unless it is the horror associated with the behavior of "unnatural" children—so much as it is exasperation and a sense of colonial/parental irritation.

In stories of both leaders' disturbed childhoods, for instance, there is a constant tension between their future power and their future humiliation. Both lived out not just their years of tyrannical rule, but also their eventual fall in repeated childhood episodes. Likewise, both combined the "savage cunning" of the uncivilized child with an inability to perform the most basic functions of the budding civilized adult. In the case of Abdülhamid, for example,

> the youthful misanthrope avoided his brothers' society and took no part in their games. Most of the time standing alone in some dark corner, he would watch them laugh and play with a fixed stare and with an expression in his eyes of infinite sadness except when fear or malice lit them up with a fugitive flame.... [S]tudious and diligent as was his elder brother Mourad, so Abdul Hamid displayed little aptitude for books.[50]

In this scenario, there is no question that Abdülhamid has power of a sort, coded in his "standing alone," in his refusal to take part in the games of the other children. At the same time, however, the eyes with which he watched these games—the body language that tells so much more than any articulate speech—expressed sadness and even fear. Moreover, his inept approach to books, his inability to replace his natural inclination toward solitude with adult skills and education, underlined the extent to which this "standing alone" resulted from a humiliating inferiority rather than any genuine superiority. Indeed, the passage continues, "as is well known, he is today practically uneducated and ignorant even of his own tongue; and although he has tried several times to improve it, he has never been able to restrain the excessive independence of his orthography."[51] It is not just that as a child Abdülhamid suffered difficulties playing or learning to read and write, in other words. He is still wrestling with these problems—the "excessive independence of his orthography," understandable and even quaint in a child, continues, abnormally, to plague him as an adult and a leader.

Whereas Abdülhamid spent his childhood in a royal family at the cosmopolitan center of an empire, Saddam Hussein grew up impoverished in a rural village. Despite these differences in chronology, culture, and class, however, the defining and telling characteristics of Saddam Hussein's childhood are nonetheless almost identical to those of Abdülhamid's. He, too, was abnormal, suffering excessive humiliations, and manifesting an inappropriate desire for power. He, too, had a certain native cunning that was nonetheless overridden by his lack of a civilized education. One particularly graphic account plays up these themes in an almost painful manner:

> illegitimate, whipped, sexually abused and ridiculed for his illiteracy, the young Saddam possessed a pathological hatred of those around him. In his teens he committed his first murder and discovered the brutal truth: power's won through blood and fear. . . . [I]nstead of being sent to school, the boy was made to tend the sheep and do menial tasks around the house. At night he was sent out to steal from nearby farms. . . . [B]y now, at the age of about 14, Saddam needed, in the modern argot, "respect." A "son of the alleys" who didn't even know how to spell his name, he would have had to sit in classes with five year olds and was ridiculed by pupils his own age for his poverty and backwardness.[52]

The constant fluctuation in this passage between power and humiliation, between savage aggression and innocent victimization is obvious. On the one hand, Saddam Hussein learns early the "brutal truth" about power—and he makes use of this truth. On the other, he is humiliated and abused—sexually, physically, and psychologically. On the one hand, he wants respect and makes an effort of will to overcome his "backwardness." On the other, despite this effort, he is infantilized even at age fourteen—put into a class with five year olds—and still unable to read and write. Like the childhood of Abdülhamid, the childhood of Saddam Hussein not only set the foun-dation for his future role in the narrative of the corrupt leader, but was also collapsed into this narrative. Both leaders were simultaneously children and adults, exhibiting infant versions of their future telling physical and mental characteristics, but also failing in the end to put this infant stage behind them.

Indeed, the trope of infantile sexuality that runs throughout the corruption narrative in general is a key component to descriptions of the two leaders in their adulthood. Both are displayed as attractive in their innocence, naiveté, and savagery, but both are also disturbing in this regard. Both are cast as children in need of discipline from a colonial parent, but children whose lack of *self*-discipline, whose inability to curb their irrational desire leads one to wonder whether straightforward (and spectacular) punishment might be more effective. Finally, both exhibit a childlike capacity for revelation and deception, for openness and duplicity.

An 1895 article ostensibly about Abdülhamid's diplomatic correspondence with the British foreign minister, for example, chooses to focus not on the contents of the exchange, but on the strangely innocent mindset that apparently prompted the sultan to initiate it: "there is a naiveté about the Sultan's letter to Lord Salisbury asking him to make a speech, and this time in defense of him, that is at the same time pathetic, amusing and exasperating."[53] Abdülhamid is in no way threatening in this passage. He is indeed naïve, pathetic in his inability to understand the role that Lord Salisbury plays in the organization of world affairs, but unlikely to benefit at this stage from any education in that regard. Again, it ought to be emphasized here that the event being described is an exchange between a political leader and a foreign minister. It is presented, however, as a dialogue between a charming, but petulant, child on the one hand, and a patient, if frustrated, parental figure on the other.

Although the violence of Abdülhamid's regime, his despotism, and the suffering that his rule inflicted upon the Ottoman population are the usual features of writing about the sultan, in other words, his capricious innocence and amusingly bewildered and bewildering behavior are nonetheless strong—and often privileged—subthemes. But it is not just that his "vanity" gets "flattered" in political correspondence,[54] that he possesses an "overweening infatuation" for this or that political ideology, or that the advances of members of the diplomatic community can "turn his head" like that of a confused young girl.[55] Abdülhamid in a very basic way is girlish whether he is enacting violent legislation or reposing in his domestic sphere. Even articles that set out to portray a "positive" image of the sultan rely on these tropes. One writer, for instance, writes with some hyperbole:

> bashfulness not less instinctive than the gazelle's, simplicity so credulous as to be virginal and that inexpressible delicacy of soul from which all comprehension of the unrefined seems eternally excluded, cloth the personality of the Turkish Sultan. . . . [F]or flowers the Sultan has a passion in which he is swallowed up, swept away, lost . . . but he is the easiest Sultan to shock. . . . [T]here is in Abdul Hamid," writes Mr. Mijatovich, "a peculiar modesty, timidity and tenderness which are quite womanly. . . ." [T]hus does Mr. Mijatovich pull asunder the rose of his sub-

ject, petal by petal, and ever it exhales the same entrancing essence. . . . [I]t is when some pet parrot has perched upon his forefinger while he toys with the ear of a fawn that the infantine spontaneity of the Sultan's predisposition to love overcomes the natural melancholy of his temperament.[56]

There is nothing obvious to indicate that this passage is intended ironically. Whether or not it *is* to be taken at face value, however, the point to be made is that the same themes that run throughout the "political" reportage on Abdülhamid run throughout the more overtly biographical or hagiographical pieces as well. The sultan is delicate, simple, virginal, and "infantine." In the same way that he succumbs to overweening infatuation for new ideologies, he is swept away and swallowed up in his love of flowers. Just as he is girlish in his vanity, so, too, is he womanly in his modesty, timidity, and tenderness. Again, identical points are made in this piece as were made in those earlier. Whereas previously, however, Abdülhamid's infantile behavior is "exasperating," here it inspires both "tenderness" and the desire to "pull asunder the rose of [the] subject, petal by petal." The childlike nature of the sultan, that is, extends even to a child's openness—with nothing to fear from revealing all.

The majority of writing about Abdülhamid was not quite so enamored of him. But even those who explicitly set out to demonize the sultan occasionally played with the trope of innocent, as opposed to malicious depravity. As one biographer notes in describing the Sultan's inappropriate use of state funds, for example, "Abdul Hamid has the building fever, an innocent mania among Orientals, who believe that the more a man builds the longer he will live."[57] A second is more blunt:

> our friend-guide tells us curious tales in a lowered voice of the terrors of the self imprisoned monarch, himself a terror (as all autocratic sovereigns must be) to all around him, who yet finds childish pleasure in constructing kiosk after kiosk, and entering into the smallest details about doors and windows like a self-enriched Cockney who builds himself a little "'ouse upon the Thames.'"[58]

In the first passage, Abdülhamid is quite definitely causing damage with his behavior, but we can almost forgive him his destructive tendencies given the innocence of his desires and the culturally specific Oriental nature of their manifestation. In the second, the childish nature of the sultan (and, for that matter, the working-class Cockney made good) becomes explicit—set up in direct contradistinction to the terrors undergone by both Abdülhamid himself and his subjects. The nightmarish quality of the sultan's rule is undoubtedly horrific, but it is tempered, made attractive, indeed eroticized by the depraved yet innocently infantile mentality that apparently produced it.

One hundred years later, we can almost, but not quite, forgive Saddam Hussein the same sort of inclinations. The Iraqi president's "building mania"—again, different, more sinister, but also somehow more naïve than any European or North American interest in residential construction—is a recurring theme in discussions of his corrupt rule. Like Abdülhamid, however, Saddam Hussein was almost charming in his love of his new houses and mansions. He is, for example, described in one piece as possessing "two dozen palaces, between which he flits daily to avoid risk of detection";[59] almost as evocative of childhood shenanigans is the president's "latest efforts to wriggle out of arms-control inspections," described in a second article.[60] "Flitting" and "wriggling" are not activities one ordinarily associates with proponents of the "gangster rule" that is late twentieth-century Iraqi governance in most analyses. Such portrayals of Saddam Hussein, however—a leader without question destructive, but somehow also exasperating and amusing—are too common to be ignored.

Indeed, a final passage, ostensibly describing Iraq's 1991 invasion of Kuwait, collapses Saddam Hussein's childhood desire and adult irrationality into an almost seamless formulation:

> this was the first of Saddam's monumental follies. The peasant boy who had sat at his uncle's knee and heard the stories of Nebuchadnezzar, who captured Jerusalem, and Saladin, who defeated the Crusaders, sought to become an incarnation of these immortal heroes of the Arab world.... Under pressure from Saudi Arabia in July, Kuwait agreed [to Iraq's demands]. Saddam invaded anyway. On Aug 2, 1990, the Iraqi army rolled south and Field Marshal Saddam blithely declared the emirate his 19th province. He convinced himself that he had stunned the world with an irreversible coup.[61]

Not just one who flits and wriggles, Saddam Hussein is here also blithe and prone to folly. More to the point, however, his apparent motivation for the invasion of Kuwait had nothing to do with economics or politics. It had, instead, to do with memories of stories that he, infantilized once more, had heard as a child/peasant (if not a child/Cockney) "at his uncle's knee." Likewise, unable or unwilling to understand the dictates of diplomatic exchange, Saddam Hussein ignored Kuwait's efforts to negotiate and simply did what he wanted "anyway." Like Abdülhamid and his exasperating attempts at correspondence with Lord Salisbury, his girlish love of flowers and German "attentions," and his childlike mania for building

Celebrating the Corrupt Leader 61

houses, Saddam Hussein, too, is known not just for his diplomatic, economic, military, or political policies, but the silly, capricious, and maddening style in which he enacts these policies. With their capers and their antics, both leaders attract a distinctly colonial, if also desiring, gaze. They undoubtedly get what they deserve, but their punishment, and the spectacle of such punishment, involves the same forbearance and irony that the punishment of children—and its spectacularization in nineteenth-century fairy stories and twentieth-century sit-coms—inevitably sparks.

The two leaders do, though, quite definitely get what they deserve. While they are undoubtedly innocent and even attractive in their depravity, they are also a threat—perpetrators of the very behavior by which they are themselves victimized. Portrayals of Abdülhamid and Saddam Hussein repeatedly play up the simultaneously threatened and threatening aspects of their personality and, given the genre, by extension their rule. In the case of Abdülhamid, this usually appears as a commentary on the sultan's corrupt and lawless personality/state and then an exegesis on his constricted, terrified personal existence. In one passage, for example, we learn that "His Majesty the Sultan of the Ottoman Empire is a most high and puissant monarch. His will is law, and his nod is death. . . . [B]ut social power he has none. His life is passed in an endless round of official drudgery, nay, positive servitude,"[62] whereas in a second, "his judgments, wishes and desires are controlled by bonds that he cannot loosen, much less rend asunder; and . . . he is surrounded by conditions that render him powerless to obey with alacrity the behests of Europe."[63] Abdülhamid is, in other words, a good child, in that he seemingly *wants* to obey the behests of Europe. But he is powerless, controlled, in bondage, and in servitude—he is victimized by the very "will" that he embodies. It is in fact difficult in these passages to discern where "law" ends and "raw power" begins. What we do understand, however, is that the corrupt situation that the sultan oversees forces him into the victim/victimizer role—he is childlike in his capricious will but also childlike in his inability to maintain even a most basic social power.[64]

Saddam Hussein was similarly trapped, himself victimized by the abuses he inflicted on his population. Although it is a given, for instance, that "for much of his 65 years, Saddam has been beyond the ability of anyone to deal with,"[65] that his recalcitrance led the watching world in effect to throw up its collective parental hands, one can almost read this behavior as a cry for help. "Once he was established in power," for example,

> Saddam's overwhelming vanity and constant sense of insecurity ran wild. Iraq was plastered with pictures of the dictator, even on Iraqi watch dials. A 19-volume official biography became mandatory reading for government officials and Saddam commissioned a six-hour film about his life called The Long

Days. . . . [B]ut in the end Saddam's diplomatic dancing, displays of defiance and macho rhetoric accomplished little.[66]

Although there is a distinct sense of disapproval in the presentation of this behavior, it is nonetheless predicated, first of all, on Saddam Hussein's "constant sense of insecurity," and not on any more sinister, conscious program. The president's attempts to create political and aesthetic structures in support of his style of rule, as well as his diplomatic policy (or "diplomatic dancing") are instead portrayed here as nothing more than the overcompensation of a troubled child. His "will," like that of Abdülhamid's is not his own—it is in bondage to his unconscious fear, vanity, and insecurity. Indeed, all of his frenzied attempts at control lead in the end to nothing, they "accomplish little," and like a child Saddam Hussein is left still pained, still powerless, and still under the concerned watch of the parental world.

The infantilization of the corrupt Sultan Abdülhamid and the corrupt dictator Saddam Hussein fits cleanly into the larger corruption narrative of the late nineteenth and late twentieth centuries. In these portrayals, both leaders attracted a straightforward colonial gaze, aiding in the conflation of working-class, peasant, nonwhite, and childlike misbehavior. Both also attracted a commercial gaze, playing up the fascinating deviance, innocence, bewilderment, and savagery of the celebrated and sexualized child of fairy tales, sit-coms, and child pornography. The implied punishment of their naïve, amusing, but nonetheless exasperating infantile behavior was the parental punishment that plays such a key role in all three genres.

At the same time, however, like the sharpened focus on intimate aspects of the corrupt leader's life and body, the sharpened focus on the corrupt leader's infantile nature also tells a morality tale about the role of law in corrupt and noncorrupt states. The corrupt leader's "will is law." But his will is also not his own, is coerced, is in bondage, is servile, and is irrational. And law as a rational, self-contained, active, positive force is obviously inconceivable when its embodiment can control neither his own impulses nor the environment which he created. Indeed, the logic of the narrative of the corrupt leader is inescapable: the state is corrupt because the will of the ruler is law. The state is also corrupt because the ruler is a child with no conscious control over his will/law. The child/ruler must therefore be punished both for his tyrannical control over the functioning of the state and for his inability to make even the most trivial decisions regarding this same functioning.

Body Doubles and Doubled Bodies

In an important passage in *Homo Sacer*, Agamben discusses the relationship between the wolf-man or werewolf and structures of biopolitical power.

"What had to remain in the collective unconscious as a monstrous hybrid of human and animal, divided between forest and city" he argues, is

> in its origin the figure of the man who has been banned from the city. That such a man is defined as wolf-man and not simply as wolf . . . is decisive here. The life of the bandit, like that of the sacred man, is not a piece of animal nature without any relation to law and the city. It is, rather, a threshold of indistinction and of passage between animal and man, *physis* and *nomos*, exclusion and inclusion: the life of the bandit is the life of the *loup garou*, the werewolf, who is precisely *neither man nor beast*, and who dwells paradoxically within both while belonging to neither. [italics in original][67]

The monstrous, in other words, defines for us not only what belongs to the realm of law and what belongs outside of it (if nonetheless still included). It is also manifested physically in the figure of the dehumanized man and the humanized beast. When the corrupt leader is celebrated as a monster, therefore, a specific legal meaning is attached to this celebration. When Abdülhamid, for example, is described as "on his way to the mosque, with the inscrutable look, partly that of a hunted animal, partly that of mere *ennui*, in his half closed, coal-black eyes,"[68] when Saddam Hussein is described as a "boy monster," the result is a distinct affirmation of the included/excluded "sacred man." At the same time, the corrupt leader, *as* a being existing on the "threshold of indistinction," also emphasizes the inadequacy of law in determining what is (and ought to be) inside of the body politic and what must be expelled. The repeated recourse to themes of miscegenation, incest, animal ferocity, insanity, disease, and contagion thus turns the corrupt leader into a symbol of both contamination (the outside seeping in) and purification (the inside expelled out).

Discussions of Abdülhamid and Saddam Hussein, for example, often begin with stories of their illegitimate, incestuous, or "mixed" parentage. Such biographical accounts usually cite first what is conventionally believed, and then go on to expose the "secret" of these leaders' "real" background. In the process, conventional wisdom is by no means discounted. Instead, additional parents are added to whichever two are commonly thought to have spawned the monster, and each leader is left with the blood of multiple, equally horrific types flowing in his veins. The immediate result of this move is of course to turn personal illegitimacy into a metaphor for political illegitimacy—something certainly not new in (for the most part liberal) attacks on (for the most part "undemocratic") leaders. The incestuous background of the sovereign leads inexorably to the incestuous relationship that this same sovereign eventually tries to force onto an unwilling nation. The extent to which this mixing of blood occurs in the case of the corrupt leader, however, the extent to which it leads to bestial behavior, cannibalism, or ferocity, and finally the extent to which it is set up against the rationality of legal text is, I think, relatively unique. The message in nearly all of these discussions—sometimes implicit, but often explicit—is that corruption is inside and biologically dangerous, that the only way to expel it *and* contain it is via the purifying force of the law.

The relationship between Abdülhamid's confused parentage and his violent, corrupt rule is something that recurs repeatedly in biographies of the leader and accounts of his political decisions. The sultan's policies against eastern Anatolian Armenian populations, for example, have nothing to do with politics or ideology per se in these accounts. Rather, they are the horrific result of Abdülhamid's blood outing itself, a political manifestation of the sultan's monstrous mixture of Armenian and Turk, aristocrat and peasant.[69] The inappropriate intimacy, the confusion of inside and outside, the fear that accompanies incest and miscegenation are inextricably linked to Abdülhamid's policies—given his biology, the sultan could not help but attack good order and appropriate legal hierarchies. As George Dorys, Abdülhamid's self-appointed unauthorized biographer, notes,

> several stories are current regarding the paternity of Abdul Hamid. According to some his father was an *aïvaz* (the Kurdo-Armenian type of Abdul-Hamid has given some color to this story) or Armenian cook in the palace of Abdul-Medjid; according to others, the present sovereign is the son of Garabet-Effendi-Balian, brother of the late Serkis Bey. . . . [T]hese stories are doubtless apocryphal; if there is really Armenian blood in Abdul-Hamid's veins, it comes from his mother's side.[70]

Abdülhamid, in other words, is—even if only apocryphally—Turkish, Kurdish, as well as Armenian; he is the son of a cook and an adulterous bureaucrat as well as the son of a former sultan. The fact that Abdülhamid's mother could conceivably have copulated with all of these various types implies that his parentage is in actuality completely up for grabs—racially muddled as well as diseased[71] by virtue of his heredity and blood. In a basic, biological way, therefore, Abdülhamid is contaminated—both he and his government exist in a space on the threshold between the realm of law and the realm of blood.

Indeed, as time passes, the exposure and exhibition of Abdülhamid's biological monstrosity and impurity, his resituation within indistinct space, become necessary adjuncts to larger lessons about the nature of his corrupt rule. As a *New York Times* article from June 1909 on a "condition surpassing fiction" notes,

> to understand what a sensational affair [the removal of Abdülhamid from power] has been, we must bear in mind the fact that for thirty three years Abdul Hamid has been a veritable ogre, living on the flesh and blood of the Ottomans. Into his horrid den at Yildiz he has decoyed the best of the Osmanli and devoured them. . . . [N]ow that this hoary monster has fallen, his lair, littered with evidences of a thousand crimes, undermined by secret passages and provided with all the mysterious chambers, labyrinths, trapdoors, etc. which we should expect in the house of a man who has all his life employed a whole staff of translators to render into Turkish all of the low class, sensational novels of intrigue and crime that are written in Europe.[72]

The parallelism between the "sensational affair" that is Abdülhamid's rule and the "sensational novels" that Abdülhamid likes to read first places the sultan into the half-real, half-fictional space that likewise surrounds Saddam Hussein. Abdülhamid is an ogre, a cannibal, and a monster, while—given his apparent ability to act as a decoy—also something of a siren. It is above all his inappropriate feeding habits—the displaced and disfigured sexuality associated with consuming the flesh and blood of both citizen and human being—that code as politically reprehensible. Moreover, just as Abdülhamid's clothing contained weird crevices and strangely placed orifices, his "lair" also contains mysterious chambers and labyrinths, inviting exploration and exposure. In the end, however, what is at stake is an issue of corruption and class. The sultan employs his translators inappropriately, and the reason that this employment is inappropriate is that their focus is not on law, politics, or diplomacy, but on "low class" and "fictional" intrigue.

Indeed, Abdülhamid's inappropriate (sexual, physical, and biological) relationships with his translators and his citizens are rivaled only by his violently inappropriate interactions with liberal concepts in the abstract. In addition to "stifling budding liberalism," for instance, he

> cut the throat of independence in the cradle, seized power by intrigue, kept it by force and cunning and concentrated it by violence. He has paralyzed patriotism, gagged truth, and put in chains independence of thought and conscience; he has massacred entire populations of his Empire, parts of which he has also traded over to the foreigner.[73]

This mutant, mixed-race, diseased child of unknown parents, in other words, is congenitally unable to allow the noble purity of infant liberalism and infant independence to survive. And so he strangled one and cut the throat of the other. This (sexually) deviant cannibal with his fixation on pockets and crevices could not engage normally with feminized "power," "patriotism," "truth," "thought," and "conscience." Therefore, he inflicted his sadomasochistic fantasies on them, seizing and intriguing one, paralyzing another, gagging a third, and chaining up the last two.

Abdülhamid's political corruption here, his inability to function according to reason or law, is thus tied inextricably to his sexual and biological impurity. His relationship to his citizenry involves an intimacy gone out of control—and an intimacy that is and always has been maintained in his contaminated and diseased blood. It is in fact worth pointing out that the final two examples of corrupt behavior in this passage are quite concrete, and a distinct departure from the abstracts with which it begins. In addition to his disturbing relationship with liberalism personified, Abdülhamid has also denied the right to life to portions of his population and has lost Ottoman land to colonizing states. But these policies cannot exist in their own rhetorical space. Rather, it is Abdülhamid's personal and biological placement in "sensational" space, his existence as half-man, half-animal, that makes these concrete examples meaningful.

In their uniform, stylized presentations, these flashpoints also make the narrative of the corrupt leader *mobile*—applicable to any and all circumstances, and thus doubly meaningful when they are applied, for example, in the late twentieth century to Saddam Hussein's corrupt rule. Indeed, rarely an interview or an article on the Iraqi leader was written in the 1990s and into the 2000s without some mention of his incestuous/miscegenated background, his contaminated/contaminating nature, his existence both inside and outside of law and politics, and the consequently inevitable violence of his policy. Like Abdülhamid's, Saddam Hussein's birth, stories of it, and what it means in terms of both blood and politics are a running theme in articles and biographies. In one account, for example, we are told that

> the most common story holds that Saddam's father was killed by bandits or by bargemen defending their goods from raiders. Another report suggests that he was murdered by relatives of Saddam's mother for getting her pregnant outside marriage, and that she was so distraught at the prospect of being a single mother that she tried to throw herself under a bus, shrieking: "I am giving birth to the devil!" Whatever the truth, Saddam grew up without a natural father, and since his mother could not afford to clothe and feed him, he was sent to

live with her brother, Khairallah Tulfah, who lived in the provincial town of Tikrit. . . . [T]here are rumors that Saddam was caught and spent time at a juvenile detention centre, and others that his stepfather subjected him to sexual abuse—a not uncommon occurrence in these primitive conditions.[74]

In a much more overt way than in the nineteenth-century accounts, that is, the monstrosity of being a child without a "natural" father ("I am giving birth to the devil!") is played up in this twentieth-century discussion of the corrupt leader. Likewise, the supposed contradiction between law and liberalism on the one hand and arbitrary violence on the other—invoked by the parallelism of juvenile detention centers and incestuous abuse—emphasizes Saddam Hussein's existence in exceptional space almost more clearly than similar narrative structures in stories of Abdülhamid. The reason that incest and unnatural birth *can* happen here is that the environment is exceptional—"primitive," outside of the bounds of modern liberalism, and populated by bandits,[75] raiders, and murderous relatives.

Likewise, the sexual purity of Saddam Hussein's mother is questioned far more explicitly in this passage than that of Abdülhamid's mother. As a result, both the insidious mixture of the Iraqi leader's blood and his apparently pathological need to purify himself or his state, to expose and to hide, becomes much more overt. As a second reporter notes in a discussion of Saddam Hussein's military policy, "the only known employment of his mother, Subha Tulfah, was as a clairvoyant. Some Iraqi men would later suggest she also was a prostitute. . . . [S]uch are the ways of a dictator—one with a peasant's blood and a survivor's soul."[76] Military and political policy here are tied back first to Saddam Hussein's confused paternity—his mother was a prostitute (and/or dabbled in the occult), producing "unnatural" offspring—and second to his "peasant's blood," which, as we learned earlier, was almost certainly incestuous.

It was not just Saddam Hussein's birth that produced a confused overlap between what should be inside and what should be exposed or expelled, however. His family life and his equally monstrous offspring—often explicitly referred to as "spawn"—are also portrayed as "manifestations" of his corrupt nature and state. We are repeatedly told, for example, that Saddam Hussein married his first cousin, a situation that is meant to explain his style of rule.[77] Indeed, Saddam Hussein's two sons, Uday and Qusay, receive nearly as much attention as the leader himself, almost always as living morality tales about the simultaneously contaminating and purifying nature of incestuous corrupt rule. It is worth quoting two versions of this conflation of the biological and the political, the legal and the spectacular at length. The first is from a May 2003 article in the magazine *Vanity Fair*. It begins,

> in the traumatized country that is Saddam Hussein's Iraq, the most visible manifestations of the dictator's power have for some years been his elder sons, Uday, who turns 39 in June, and Qusay, 37 in May. Since the 1991 Gulf War, Saddam has kept himself largely hidden, moving furtively from palace to palace, seldom spending consecutive nights in the same bed, and often relying on body doubles for public appearances. But Uday and Qusay are everywhere, perfectly embodying in their very different personalities the two sides of their father's conflicted nature—Uday the unstable, capricious megalomaniac, the sadist who kills on a whim; Qusay the ruthless strategist and organizer, the enforcer who kills when it is the way to achieve measured and rational objectives. . . . [O]ne of the themes of the propaganda issued on behalf of Iraq's self-styled "uncle," Saddam Hussein, is that of the dictator as family man. . . . [A]ccording to the defectors, who knew the boys at school, these images were a sham. . . . [U]day's father was usually absent, and there was no one to control him," one of the defectors says. "It was not like a normal family" . . . . [O]ne afternoon, he overheard Saddam's daughter Raghad complaining to her mother about one of her teachers. He understood the beginning of her remark—"If you don't tell the bitch to fuck off, I'll . . ."—but not the Arabic phrase which followed: "Shug kussha." . . . [S]omewhat later, Karem acquired a translation: Raghad had threatened to rip out her teacher's vagina. At the time, the girl was seven or eight. "It gave me something of an insight," Karem says. . . . [U]day was never to achieve this grounding. Like most of Saddam's inbred family, he married a relative, his cousin Saja Barzan Tikriti. Their union, in 1990, lasted 10 days before she fled to Switzerland. She has never spoken of what transpired. Later he married another relation, Hanan, the daughter of the sometime Iraqi defense minister Ali Hassan Majid. His failure to father a child may help explain his promiscuity. Once, says one of the defectors, after tests established he had an abnormally low sperm count, he abstained from sex for an unprecedented 10 days, in the hope that this would boost a subsequent test's results. The stratagem failed.[78]

Once again, it is the curious conflation of outside and inside, of blood, sex, and politics that makes this attack on Saddam Hussein's rule effective. The first image is of a "traumatized country," an abstract liberal portrayal of the nation-state in agony. The reason that the country is traumatized, however, has nothing to do with politics or for that matter even with biology. Instead the country is a victim of their overlap—the illegitimate sovereign's offspring are manifestations not of Saddam Hussein himself, but of his simultaneously personal and dictatorial power. The monstrous results of Saddam Hussein's incestuous relationship are presented here, in other words, not as biological forces, not as political forces, but as biopolitics in action, fleshy embodiments of the leader's will (and presumably his law).

At the same time, the repeated invocations of incest—Saddam Hussein as the product of incest and the recipient of incestuous abuse, the incestuous marriage of Uday, the monstrous mutant daughter, also a product of incest, who wants to inflict sexual violence on her teacher, the impotence/sterility of the monstrous mutant son, likewise the product of incest—are all then tied back to the victimized state. Saddam Hussein is Iraq's uncle, but he is really only a "self-styled 'uncle'"—an uncle who forces himself, like Saddam Hussein's own uncle Khairullah, on an unwilling state. In the same way that Saddam Hussein's uncle took advantage of him in "primitive" Tikrit, the leader here is taking advantage of Iraq as an abstract, producing nothing more than violence and impotence, attempting to exorcise his own impurities by turning his entire country into a quasifictional caricature of his family.

Saddam Hussein himself, however, is unable to position himself in any space but the exceptional one in this narrative. He, like Abdülhamid, hides—he keeps himself away from the gaze of the public, and remains "inside." But he also reproduces himself in public, outside, making use of both body doubles and his avatar sons. He is thus both present and absent as political leader, "unnatural" as a leader in the same way that he was "unnatural" as a present/absent father to his sons. In this presentation of Saddam Hussein, the leader both exists and does not exist, is powerful, but also contaminated and diseased—in a very basic way operating in direct opposition to the liberal rhetoric of legal transparency.

A second discussion of Saddam Hussein's sons as manifestations of corrupt political rule plays on similar themes. In July 2003, ABC News ran a biographical report about the "former Iraqi leader," and his family on *Primetime Live*. It is once again worthwhile to quote it at length:

> CHARLES GIBSON (off camera): Well, listen to this, just for a moment. Brutal, calculated, spoiled, depraved, deviant, embarrassing, criminal, jealous, insane. Over the years, an enormous amount has been written about Uday and Qusay Hussein, almost always using words like those. Some of

their reputation for brutality was legend, but most of it well deserved. . . .

BRIAN ROSS (voice-over): American authorities had a wealth of evidence of Qusay's brutal and violent behavior, including this videotape, smuggled out of Iraq by a defector and obtained by ABC News. It shows Qusay calling the shots at a bizarre cult-like performance in Baghdad six years ago.

PROFESSOR FAWAZ GERGES, Sarah Lawrence College: What is fascinating about this scene, Qusay was not a passive spectator. He took an active interest in the bloody rituals and he seems to be enjoying the bloody rituals.

BRIAN ROSS (voice-over): Professor Fawaz Gerges, a leading authority on Islamic affairs, says men seen on the tape actually pierce their bodies and heads with lances and swords. . . . [I]t was a father's dilemma, what to do with the wayward son. In this case, Saddam Hussein's son Uday, accused of murders and rapes too numerous to count. For Saddam Hussein, the answer was easy, put Uday in charge of Iraq's Olympic athletes, where he more than lived up to his reputation as a twisted maniac. . . .

PETER GALBRAITH: He allows his eldest son to be a killer, to be a thief, to be a torturer, to be a rapist. This is not possible in any democratic country.

BRIAN ROSS (voice-over): But the real horror story about Uday was what happened at night in Baghdad, the bizarre sexual behavior and rapes for which he became notorious. . . . [U]day was the first child of Saddam and Sajida Hussein, who are cousins. His younger brother Qusay was less well known but emerged as a top military adviser to his father and Uday's rival for power and attention.

PROFESSOR AMATZIA BARAM, University of Haifa: Very angry that his younger brother got all this power.

BRIAN ROSS (voice-over): Professor Amatzia Baram of the Brookings Institute and Haifa University says Uday's flash temper and lustful kinks were well known in the Arab world.[79]

The argument that is being produced in this clip is not a particularly coherent one, but leaving aside the various slippages and the strange conflation of "Islamic affairs," self-mutilation, and what the "Arab world" knows, a few relatively meaningful themes can be drawn out of it. Most important is the repeated switch in focus from the monstrously biological to the monstrously political. We are told first about Uday and Qusay's personal deviance and brutality. Immediately, however, the "brutal, calculated, spoiled, depraved, deviant, embarrassing, criminal, jealous, [and] insane" personalities of the two leave the realm of the personal and enter the realm of the political and legal—what is of particular importance is that "American authorities" had "evidence" of this behavior. What exactly "American authorities"—the abstract representatives of a presumably legal or legalesque system—wanted to do with this "evidence" is a bit unclear. But what is not unclear is the importance of the exchange between the rational as it is manifested in American legal and political structures and the spectacular as it is manifested in the public's right to know. The tape moves quickly from Qusay himself to the "Iraqi defector" to "American authorities" and then finally to ABC News. Qusay is thus represented, by virtue of his monstrosity and deviance, as a perfect porn star, an object of curiosity to both a legal and a "popular" gaze, operating in an exceptional, lawless space, both inside (on television screens across America) and outside (by virtue of both his geographical displacement and deviance).

Qusay's occupation of this space is further reinforced by the commentary of the "expert," Fawaz Gerges. The expert tells us first of all what is "fascinating"—not only appropriating narrative power from Qusay himself, but also alerting the audience as to what should be titillating and what should not. He then plays further upon the theme of inside and outside, invoking even the blood imagery of the incest/miscegenation stories. Qusay is not "just a spectator"; he participates. He is thus in the same place as both the "real girl" of pornography and the sacred man of law, both inside and outside, both in control of the narrative and violently constrained by it. Moreover, what he is participating in is a "bizarre cult-like performance," a "bloody ritual." Qusay's behavior is first spectacularized (it is a "performance"), and, second, removed from the realm law and rationality (it is bizarre, inexplicable even for the self-appointed narrators, and its meaning purely ritual). Finally, we learn the apparent moral to this story: "He allows his eldest son to be a killer, to be a thief, to be a torturer, to be a rapist. This is not possible in any democratic country." In other words, the discussion of Qusay was apparently leading to a *political* conclusion—the only barrier between "us" and the bizarre, the bloody, the violent, the deviant, the ritual, and the emptily spectacular is, it seems, "democracy."

But even this political conclusion is undermined, is folded back on itself into a new biopolitical message, in the next sentence. It turns out that faith in the protective role of "democracy" is not in fact what we should be taking away from this piece. The "real horror story" has nothing to do with what can and cannot happen in a democratic country—instead it is "what happened at night in Baghdad," the sexual escapades of the other son, and the fact that both are the product of an incestuous sexual relationship. We thus return to the point at which we started—the "lustful kinks" that are "known" by both "American authorities" and the "Arab world," the open but dirty secret, and the monstrous activities that happen under the cover of darkness.

Like the discussion of Qusay and Uday in *Vanity Fair*, that is, what we have here is an invocation of the sexual and the biological as a means of placing the corrupt leader simultaneously outside and inside the realm of law and politics. "Democracy" or "law" is set up against sexual violence—indeed it can be understood only via a spectacularization of this violence. In this way, the sexually deviant corrupt leader is contained *within* the realm of legal and political discourse. But the monstrous, bloody, and bizarre "rituals" enacted by these leaders are made explicitly "inexplicable." The narrators of the story tell us directly that they cannot understand what motivates the leader to do these things—only that such things are not possible in a democratic country. In this way the corrupt leader is also placed *outside* of law and politics—it is paradoxically also beyond the capability of legal and political vocabulary to describe or contain their behavior. The corrupt leader is too dehumanized and too much of an animal to interact with in a rational way. He must be and is contained, but he must also be simultaneously expelled.

Like Abdülhamid, Saddam Hussein as a monster and his rule as a monstrosity also played out in his inappropriate feeding habits and his violation of both nation and citizen. We might consider two *New York Times* articles from October 1, 2000, for example, as follow ups to the 1909 article on Abdülhamid's mutant appetites. The first, on "Saddam's Bomb," describes one incident in the Iraqi leader's rule as follows:

> when the video [of the executions] was finished, Hamza says, the party official turned to him in disgust and said "we are now cannibalizing ourselves. These are not people you don't know. These are your friends. One day, I might be asked to shoot you. And I would, because my own head would be on the line."[80]

In the second, "Inside Saddam's Court," we learn with reference to Saddam Hussein's sexual violence, "the rape and the payoff were insult enough. Almost as disturbing was the memory of Saddam's yellow, lifeless eyes. 'They were the eyes of death,' she told me. 'He looked at me as if I were a corpse. There was not a hint of humanity or warmth in them.'"[81] Although the cannibalistic tendencies in the first passage are displaced onto state functionaries, the trope of the corrupt leader's abnormal consumption—and its effect on what is assumed to be normal state behavior—remains in place. In this case, the cannibalistic disease, along with its erotic overtones, has spread. The corrupt leader cannibalizes his state and his citizens; simultaneously, functionaries attached to the corrupt leader—even as they are "disgusted" by it—are also drawn into this schematic, autoerotic rather than erotic self-referential "cannibalism" of themselves.

The second passage is similarly concerned with the transference of monstrous qualities from the leader to his citizens and back again. Here, the corpse-like nature of Saddam Hussein is invoked with reference to his yellow and lifeless eyes. When the leader gazes on his citizen with these eyes, the lifelessness is transmitted to her—she was looked at as if *she* were a corpse. The conclusion to the passage, however, reasserts the gaze of the newspaper reader, which in turn attributes the lifelessness ("lack of humanity") once more to Saddam Hussein. And it is here that the discussion ends. Political as well as sexual or biological necrophilia is, in other words, much like cannibalism—the only possible end to the corrupt state–corrupt ruler relationship. Like the werewolf, Saddam Hussein is portrayed here as completely nonhuman, lifeless, and cold—his effect on his state and his citizens is a simultaneously homicidal and suicidal one because he has no actual connection to them. But also like the werewolf, he is *human*—cannibalism cannot occur unless both parties are human, too similar for eating of that sort to be natural. He, like Abdülhamid, is both too similar to the civilized/human and too different from it, too attracted to it and too repelled. His physicality cannot be constrained within the bounds of normal legal process, but legal process cannot exist without his cannibalistic presence.

Whereas familial illegitimacy, mixed blood, and unnatural appetites (sexual or otherwise) play important roles in the narrative of the corrupt leader-as-monster, an equally important aspect of the trope emphasizes the strange nature of the leader's body itself. Both Abdülhamid and Saddam Hussein, for example, are portrayed in a number of accounts as personally, physically, and biologically omnipresent, multiple, or "absorbing,"[82] on the one hand, and invisible or "annihilating" on the other. As half-human, half-animal monsters in the first set of narratives, they occupied a tenuous position both outside of and inside of the law. They were constrained or defined by the gaze of "democratic public opinion," but they were also inexplicable, incapable of rational narration or being narrated, existing within the realm of the exceptional/pornographic "real girl" and sacred man. In this second set of narratives, the two leaders are instead the possessors of either multiple bodies or no body at all. Rather than existing under the gaze of the law/public opinion but being nonetheless inexplicable—rather than existing both too much inside and too much outside of liberal political structures— Abdülhamid and Saddam Hussein in these latter discussions elude the gaze of law and politics altogether. Doubling, tripling, eliminating, or expanding their physical presence, they highlight the extent to which law does not affect them—and the extent to which, therefore, their true bodies need to be found, constrained, and exposed within the legal sphere.

By reveling in their own bodily and biological monstrosity, in other words, both leaders are portrayed as effectively undermining one of the most fundamental bases of democratic rhetoric—namely, the habeas corpus[83] rights of each and every citizen. And while it is true that Abdülhamid and Saddam Hussein are described as corrupt because of their inappropriate use or abuse of legal structures—their "undemocratic" behavior and policy—the biopolitical nature of modern democracy is such that their monstrous spreading, multiplying, and physical doubling quickly ceases to be merely a *metaphor* for this corruption, and soon becomes a distinct and concrete example of how their rule is illegitimate. Indeed, the media fixation on the body double can be understood only if we likewise understand that physical multiplicity codes as a direct attack on legal structures in these analyses.

Abdülhamid's reliance on body doubles, for example, is a common theme in discussions of his corrupt rule. At the same time, though, I want to focus more in this section on the various ways in which Abdülhamid's body *imperfectly* reproduced itself, and how this played out in critiques of his governance. Although the sultan frequently relied on "exact" doubles, in other words, I think a discussion of his use and abuse of multiple bodies both bigger and smaller than "life" are of equal interest. In an 1897 analysis of Abdülhamid, his body, and his corrupt rule, for example, we learn that the Ottoman government is "much fettered by the absorbing tendencies of Sultan Abdul Hamid," that this "corruption and intrigue of the centre [has] spread to the provinces," and that it is therefore "expedient to enlighten public opinion as to the nature of the cancer which is poisoning the life-blood of Turkey, and which, until it is eradicated, renders hopeless all reform."[84]

This analysis is not just a liberal criticism of the backward "tradition" by which the monarch's body represents the state.[85] More than that, it is a twist, again, on the notion of habeas corpus. Abdülhamid is being indicted in this passage as a criminal, not just as a monarch, but his crime is his refusal to possess a body that can be constrained and defined by law. It is not the function of "sultan" in the abstract that "absorbs" and "fetters" the central government—it is the specific person of Abdülhamid himself, his body that encompasses and absorbs, this person that prompts the geographical spread of corruption. Indeed, this metaphor for inappropriate state function is an explicitly biological one, invoking blood and cancer as well as the liberal public's right to know about such things. The linkage that exists here between biology and politics therefore relies quite completely on the notion that Abdülhamid's body is illegally indistinct. The sultan is cancerous, his state is cancerous, but this is the case not because each is displaced onto the other in a medieval or early modern notion of kingship; rather it is that the sultan's body is too great to be contained within legal discourse on the one hand, or the enlightened discourse of public opinion on the other.

It is not just that Abdülhamid's body expands in monstrous ways, however. Imperfect reproductions of Abdülhamid and his relationships with these reproductions also play up the sultan's corrupt, destabilizing relationship to law.[86] At one point in his unauthorized biography of the sultan, for example, Dorys relates the following story about Abdülhamid's court jester:

> his master used to throw him into the water, rub black all over his face, and play on him a thousand tricks of this kind. Ali knew better than to complain, knowing well that all these little humiliations were usually followed by presents more or less liberal. Sometimes the pleasantries of the Padishah assumed a grotesque and trivial character absolutely incompatible with the idea that one has usually of the dignity of a sovereign.[87]

The symbolic (and grotesque) relationship between monarch and jester, between appropriate rule and disordered rule is one that has been discussed in detail elsewhere.[88] Here, however, what we have is a situation in which, once again, it is the overlapping physicality of the sultan and the jester, the fact that Abdülhamid tries to humiliate Ali, but that in the end it is his own behavior that is "grotesque and trivial," that is important.[89] The reader is invited to confuse the degradation of the corrupt leader with the degradation of his humiliated follower, to confuse even the grotesque quality of the jester with the damaged dignity of the sovereign. In the process, the bodies of the two overlap, and the same legal chaos that is caused by the use of "exact" doubles is caused by this imperfect reproduction of sovereign power and physical presence. The humiliated body of the jester represents too perfectly the humiliated character of the sultan, and separating the two for the purposes of a rational, legal process is impossible.

Saddam Hussein's use of body doubles receives as much attention as that of Abdülhamid. Indeed, it is often argued that it caused "difficulties for the [Iraqi] state-owned media's daily reports on Saddam's itinerary."[90] Once again, however, what I would like to focus on here are the *im*perfect reproductions of the corrupt leader and how they emphasize the troubled relationship among law, the monstrous, and the public's right to know. It is in particular Saddam Hussein's ability repeatedly to replicate himself, physically and biologically, in the form not only of his own doubles, but in the form of his avatar sons, their doubles, and their doubles' doubles, that comes to represent the illegitimate, "lawless" violence of corrupt rule. In the same *Primetime Live* discussion of Uday and Qusay Hussein, for example, we come to a strange interview with the former's double:

> BRIAN ROSS (voice-over): People tried to kill Uday. He walked with a limp after being wounded in an assassination attempt eight years ago. And he long had a body double trained to take a bullet for him. Were you a good double?
>
> LATIF YAHIA, body double for Uday Hussein: I was good double for one person.
>
> BRIAN ROSS (voice-over): Now in exile in London, Latif Yahia served for more than five years as Uday's double. As seen on this old videotape, Yahia was given the same French suits, after shave, and even had plastic surgery on his chin to make him a convincing Uday. Yahia on the left, Uday on the right. They even had the same barber. And, Yahia says he, too, saw the brutal side of the man.
>
> LATIF YAHIA: He picked one girl, she's pregnant, and he touch her. And, this is Uday. Uday, he can't sleep with a woman if he don't hit her and see the blood come out of her.
>
> BRIAN ROSS (off camera): So that for him is the sexual excitement?
>
> LATIF YAHIA: Yeah, the violence.[91]

The obvious question to ask with regard to this interview is what viewers are supposed to get out of it. On what subjects can a body double be expert? What is the purpose of engaging him in conversation? It becomes clear given the tenor of the questions and answers that, essentially, Latif Yahia is supposed to continue playing the (imperfect) role of Uday Hussein, representing (again imperfectly) the corrupt nature of Saddam Hussein's leadership. Brian Ross is eliciting a confession from Latif Yahia/Uday Hussein concerning the sexualized violence of Saddam Hussein's rule. ABC News, in other words, has managed to constrain and exhibit at least one *corpus*, and is in the process of producing the legalesque spectacle of confession/interview for the sake of the public's right to know.

At the same time, however, throughout the conversation, it is made clear that although the body of Uday Hussein exists and has been captured in one sense, in another, his body is completely "free"—given that Uday had been killed at this point. Reproduced in the transcript of the interview, therefore, is Latif Yahia's imperfect English, with its dropped articles and subject/verb disagreement. Likewise reproduced is the imperfect nature of Latif Yahia's knowledge—he did see "the brutal side of the man," but he could not have seen all sides of him. As a result, the interview is in the end unsatisfying. It plays up the physical duality—multiplicity—of both Uday Hussein and his father, and in the process it emphasizes their continued disregard for the law.[92] The multiple bodies of Saddam Hussein, expanding to an overwhelming size and contracting to nothing, thus create an unresolved tension between biology and law, in which the triumph of law can only happen, first, with the discovery and capture of the "right" body and, second, with its exhibition to scale and in detail.

A second aspect of Saddam Hussein's monstrous self-replication and doubling occurs in the repeated recourse to his corpse-like, inhuman nature. Earlier, the eroticism of the active living corpse, the corpse-like nature of the passive woman/citizen, and the (sexual) violence implicit in the corrupt leader/victimized citizen relationship became an important theme in the narrative of Saddam Hussein. In *The New Yorker* article "Saddam's Ear," a similar discussion of the corrupt leader's body shows up. We are told, for instance, that

> It seemed to me that there were uncanny, rather creepy parallels between the fanciful drawings for the Soviet uber-morgue and the necromantic bestiality of the "Epic of Saddam" monument that Bashir had designed. I asked him if he thought of himself as, in a sense, Saddam's embalmer. Bashir looked at me quickly, and then looked away. He laughed, but didn't say anything.[93]

Bashir showed up earlier on as Saddam Hussein's doctor (and thus translator). Here, however, he is reproduced as not just a doctor, but as an "embalmer," the architect of the leader's monument, still flirting with the interviewer, but displaying the corrupt leader's body in a far "creepier" way. And it needs to be emphasized that the creepiness here is derived from the fact that Bashir is not telling us the secrets of the leader's "real" body, but instead demonstrating the ease with which this body can be replicated—be it as a monument or an embalmed corpse.[94]

It is the creepiness, in other words, that an audience feels in the knowledge that in addition to a "human" body, the leader also possesses a "necromantic" one—magical, occult, yet still resonant of death—as well as a "bestial" one. In this passage, the wolf-man is not a single entity, but is doubled, tripled, and quadrupled—the beast, the human, the magical, and the corpse all exist in separate but overlapping spaces. The disturbing implications of this biological replication in the realm of the law are obvious. Before, the wolf-man existed in exceptional space, defined (and therefore constrained) by the law, even if he was explicitly placed outside of it. Now, the wolf-man in his multiplicity can no longer be constrained. His *corpus* is multiple, and it can represent neither rational sovereign power nor individual liberty. Narratives of body doubling are thus indeed "creepy," horrifying even, especially within the context of liberal discourse. They also serve a distinct and specific purpose, calling out for structures of authority to place the deviant and corrupt leader back into one body, to define this body minutely,[95] to exhibit it, and therefore to reinstate the overriding power of the rational "law."

On the flip side of the monstrous nature of the corrupt leader is of course his diseased, paranoid, and mentally ill character. In the same way that the biological horrors of miscegenation, incest, the werewolf, and body doubling serve not just as metaphors for—but actual legalesque concrete evidence of—the corrupt leader's rule, his apparent fear and paranoia, his pathological, usually congenital, inability to behave in a sane manner placed him into a confused, half-rational, half-violent space as well. Both Abdülhamid and Saddam Hussein, for example, hide in terror from, and attempt to elude, the public gaze (read as law). They try to turn their twisted private worlds into public policy. They thus in turn elicit constant discussion, analysis, and debate among psychological "experts" as to the true nature of their (single) body and mind. Given the psychobiological foundation of their corrupt rule, however, it only makes sense that psychiatrists should be representing the discursive power of law in this narrative, defining, exhibiting, and eliciting confessions for the benefit of the waiting audience.

In an echo of the body-double narratives, for example, discussions of Abdülhamid's insanity and his psychobiological inability to relate to the law more often than not occur within the larger context of his relationship to his deposed, allegedly insane, imprisoned brother, Murad. As these discussions intensify, the comparison between the unjustly imprisoned, patient ex-Sultan and the terrified, corrupt reigning leader become increasingly pointed. In general, indeed, the primary theme that emerges in these stories is that whereas the insane Abdülhamid avoids the public eye—and thus implicitly the gaze of the law—the sane Murad is involved in a constant, if thwarted, attempt to engage the public, to restore appropriate liberal surveillance over the activities of the sovereign, and to represent the noncorrupt "rule of law." In a *New York Times* article from 1895 entitled "Sultan Murad's Letter: He Writes from Prison to His Brother the Reigning Sultan: On the Recent America (sic) Troubles: Mighty Good Advice from a Man Who Is Alleged to be Insane: He Is Very Progressive in His Views," for example, we learn that

> an extraordinary letter purporting to have been recently written by ex-Sultan Murad in his prison to his brother . . . has been published in the Arabic newspaper al Mushir of Cairo, Egypt. . . . [T]he editor of Al Mushir says that the letter was written on small pieces of paper, on Fridays, when he was able to evade the vigilance of his guards. . . . [he writes] "wake up from your sleep and drive away from you all the liars and hypocrites who would suck out the blood of the nation, and know that our one good friend is the nation."[96]

Against all odds, in other words, Murad attempts to talk with the public—spending Friday, when his less modern guards were at prayer, writing on scraps of paper to the newspaper, and speaking a language of law and liberalism. Although he is forcibly kept from the public view, he makes his presence known, and emphasizes in this passage his disinterested "friendship" with the nation, whose blood is being sucked out.

Abdülhamid, meanwhile, in addition to subjecting the nation to all sorts of distinctly "unfriendly" violence, attempts to hide from this same audience. His fear and paranoia produce a situation in which he is "as usual, painfully apprehensive" about venturing outside,[97] in which he "hollow[s] out a cave, to which he alone has access," to prevent public scrutiny of his "most secret documents,"[98] and in which this pathological terror of exposure and simple public curiosity becomes an increasing menace to normal state function:

> during the first few years of his reign the present Sultan showed himself to his people from time to time. . . . [S]ince then, isolated from the rest of the universe on the heights of Yildiz, defended by thick walls, barracks, and bodyguards, the *voluntary captive*, in spite of the extraordinary precautions with which he is surrounded supports with difficulty the burden of an existence filled with suspicion and terror. . . . [C]rouching at the back of a victoria . . . the raised hood of which conceals a

> steel shield between the outside leather and the cloth lining, the Sultan, with his two magnificent horses at full gallop, passes like the wind, surrounded by a living fortress of aides-de-camp and courtiers, who hide him almost from the gaze of the crowd. [italics in original][99]

The most important aspect to note about this passage is that in Abdülhamid's case, the "living fortress" can only *almost* hide him from the gaze of the crowd. No matter what he might do, or how he might try to hide himself, he is still subject to his celebrity and to this celebrity as a metaphor for legal constraint. In the apparent act of hiding, Abdülhamid is inviting the exposure that would be provided by legal structures—in much the same way that in the act of self-exposure, Murad is negating the necessity for such measures.

But since the basis for Abdülhamid's dysfunctional relationship with his nation, his citizens, and their law is his congenital insanity, more often than not it is medical and psychiatric structures rather than legal ones that frame his relationship with "the public." An article from 1899, for example, entitled "Illustrious Lunatics," is an interesting twist on the "famous characters" genre so popular at the turn of the century, and chronicles the careers of a number of well-known "lunatics" including various Roman emperors, the "Jewish Kings," Ivan the Terrible, Henry VIII, Elizabeth I, and George III. Emphasizing the biological nature of lunacy—Elizabeth I's sexual excess, for example, or their incestuous unions[100]—it concludes with a portrait of Abdülhamid as *the* most illustrious lunatic of them all. Before getting to any of these portraits, however, the article begins with a scientific and rational discussion of mental illness as a general problem, issues of registration and of accommodation for diagnosed lunatics, and what the proper role of the liberal state, in this case England, ought to be:

> when it is seen, according to official returns, that the registered insane have increased from 14,680 in England and Wales to 96,446 in less than two generations and that provisions for lunatic asylum accommodation, great as it is, cannot keep pace with the annually increasing numbers, there is a certain significance in it.[101]

There are various ways in which this passage concerning the growing number of the "registered insane" might be interpreted. I would like to focus in particular, however, on its vocabulary and tone. There is, for example, above all a faith in the rational, civilized, and scientific presentation of basic biological truths. There is a belief in statistics, an acceptance of the accuracy of "official returns," and a well-formulated, calmly presented suggestion that the disturbing trend be noted and deemed in some way "significant."

This well-measured tone begins to shift, however, when we get to the various character sketches. In its discussion of Abdülhamid, in particular, the article vacillates with increasing violence between horror at the monstrosity of his rule and a calm psychiatric analysis of his apparent motivations. The result is a process by which the vocabulary of law is first displaced and then reappropriated for the apparent purposes of medical and psychiatric narrative. Despite the painful self-consciousness that informs the modern "science" of psychiatry, and that runs so forcefully throughout this article, in other words, the inherently punitive rather than curative nature of psychotherapy becomes increasingly explicit. Abdülhamid, the article argues, does not belong in the legal-criminal space of the prison, he belongs in the exceptional space of the lunatic asylum. But this exceptional space is nonetheless quite clearly punitive as well—the sultan must be incarcerated there rather than in the legally defined prison because he is, quite basically, beyond the law. At the same time, however, it is legal rather than medical structures that are invoked to place the sultan into this new position:

> the mantle of the manslayers, to whom reference has been already made, seems to have fallen upon the shoulders of another Eastern potentate, the modern lycanthrope, or wolf-man, whose wholesale massacre of his own subjects has excited the horror and indignation of the whole world. . . . [T]o ordinary minds it seems inconceivable that the atrocious Turk has been permitted, near the end of the nineteenth century, when electricity, steam, and the newspapers keep the world informed, day by day, of what is taking place, to butcher thousands of Armenian Christians, men, women, and children, without let or hindrance, in broad daylight. It goes without saying that the army or fleet of any one of "the high contracting powers," as they are pompously called, could stop the imperial madman's career, and put him in a straight waistcoat at once. . . . [T]he question may be asked, Is Abdul Hamid mad? Judged by his life of sensual excess, and by his savage treatment of his Christian subjects, he is not only insane, but a criminal lunatic, qualified in every way to rank with the inhuman monsters of antiquity. Taking all things into account he may be set down as the most illustrious lunatic that has appeared upon the earth.[102]

The intersections among legal discourse, medical discourse, and the horror genre in discussions of the corrupt leader are made explicit in this passage. First of all, Abdülhamid is defined as a werewolf, exciting and horrific in his savage behavior. From the very beginning of the analysis, therefore, he is placed outside of the law, while nonetheless remaining under the gaze of the "whole world." This gaze, public opinion, and the role of modernity and liberalism in dispelling the "horror" are indeed made overt—the werewolf may exist, as Agamben notes, in our collective, premodern imagination, but "today," in the age of technology (electricity and steam) and surveillance (newspapers), such things need not frighten us. The brute force of European military strength could in fact easily stop Abdülhamid, but rather than punishing him with some form of imprisonment, this force is instead called upon to put him into "a straight waistcoat at once."

It is here, then, that the medical comes into play—but it is a medical, again, that is fundamentally punitive. Abdülhamid is insane and a perfect candidate for constraint within a straightjacket. But this constraint should also serve as a punishment—as something to be effected by the avenging military forces of Europe. The sultan's corrupt sex life (sensual excess) and his corrupt politics (mistreatment of Christian subjects) indeed serve as parallel symptoms of a larger illness, which is both legal ("criminal") and medical ("lunatic"). Despite the self-consciously modern emphasis on the intersection between law and medicine, however, the passage refers in the end to an apparently early modern or medieval interest in the wolf-man or the human/inhuman monster. The sultan is mad, he is a criminal lunatic, but he is also an "inhuman monster," who belongs in "antiquity." The medical diagnosis thus leads inexorably back to the realm of werewolves and bandits, threatening to modernity and the rhetoric of law, but also celebrated—highlighted and spectacularized like the "real girl," produced pornographically for the sake of both public opinion and public amusement. The celebrated spectacle of Abdülhamid as an inhuman monster constrained by the law, but still placed outside of the it, is in other words, the direct result of the overlap between a psychobiological narrative and a legal one.

Nearly a century later, discussions of Saddam Hussein followed a similar line. Like Abdülhamid, Saddam Hussein was known to hide himself, to elude the public gaze, even as he multiplied himself via body doubles. Like Abdülhamid's, this behavior in Saddam Hussein was both explicitly and implicitly made analogous to his inappropriate attitude toward law. Finally, like Abdülhamid, Saddam Hussein was the subject of much long-distance psychiatric analysis. The Iraqi president, too, invited the concern of the medical establishment—he also supplied an arena for discussion in which medical and legal narratives could overlap. And in the end, he, too, was placed, as a result of this overlapping, conflicted identity, into exceptional space, punitive but not, legal but not, medical but also not.

First of all, Saddam Hussein's paranoid attempts to elude the public gaze—his desire to hide, to keep himself away from legal, popular, and political surveillance—are linked, like those of Abdülhamid, to both his apparent mental illness and his corrupt rule. Saddam Hussein's construction of palaces, for example, is held up as "corrupt" in a number of mainstream and less mainstream discussions of Iraqi politics, but it is likewise described as a "building mania," arising from a pathological need to disguise himself. Indeed, this relationship between the hidden and the exposed, the insane and the corrupt, places leaders like Saddam Hussein into their own special world:

> by this stage in his long career Saddam had developed a siege mentality. He had always taken his security to ludicrous extremes, but by the mid-1990s the sixty-something tyrant—his precise date of birth has never been established—had become almost dysfunctional in his obsession. Saddam spent most of his time at Baghdad's Presidential Palace, which by the 1990s had become a massive, sprawling complex of about one thousand acres.[103]

Although the passage starts out with Saddam Hussein's "career," it quickly replaces this legal/political issue with psychobiological ones. Personal and public security in Iraq were not about politics, they were about the president's "mentality," his "dysfunction," and his "obsessions." Likewise, the reason that Saddam Hussein spent most of his time in his presidential palace—a site that is turned monstrous by association, "massive," and "sprawling"—is not that it is where he worked or where he performed the public function of president. It is that he needed to hide and that he imagined himself "under siege." Saddam Hussein is thus hidden both physically and psychologically. There are secrets to be discovered—if nothing else, "his precise date of birth"—and these secrets are being deliberately kept both in the physical space of the presidential palace and the psychological space of Saddam Hussein's troubled personality.[104]

Psychiatrists, lawmakers, and newspapers worked together to unearth these secrets. Two articles from 1991 and 2003, for example, both relying on the medical expertise of the psychiatrist Jerrold Post, reproduce the "illustrious lunatics" narrative in more or less complete form. In the first,

> a detailed psychological study of Mr. Hussein, given in Senate testimony, depicts the Iraqi President as not clinically insane, but suffering from "malignant narcissism," a severe personality

> disorder that leaves him grandiose, paranoid and ruthless. The study was prepared by Dr. Jerrold Post, a professor of psychiatry and politics at George Washington University. . . . [M]any experts question whether it is possible to draw useful conclusions about people from a distance . . . but Dr. Post said there was evidence to show that Mr. Hussein meets the four conditions Dr. Kernberg set for a diagnosis of malignant narcissism: an extreme sense of grandiosity, sadistic cruelty, suspiciousness to the point of paranoia and an utter lack of remorse. . . . [D]r. Post sees paranoia in the Baathist Party ideology that Mr. Hussein has embraced. "Saddam Hussein says with sincerity that the problems of the Arabs came from the imperialist West, from the Jews, and from the Persians," he said. . . . [F]or a dictator it typically takes the form of "if you're not with me, you're against me."[105]

Again, the rhetoric in which this analysis is couched is a rhetoric of calm, scientific, medical reportage. Indeed, the apparent purpose of the article is to raise the question of whether long-distance psychiatric diagnosis is even something that is possible or desirable. Despite this apparent analytical distance, however, the article immediately places Saddam Hussein into the same legal/nonlegal space occupied by Abdülhamid one hundred years before. Saddam Hussein may not in fact be clinically insane, but he is nonetheless "suffering" from a personality disorder—a notion that in turn implies that the medical establishment should attempt some sort of "cure."

Rather than discussing such possibilities, however, both the psychiatrist and the newspaper produce the same slippage between the politicolegal and the medical that occurred in the "illustrious lunatics" piece. It is not just that Saddam Hussein is personally disturbed, it is that Ba'thist ideology as a whole—a political philosophy espoused, discussed, and critiqued by thousands of intellectuals in the Arabic-speaking world over the course of the twentieth century—is "paranoid." Far more overtly in this case than in the nineteenth century, the political "not liberal" is equated here with the medical "not sane," and the forces of liberalism are implicitly called upon to cure/punish the corrupt leader who exhibits both tendencies. Saddam Hussein's politics, his political corruption cannot be separated from his mental illness—he must therefore be constrained legally, but "treated" in a realm outside of, beyond the realm of the law. He must be understood according to a biopolitical rhetoric, but contained within a legally defined not-legal space. Twelve years later, the 2003 article makes this point with far more force:

> Psychiatrist Jerrold Post, who has profiled Saddam for the CIA and updated his take on the Iraqi leader in a recent essay,

Celebrating the Corrupt Leader

is among those who believe Saddam's last stand could be ugly, assuming he still has a stash of chemical and biological weapons at his disposal. "He can bob and weave, but he becomes dangerous when he is backed into a corner," the Christian Science Monitor quotes Post as saying. . . . [P]sychiatrist Post says Saddam's traumatic childhood, including the beatings and the realization he almost wasn't born, are at the root of the Iraqi President's malevolent personality. "These early experiences can be seen as profoundly wounding Saddam's emerging self-esteem," Post wrote in a recent essay. In effect, Post and co-author Amatzia Baram, an Israeli historian, argue Saddam grew up believing the only reliable means of survival was ruthless force. "People who are abused as children often become abusive themselves, and he did it on a larger scene, a national and a regional scene," Post told Times Online earlier this year. "In Saddam's case, he has been able to shape the social system so that it mirrors his own psychology. He has no father, and he then becomes father to this nation. The sort of violence that was shown him, he shows to the people around him to keep them under control. He says: 'Never again will I yield to superior force.'"[106]

In this passage, every aspect of the narrative of the monstrous, diseased, and pathological corrupt leader comes together in the apparent name of law and psychiatric health. Saddam Hussein is defined, first of all, by the half-medical, half-legal expertise of Jerrold Post—a figure attached simultaneously to the hospital and to the CIA. Moreover, in the process of reading this portrait/profile we learn the following: like a beast, Saddam Hussein gets dangerous when backed into a corner; like a mutant, he almost was not born; with his monstrous, larger than life presence, he shapes the state to mirror his own psychology; given his unnatural, fatherless birth, he commits acts of (incestuous) violence on the nation. He then, finally, translated through Post, invites and provokes the extension of power networks and surveillance systems with his cry, "never again will I yield to superior force."

Every element of Saddam Hussein's personality—including the rhetorical arena in which it was constructed and produced for public consumption—places him into a legally defined exceptional space. The law is ever present in this discussion, but it is present only as a means of defining Saddam Hussein as "outside" of itself. As a mutant, incestuous, violent, and insane beast, the corrupt leader is in this narrative emphatically both productive of and constrained within exceptional space. This space, however, like the pornographic space of the "real girl," is one that is under the constant, titillated gaze of public opinion (read as law). The celebrity of the corrupt leader is therefore also an essential element to his monstrous nature, his existence operating both inside and outside the law.

The *biological* character of the celebrated monstrous mutant is equally important and equally necessary to the eventual dénouement of the story. Given the fact that it is his biology, his physicality, his fleshiness, his genetic traits, his offspring, his every celebrated move that defines the corrupt leader as, in fact, corrupt, the "confession" of this leader, his exposure, must include similarly minute characteristics. It is thus not the articulated confession of the realm of law that is eventually extracted from the fallen tyrant, it is instead the involuntary shudder of the protagonist of the melodrama, the shuffling testimony of the *Muselmann* in the camp, and the death throes of the pornographic "real girl" at the end of the snuff film that drive the apparently politicolegal narrative of "corruption unmasked" and "corruption contained."

Confession

When the U.S. military captured Saddam Hussein in late 2003, they immediately turned him over to a corps of doctors, who gave him a full medical examination. The film footage of "Saddam's Physical," reproduced thousands of times in hundreds of contexts, shuttled around the world, turned into stills and prints, quickly became the most resonant and recognized symbol of America's "triumph" over the corrupt leader—of American "presence" in Iraq. CNN anchorman Wolf Blitzer had this to say about the strangely compelling spectacle of Saddam Hussein's trip to the doctor: "and Barbara, as we saw the video, the dramatic video of the tongue depressor going in Saddam Hussein's mouth, clearly with a full beard, a beard that showed a lot of gray in that beard, they weren't just checking his tonsils or anything. They were looking for DNA."[107]

The idea that a routine medical examination should be described as "dramatic" deserves some attention. Why should Blitzer find the tongue depressor moment so worthy of exegesis, and why should the tongue depressor moment be reproduced so frequently in the weeks that followed—rivaled only by the footage of Saddam Hussein being shaved? The basic answer, clearly, is that the tongue depressor entering the leader's mouth produces the money shot in the corruption narrative. Quite literally, the orifice of the now powerless leader, surrounded—as Blitzer notes—with hair, is being penetrated by superior force. There is nothing metaphorical here—it is more overt even than the discussion of Abdülhamid's fixation on "pockets"—the triumph of law over corruption occurs at the precise moment that liberal, rational structures penetrate, open, and expose the corrupt leader's sexualized interiority.

There is more going on in the climax to this story, however, than simple pornographic titillation. Blitzer also focuses on the fact that "they weren't just checking his tonsils or anything. They were looking for DNA." And it is here that the complexity of the confessional moment, the exposure, exhibition, and release, comes into play. It is not just that in the modern period political power becomes biopolitical power and is thus sexualized—that a defeated enemy, population, or nation-state must be raped into submission. It is also that the nature of the corruption narrative, and the narrative of the corrupt leader especially, requires this overtly pornographic conclusion. Throughout, the corrupt leader is defined as a celebrity. He is our intimate friend, and his clothing, physicality, and fleshiness become objects of our fascination. He is understood using a vocabulary of flesh and sex rather than a vocabulary of law. Likewise, his childlike/savage nature is understood as an inability to control his will, to distinguish between fantasy and reality, and in a basic way to create a coherent self. He needs a superior narrative force to put him into his proper place. Finally, his monstrosity is similarly a psychobiological (rather than political or legal) monstrosity, in which his mutant, multiplying, expanding, and contracting body is both exposed and hidden from view—simultaneously celebrated and protected by a pathological medicalized paranoia from the public gaze.

The corrupt leader is, in other words, defined and understood according to flesh rather than according to law. His confession must therefore be a biological, physical, or sexual confession rather than anything verbal or articulate. Likewise, the information contained in this confession must be above all biological information. Blitzer's parallel focus on Saddam Hussein's DNA *and* the penetration of his orifices thus makes a great deal of sense. Given the narrative of the corrupt leader that occurs prior to his actual capture and confession, given the extent to which he is *already* defined as inhabiting exceptional space, there is nowhere that he can end up *except* in the space of the "real girl." His every biological function will be monitored, his every sexual and physical movement will be surveilled, placed under the gaze of the public, and this will be rightly so because law, the leader's departure from law, and his (sexualized) violation of law have already been very literally embodied in his physical function. The simultaneous penetration of Saddam Hussein's orifice and search for DNA is simply biopolitical control on the microscopic level—DNA is the smallest unit of biological knowledge, and the liberal state will expose it, understand it, and then, via CNN, broadcast it to a waiting public.

The confession of the corrupt leader in this way relates directly back to the various ways in which he was narrated prior to his capture. As our intimate friend, his confession must be intimate, sexual, and physical. Accounts of the confession must focus on body language and inarticulate signs or excretions rather than on anything the leader might say or write.

The corrupt leader's clothing or lack thereof is also of extraordinary importance in understanding his crime, and so it, too, receives a great deal of detailed attention. Likewise, one of the most titillating aspects of the confession is the tension that occurs between the captured, infantile, and usually "defiant" leader's (doomed) attempt to control his own narrative and the abject submission implied by the fact that *everyone* except for him has actual narrative control.

This fight over discursive power and its implications in terms of law lead in turn to the notion of the "bar of public opinion"—invoked explicitly in both the confession of Abdülhamid and the confession of Saddam Hussein. Finally, the most overtly totalitarian aspect of the relationship between the corrupt leader and liberal power is the attempt to contain his monstrosity. The leader's body—both dead and alive—is repeatedly displayed, manipulated, penetrated, and constrained. Body doubles, explicit and implicit, serve as parallel confessors to the leader himself, playing up the extent to which the leader's "real" body (and bodies) are under the control of legal power. Finally, the lair, pit, hole, or harem from which the corrupt leader was extracted and captured is the object of much fascination—the detritus of the leader's physical life left there serving as a further metaphor, or simply as further evidence, of his embodiment of lawless, inhuman violence, its penetration a symbol of legal transparency.

Abdülhamid II's reign came to an end in late 1908, when the Young Turks successfully led a political coup against his government. After raising a military force in the European provinces of the Ottoman Empire, the Young Turks marched to Istanbul, met almost no resistance, and informed the sultan that he would be abdicating the throne. Like the narrative of Saddam Hussein's capture, the narrative of Abdülhamid's capture eventually came to focus repeatedly on one or two key stylized moments—moments that were reproduced, reconfigured, and discussed ad infinitum in the media coverage of the event. One of these was the "interview" that occurred between the sultan himself and the Young Turk delegate who entered the palace to tell Abdülhamid his fate. This conversation continued to pop up in newspapers six and seven months after the original coverage. The most straightforward *New York Times* account of Abdülhamid's reaction to the news that he would no longer be sultan, inclusive of most of the elements that attracted attention and repetition, goes as follows:

> a convulsive shiver passed rapidly over his body and across his face.... [A]t this moment, the Young Prince begins to weep. He tries to restrain himself, but cannot, and hides himself behind the screen where he breaks into bitter sobs. The Sultan turns to look at him, then for an instant we see two tears trembling in

his cruel eyes, perhaps the only tears of his whole life. . . . [F]or a second time a shudder passes through the body of Abdul, who salutes us twice, humbly carrying both hands to his forehead, and we retire. The interview lasted eighteen minutes.[108]

Although the interview lasted for (precisely) eighteen minutes, the complete article reproduces only two articulate sentences from the Sultan—first he asks if he is going to be killed, and second he asks to be taken to the Çırağan Palace with his family. The rest of the article discusses what the interior of the palace looks like, what, more important, Abdülhamid's physical responses to his situation were, and finally the Young Turk delegate's translation of these responses for the benefit of the reading public.

The sultan, in other words, is understood in this article as a being who can tell us things only via body language—a being, as Linda Williams notes, integral to the realm of sadomasochistic pornography and melodrama. The feminized sultan convulsively shivers and shudders, there is unrestrained weeping and trembling, and then finally there is humiliation and withdrawal. The confession of the corrupt leader is placed squarely into the realm of pornography and, given the widespread play that this discussion of the leader received in various media outlets, into the *celebrated* realm of pornography. It is not just a sexualized politics that is being described here, it is a pornographic politics—in which the leader becomes a star and in which the audience, the public, becomes an essential component of the larger message.

When we get to depictions of Saddam Hussein's confession a century later, both the body language and the fascination with body language become more overt, with headlines such as "Saddam Hussein's Body Language Reveals Secrets" making the rather obvious point. Arguably, both also become more sadistic. A CNN report on Saddam Hussein's original court hearing in Iraq, for example, ostensibly about the leader's "statement," focuses almost exclusively on what the leader does not, or cannot, "say." Indeed, it is only after many thousands of words on Saddam Hussein's physicality that the transcript of the exchange between him and the judge is produced for the audience. John Burns, the reporter covering the trial notes,

> where we were, a lot of nervous gestures, hand to the side of the face, hand to the moustache, rubbing his brow. I took down a list of—of the—of the moods that I thought I saw him pass through in the course of all of this, if I can find it. He talked—he seemed to me to go from—just a minute—from initial nervousness, anxiety, disorientation, to irritation, anger, and eventually defiance. And I guess you've seen the—the tapes of

that. . . . [I] could give you more, if I took the time, on the precise gestures, but if you want me to just go to the text, I'll do that. Just a minute. I also, by the way, have some reaction from the Iraqi officials who were there who were principally Rabii and Salem Chalabi, which we can get to later on. We have finger frequently raised to the left eyebrow. His voice sounded initially slightly broken. You know, he always had that sort of middle pitch voice which didn't sound like the voice of the brutal dictator to me ever. Today, it sounded even less like that to begin with. He sounded husky. He had that slight Tikriti lisp—lisp. And he looked initially and sounded very much like a broken man. Scratching his forehead, hands (unintelligible) on his cheek, finger against his lips. You know the charges, I suppose, do you? . . . [M]odulation of the voice, sentences that trailed off, these hand gestures all the time? Hands, like this, like this, on his knees, to his face. Nervous gestures.[109]

What is interesting here is the repeated offers to "go to the text," and the repeated extent to which the "text" actually gets no attention. Instead, Saddam Hussein's gestures and tone tell Burns what is really going on. We learn not just his state of mind—dissected in great detail—but also his broken character, the fact that he is no longer a brutal dictator, the fact that he is from Tikrit, and again, above all, the fact that he is constrained by the law, and is no longer in control. These gestures are all involuntary, all betray the interiority of Saddam Hussein to the watching public.

Moreover, such body language is equally telling when it is repositioned within a sartorial framework. Much like pornographic narratives, the narratives of the corrupt leader's confession also focus on his state of dress or undress—initial titillating dishabille inviting an eventual violent stripping and exposure. When the Young Turk delegate arrived in Abdülhamid's presence, for example, he was "shocked" at the state of the sultan's clothing: "we thought we should find him in full uniform, in order to undergo with the dignity of his rank the sentence of the nation. He was dressed as a civilian with negligence that betrayed haste and agitation. He had not tied the knot of his black cravat, which was held together by means of a pearl headed pin."[110]

One hundred years later, U.S. anchormen were equally shocked at Saddam Hussein's neglected wardrobe:

> BLITZER: You make a good point. He looked like a vagrant. He certainly looked like a homeless person, the way he came across, obviously. And I guess it's fair to say he was a homeless person.

COHEN: Well, he was very much on the run. He was a fugitive. He looked both hunted and even haunted, as you look at those photographs, the images of him being examined by physicians to determine his state of health. And I think that stripping away—the old expression, the emperor has no clothes. Well, now we have a situation in which a dictator clearly has no power. He has been—that mask of authority of power has been ripped away forever.[111]

In both cases, the corrupt leader's dress tells us as much as his body language does about his state of mind—in the case of Abdülhamid, "agitated," and in the case of Saddam Hussein, "haunted." More than that, however, this initial focus on the leader's dress—and relative undress—also serves as the equivalent of a pornographic full-body pan. The gaze of both the Young Turk delegate and the television anchormen, which in turn represents the gaze of the public, focuses in detail on sartorial slippages, areas of exposure that invite initial penetration. The sultan's tie was not knotted—it was instead held (inadequately) together with a pin. The Iraqi leader's clothing betrayed his homelessness, his weakness, the absence of a protector to prevent this sort of attention. And in the end, CNN makes clear what this inadequacy of dress will lead to: a "stripping away," the explicit removal of clothing, and the ripping away of a mask—all indicating most forcefully that the leader is now situated within a pornographic frame. Like body language, therefore, the disarray of the confessing leader's clothing serves not just as a metaphor for the triumph of law, but as an actual, explicit statement about the simultaneous power, seduction, and weakness of corrupt rule.

Likewise, the captured leader's infantile, defiant attempts to produce a self-narrative in opposition to that being produced for him by the "law" serve not only as a metaphor for his lost power but, again, as concrete evidence of his disrespect for legal structures. Saddam Hussein, for example, is portrayed after his capture as an individual obsessed with maintaining narrative control and as one who must therefore submit to narration (standing in for "law") in all things. Over and over, images of Saddam Hussein are presented to the "public," and over and over it is someone else who speaks for him. CNN's interview with Jerrold Post—by 2003 known as "Jerrold Post, Saddam Profiler"—about Saddam Hussein's day in court, for example, produces repeated twists on the "body language" genre. Needless to say, the courtroom context received little attention in the discussion except to the extent that it emphasized the narrative power of legal structures.

PAULA ZAHN, host: The sight of Saddam Hussein sitting in front of an Iraqi judge and the sound of his combative words were undeniably compelling, but his expressions and gestures and body language may reveal a lot about his state of mind. Our producer, Brian Todd, sat down with a psychological profiler for a closer look at how Saddam handled himself in court today.

BRIAN TODD, CNN producer (voice-over): Reporters described him as nervous at first, taking awhile to hit his stride. But once the defiance kicked in, it was vintage Saddam Hussein. We brought in Dr. Jerrold Post, founder of the CIA psychological profiling division, who later did his own profile of Saddam, to give us his take on the man's performance. (on camera) I want to ask you first about his appearance overall. I think that struck a lot of viewers, just seeing the way he looked in the courtroom. What is your take on his appearance?

DR. JERROLD POST, Saddam profiler: I'm really struck. This is Saddam in command. He looks intense, focused, he's concentrating and he's even almost—he gives an appearance here of almost lecturing to the judge. What a remarkable contrast, this decisive man in charge is with that amazing image we saw emerging from the spider hole. Look at this compliant little man in a sense, obediently opening his mouth for the dental exam and then submitting, indeed bending his head for—while they search for lice. This was a Saddam that had never been seen before. Yet, I really want to emphasize this is the core Saddam psychologically. Underneath that fierce facade, this is the man he has spent a lifetime defending against.

TODD: I also wanted to ask you about the beard and the symbolism here. At one point in detention, the beard came off. He has made a decision to grow it back and in a certain way. What is your take on the symbolism of the beard and what he's trying to put forth?

POST: I'm struck by it. Here he is, thoughtfully stroking his beard, concentrated focus, rather dapper in many ways. And I see a person who is quite conscious of his appearance.

TODD (voice-over): At one point, before a judge many years his junior, Saddam senses something, bears down, gathers his bravado and seems to take over the proceedings.[112]

In this scenario, Jerrold Post is of course replaying the role that he had been playing for the past fifteen years in the larger narrative of Saddam Hussein as corrupt leader. There is, however, a slight shift in the tenor of his analysis—rather than looking at Saddam Hussein's life writ large and drawing conclusions from this about the leader's "psychological" state, Post is now focusing on minute details of his physicality. The tongue depressor/dental exam is revisited, the facial hair is deconstructed, each gesture and look is captured and narrated. And indeed, these things are *narrated*. This is not a psychological evaluation—this is inner monologue exposed to public view. Saddam Hussein is not in this passage a "malignant narcissist" who suffered from childhood attacks on his self-esteem. He is, variously, "in command," "intense," "focused," "concentrating," "compliant," "thoughtful," and "conscious of his appearance."

But he is also, and above all, in a constant battle with "law," constantly attempting to "take over the proceedings"—"defiant" and even "lecturing to the judge." This battle over narrative power is not just a raw power struggle, therefore, it is also direct evidence of Saddam Hussein's corrupt, lawless nature. As Paula Zahn makes clear when she introduces this exchange, it is inappropriate for Saddam Hussein to *say* anything at all—the "sound" (rather than meaning) of his "combative words" may have been compelling, but it is his body that is really at issue. The fact, in other words, that Saddam Hussein is in a courtroom is important only to the extent that it plays up the abstract battle that he, as a corrupt leader, has always fought with "law" broadly defined. The corrupt leader is by definition not someone who exists within the realm of law, he exists within the realm of celebrity, and his attempts to maintain narrative control indeed prove that such is the case.

As a result, however, it becomes the duty of the public standing in for "law" to constrain and to define the leader—to force him into the realm of the "real girl," to remove his voice, and to substitute an appropriate narrative in place of it. It is thus not just professional profilers like Jerrold Post who are called upon to engage in this intimate sort of relationship with the leader; it is also the liberal "everyone" embodied in the "man on the street." Only when this "everyone" has spoken for the corrupt leader, only when "everyone" has placed the corrupt leader into exceptional space, can law truly have triumphed. This process is made clear, for example, in the way in which Paula Zahn introduces the "body language" piece.

PAULA ZAHN, CNN anchor (voice-over): The defendant.

SADDAM HUSSEIN, former Iraqi president (through translator): I am Saddam Hussein, the President of Iraq.

ZAHN: He was belligerent.

HUSSEIN (through translator): How could you defend these dogs?

ZAHN: He was defiant.

HUSSEIN (through translator): I speak for myself.

ZAHN: Tonight, Saddam Hussein gets a dose of Iraqi justice.[113]

It is not just the jarring juxtaposition of Saddam Hussein's testimony and Zahn's exegesis. It is also the things that are defined as "belligerent" and "defiant" in this passage that are startling. In particular, it is made clear that the simple act of *having* a voice ("I speak for myself") is not only "defiant," it is also something that invites and provokes "Iraqi justice." The corrupt leader's confession simply cannot happen in his own voice—it must, by virtue of the way that he has been constructed over the previous decade, be displaced by the public's and, like a child's or an infant's, be seen but not heard. The final appropriation of Saddam Hussein's narrative, his final infantilization, and his final placement into the realm of the "real girl" indeed approaches the hyperbolic:

MOOS: No more Rip Van Winkle, this time Saddam Hussein had a lot less beard to stroke.

UNIDENTIFIED MALE: He looked like he had been fresh out of a spa treatment or something.

UNIDENTIFIED FEMALE: He's not bad looking. The guy is not a bad looking guy. He didn't look scruffy.

UNIDENTIFIED FEMALE: He's not my type but I just think he looked healthier than I expected him to look.

MOOS: Anyone hoping to see Saddam Hussein locked up as securely as Hannibal Lecter.

ANTHONY HOPKINS, actor: Love your suit.

MOOS: Instead saw an unshackled man in a suit.

UNIDENTIFIED FEMALE: I think he looked way too good. And he was very arrogant. The way he lectured the judge, and I worry that—I just hope that he gets the punishment that he deserves.

UNIDENTIFIED FEMALE: That look of the pointing of the finger.

MOOS: Pointing not just one, but two fingers. . . .

UNIDENTIFIED MALE: You know, you clean him up and the guy is on the cover of *Time* magazine. You know what I'm saying? The sexiest man of the year for *People*, maybe?

MOOS: Sexiest, no, but for those hoping that the fallen dictator would appear crust (sic) fallen.

UNIDENTIFIED FEMALE: The look in the eyes, like, he's the same guy.

MOOS: For *Paula Zahn Now*, this is Jeanne Moos.[114]

First of all, we have an amalgam of "unidentified males" and "unidentified females"—representatives of the mass of liberal "citizens"—who comment for the most part on Saddam Hussein's physicality and grooming. There is then a jump to the (fictional) Hannibal Lecter and a concomitant conflation of the "fictional" with the "real," when the comment of the person defined as the (real) "Anthony Hopkins, actor," rather than the (fictional) "Hannibal Lecter," is weirdly interspersed among the comments of the "real" unidentified males and females. This confusion of the realm of the real with the realm of fantasy in turn sets the groundwork for the more legal commentary of the worried unidentified female, who hopes that Saddam Hussein will get the punishment he deserves. Finally, the legal gives way to the celebrated with the penultimate ironic comment on Saddam as celebrity in *Time* or *People* magazine. It is only at this point then that we are then finally reminded of the existence of the "real" Saddam Hussein—that, from the look in the eyes, he is undoubtedly the "same guy."

This passage, in other words, repeatedly produces and reproduces Saddam Hussein as corrupt leader—he is defined, constrained, and exhibited in myriad, varied, and occasionally simply strange ways by liberal public opinion standing in for law. The minute discussion of his physicality and flesh indicates the totalitarian nature of both his rule and his punishment. The confusion of "real" and "fictional" places him further into exceptional space, into the realm of the real girl, where it is precisely the discourse of law that allows for anything (lawless) to happen.[115] Finally, the conflation of Saddam as celebrity with Saddam as "the same guy" closes the circle—the corrupt leader can be understood and therefore judged *only* as a celebrity, his existence, legal or otherwise, defined *only* against the narratives that his (adoring) public produces for him.

As a result, the corrupt leader—in this case, both Abdülhamid and Saddam Hussein—is quite literally brought before the "bar of public opinion." This is not just a metaphorical moment. Indeed, given the narrative of corruption and the leader's role in it, "the bar of public opinion" is, I want to emphasize, the *only* arena in which Saddam Hussein or Abdülhamid can have any relationship with law or legal structures at all. As early as 1901, Abdülhamid's unauthorized biographer, Dorys, was hailed as one who "drags the Sultan to the bar of public opinion and presents him in an altogether new and startling light."[116] At the time of his actual abdication in 1908 and 1909, newspaper headlines ran along the lines of "When Turkey's Sultan Faced His Masters," and "Sultan Faces His People: Drives to Selamlik in Open Victoria While Throngs Line Streets."[117] In a very basic way, therefore, Abdülhamid was defined as an individual who could interact with law only as it was channeled through his people, his masters, the bar of public opinion.

Similarly, in 2003, *The Guardian* ran a bewildering article ostensibly about Saddam Hussein's relationship to law. In it, a vast array of celebrity equivalents to the unidentified males and females of the Paula Zahn piece each in turn discussed his "legal" status.

> Now what for Saddam? Now the difficult bit: After the cheers come the questions. Who will try Saddam for his numerous crimes? And where? Can any Iraqi court give him a fair trial? And should he face the gallows? We asked 15 people with very different perspectives how the fallen Iraqi dictator should be brought to justice: the Nuremberg veteran Gitta Sereny; the ex-minister Michael Portillo; the historian Ian Kershaw; the neocon Thomas Donnelly; the Eichmann prosecutor Zvi Terlo; the Iraqi journalist Mustafa Alrawi (sic); the Kurdish politician Barham Salih; the blogger Salam Pax; the prisons inspector Sir David Ramsbotham; the war crimes prosecutor Richard Goldstone; the Iraqi ex-pat Dr. Nadje Al-Ali; the barrister Baroness Helena Kennedy; the Arab editor Abdel Bari Atwan; the human rights campaigner Kate Allen; the anti-Pinochet lawyer Hugo Gutierrez.[118]

Again, in both scenarios, the "bar of public opinion" is not simply a rhetorical notion. The celebrity of the corrupt leader has created a situation in which "everyone" is an expert on him, in which the public gaze *is* the law. The earlier portrayal of the infantile leader as one who was corrupt both because his will was law and because he could not control his will, both because he could not create a coherent self-narrative and because he could not distinguish between reality and fantasy, meant that his confession and "trial" had to exist in the same lawless, out-of-control, fictional, and incoherent space. The inappropriateness of the corrupt leader *speaking*, rather than twitching, shuddering, or crying, the similar inappropriateness of his attempt to narrate rather than be narrated is played up because the corrupt leader exists to define the realm of "law" from the realm of "not law." He, along with the corruption that he "spawns," belongs and will always belong in the latter, his existence in exceptional space in and of itself reinforcing the power of rational liberal rhetoric.

Nothing demonstrates the inextricable linkage between liberal or legal rhetoric and biopolitics, between law as rational structure and law as spectacular, popular display, however, like the hyperbolic discussion of habeas corpus that occurs around, and in fact stands in for, the eventual confession of the corrupt leader. The corrupt leader's body is fundamental. His flesh and physicality are key. It is thus not arbitrary that Prince Johnson demonstrated Samuel Doe's illegitimacy via a repeated display of the latter's live body, his live tortured body, his dead body, and then eventually his dead disinterred body. Nor is it arbitrary that British newspapers were particularly disgusted with Johnson's "excuse," that he "knew how to please the mob." Johnson's reliance on public opinion rather than law, his demonstration of political power in the form of minute physical control over his now illegitimate rival flew in the face of classical liberal ideas about appropriate political violence. It was also an integral part of the corruption narrative, appropriated and displayed by the global media even while they condemned it.

This display of the body of the corrupt leader—a simultaneously biopolitical and liberal reaction to corrupt rule as it is embodied in the doubling, tripling, expanding, and contracting monstrous flesh of the leader—already had a long history by the end of the twentieth century, however. The *New York Times* of 1908 and 1909, for instance, was fascinated with the deposed Abdülhamid's now "life-sized" body, as well as with what his former doubles might be able to say about (or for) him. In an article from 1909, for example, Francis McCullough wrote:

> with his bent form, his hooked nose, his ashy face, his faded overcoat, and his tottering steps, the old Padishah resembled a perfect Shylock on the stage. Despite his dyed beard he looks his full 68 years, even when seated in his carriage, but when walking, or rather shuffling about, he looks 20 years older.... [A]bdul Hamid looked like a man who expects corpses to rise from the grave and denounce him. Dazed, horror stricken almost, the aged Sultan looked downward as if he saw something supernatural, unseen by all else.... [I] watched the Sultan narrowly.... [T]hat pale, worn face was absolutely impassive.[119]

The coming together of Abdülhamid's now contained, now displayed physical form—"watched narrowly" by the reporter, and barely able to move, "shuffling about" rather than walking—with early twentieth-century anti-Semitic discourse is an effective rhetorical move. But it is not simply a conflation of the Oriental as external other and the Jew as internal other. By displacing the physicality of the corrupt leader onto the physicality of the Jew—and the explicitly spectacularized Jew ("on the stage")—the relationship between the liberal idealization of law and the totalitarian focus on bare life is made clear. Both the corrupt leader and the Jew inhabit—or will eventually inhabit (explicitly as the *Muselmann* or Muslim)—a space defined not by law but by biology. The habeas corpus effect here is therefore one in which "having the body" is an end in and of itself. Once the body is constrained, displayed, and regulated, once it is defined as outside of rational structures, the work of "law" is complete.

Indeed, it is not even necessary to have the "real" body of the Sultan in these legalesque accounts—it suffices simply for there to be *a* body. In the same way, in other words, that Uday Hussein's body double served as a confessant for Uday Hussein himself, various doubles likewise serve as substitute confessants for Abdülhamid as well. We learn, for example, that,

> after spending a week in this city in hourly dread of being arrested and sent back to Constantinople to answer for his crimes against the Turkish people, Zia Bey, formerly a chief spy of Sultan Abdul Hamid's, said to be a former head of the secret police, who fled from his country when the Young Turks gained control of the government, sailed for London last Wednesday. . . . [Z]ia Bey, in his interview with a reporter for the *New York Evening Post* [said] . . . "I am Zia Bey, the chief spy of the Sultan, the wretch, the rascal, the mischief doer. I have been cruel, heartless, and done many things which a man of conscience would not do. Do you blame me? I was brought up in that life. From my childhood I saw plotting against the other. I saw graft and cruelty and followed in the steps of others for my own promotion. . . . [T]he Sultan is an intelligent man, but he is suspicious, selfish, cruel and corrupt."[120]

The unreserved abandon with which Zia Bey confesses his secrets makes this statement almost embarrassing as a stand-in for what the far more difficult Abdülhamid might have revealed. But, again, the purpose of the confession is not its content, it is its mere existence. Content, knowledge, and information are derived from the corrupt leader's involuntary body language, not from his—or his doubles'—words. The point of the double confessing is simply to play up further the extent to which the corrupt leader's body, and its doubles, are contained and controlled. It is, like the interview with Saddam Hussein's son's double, a purely physical exhibition of the captured leader's flesh.

Celebrating the Corrupt Leader 99

The extent to which it is the physicality of the body that is meaningful in this expression of liberal legal power indeed becomes clear in the "agonized" decision of the U.S. government "eventually" to display the dead bodies of Saddam Hussein's sons (as temporary stand-ins for Saddam Hussein himself),[121] and in the "shocking" revelation of the images of Saddam Hussein's hanging corpse. Unlike Prince Johnson's, the U.S. government's purpose here was obviously not to "please the mob." It was instead to work within a framework that already existed. As ABC News correspondent, Martha Raddatz noted,

> when the gunfire stopped, the US retrieved four bullet-riddled bodies from the residence, among them, Saddam Hussein's sons. . . . [T]he United States has thought about [it], Charlie. And I think tomorrow you will see photographs released of both sons, of their bodies, to try to prove to the Iraqi people that they are really dead. And it's proof they badly need, although you saw lots of celebrations today. They do want sort of eyewitness proof.[122]

The fault, if any, for this breach of civilized procedure lies in other words with the "Iraqi people," who "badly need" to see the photographs and/or the bodies themselves. But the slippage in this passage between legal terminology, with its reliance on proof or eyewitness proof, and biopolitical terminology resting in the display of flesh—of bullet-riddled bodies—makes clear the extent to which biology supersedes law in the rhetoric of the corrupt leader. It makes clear, in other words, that habeas corpus is in and of itself enough—any further trial or procedure is meaningless.

This becomes truly apparent, however, only in the eventual confession (physical display) of Saddam Hussein's own body. Once again, this display was broadcast thousands of times in the weeks following its production, and the basic purpose of it was to place him, as corrupt leader, into pornographic, exceptional, biopolitical space. That Saddam Hussein existed in that lawless arena, defined by law as outside of the law, a being with a physical identity but no legal or political one, was all the evidence needed to show that his monstrous rule was and had been illegitimate. The very first release of the medical examination deserves some further attention, however. In late 2003, CNN ran the following report on the press conference announcing the capture of Saddam Hussein:

> GEN. RICARDO SANCHEZ, U.S. army: At this time, I'd like to show you a short video. Roll the video, please. . . . [T]his is Saddam as he was being given his medical examination today. (Shouts and cheers from Iraqi media) Saddam's medical examination proved

that he had no injuries and he is in good health. (Shouts and cheers from Iraqi media) What we will see next is a picture of Saddam Hussein at the time he was captured on your left. And on your right is Saddam Hussein after he was shaved. Next slide. And here you see Saddam, a historical picture, and with him today on my left. The capture of Saddam Hussein is a defining moment in the new Iraq. I expect that the detention of Saddam Hussein will be regarded as the beginning of reconciliation for the people of Iraq and as a sign of Iraq's rebirth.[123]

The first point to note here is the apparently arbitrary moments at which we get "shouts and cheers from Iraqi media." Why would applause follow, first, Saddam Hussein's medical examination, and, second (given the apparent rhetorical purpose of the "shouts and cheers"), the fact that he had no injuries and was in good health? If we think in terms of the intersection between habeas corpus and biopolitical power, however, the timing of the applause makes a great deal of sense. The "shouts and cheers"—genuine or not—represent liberal public opinion, channeled through the media, responding to the confession of the corrupt leader.

And, I want to emphasize, the issue here is not Saddam Hussein's capture in and of itself, but the display of his body and the simultaneous display of his illegitimacy. The monstrous nature of the corrupt leader's rule as it was manifested in his body and his body doubles is indeed repeated here, parodied, but this time framed and constrained within the larger liberal discourse. There is Saddam being examined, Saddam at his capture, Saddam having been shaved, and Saddam on my left. Four different bodies, each of them controlled minutely in a different way—each of them no longer "creepy" because the doubling is now in the hands of legal structures. But once more, the legal here relies *solely* on the enframing and display of the body, and that is all. The confession of corrupt rule is embodied in flesh, not in words, not in law, not in coherent legal structures. Indeed, as Sanchez notes, it is the capture and detention of Saddam Hussein (and only his capture and detention) that "will be regarded as the beginning of reconciliation for the people of Iraq and as a sign of Iraq's rebirth." Now that the monstrous, incestuous, contaminated body of the leader has been reframed, the violated nation can once again be birthed.

At the same time, an equally effective representation of corruption contained involves the penetration of the corrupt leader's house, pit, lair, or harem, the exposure of this hidden space to public view, and the careful inventory of what we find there. This representation references in turn earlier moments in the corruption discourse, where it was these spaces precisely that hid the leader, along with his inappropriate relationship to the nation, from view. On April 28, 1909, for example, the *New York Times* ran the following description of Abdülhamid's capture: "The Sultan was left alone, save for a few women. It was necessary to seek him in the inner recesses of his private apartments, and thither the chief officials went, forcing their way."[124] On May 2, 1909, we hear a similar story from the Young Turk delegation:

> we advance and scarcely have we set foot on the great marble steps of our outer portico than the eunuchs surround us. . . . [T]o the right we perceive a large silken screen. On the wall behind it is an enormous mirror, and I note that on the opposite wall is another mirror, so placed as to allow whoever is behind the screen to see the least movement of anyone who enters the apartment.[125]

Finally, on June 6, 1909, the same newspaper ran the long article entitled, "What Was Found in the Lair of Abdul Hamid: Amazing Discoveries in the Yildiz Kiosk Following the Fall of Turkey's Sultan Reveal a Condition Surpassing Fiction."[126]

In the first passage, in other words, the chief officials force their way into the inner recesses of the palace. The interiority and privacy of the place were played up not just explicitly (in his private apartments), but implicitly with the invocation of "a few women" as representatives of domestic space. The penetration thus occurs twice—first in "real" time, when the sultan is exposed to law, and, second, in spectacular time, when he is exposed to public opinion standing in for law. It is, moreover, the description of the moment, the details set into writing, that play up the particularly intimate nature of the relationship—only when it becomes a newspaper article, does the overt control over the private manifest itself. Indeed, in the second passage, we see the futility of attempting to resist the public gaze in "real" time. The delegation is engulfed in eunuchs, it is tricked by silken screens, it is gazed at in a mirror by the invisible sultan. But when the event is turned into spectacular time, all of these things are simply further details of Abdülhamid's inner recesses, exposed and controlled. His attempt to evade the public gaze is evidence of his corruption, and it is merely something else to describe in detail, to constrain, and to exhibit. The final article from June is thus the climax to the episode. The sultan's lair is laid open, its contents described minutely, and Abdülhamid, interior and exterior, is dragged into the light—is made transparent, and therefore no longer "corrupt."

Saddam Hussein's places of residence underwent similar scrutiny, and in particular the "pit" from which he was eventually dragged into the light received much fascinated attention. Like Abdülhamid's harem, Saddam Hussein's pit represented hyperbolic interiority, and the tours that occurred following his removal from it were similarly intense, similarly intimate. On CNN, for example, we are told,

> ROBERTSON: This is the kitchen here, a sink over here, medicine, Mars bars, a flashlight, a cap, rotting bananas. . . . [T]he bedroom in here, two beds. And inside the bedroom a refrigerator, the heater. On the wall, posters. A Christian (sic) poster, Noah's Ark. The bed, crumpled bed clothing. Fresh, clean pair of boxer shorts, unused, still new. . . . [A]nd down here, a pair of shoes, unused, some water, tracksuit bottoms. Just chaos. . . . [T]his tiny hole is really small inside. It's concrete mud on the walls. . . . [I]t's very difficult to get in and out of. It wouldn't have been easy for the soldiers who discovered Saddam Hussein. He came with his hands up. . . . [A]fter that, Saddam Hussein was whisked out of the hole, pulled up, and taken away to a helicopter waiting in the field just across here.[127]

This discussion was repeated in a variety of different contexts over the last few weeks of 2003. Again, however, the point to keep in mind is the minute control that the public gaze has over the tiniest aspect of Saddam Hussein's life and interiority. The sink, the Mars bars, and the rotting bananas are exposed and celebrated. The bed and boxer shorts are the subject of intense scrutiny. The hole itself is claustrophobically small, representative of an intense, secretive interiority which hides, eventually, "just chaos." And in the end, therefore, Saddam Hussein, like Abdülhamid, is whisked out, pulled up, and reframed. He, too, is made transparent, as is his pit—he too becomes representative of law's *absolute* and *total* triumph over corrupt rule.

The confession of the corrupt leader thus in turn brings the larger corruption narrative full circle. The intimacy of our relationship with him, the infantile nature of *his* relationship to state and citizen, the monstrous ways in which his corrupt rule is physically manifested—all create a climax situated in the leader's flesh, on the one hand, and his celebrity, on the other. His body shudders, trembles, and eventually secretes involuntary evidence of his lawless rule. His celebrity fixes him in a permanently exposed and exhibited state, linking the power of public opinion to the power of law. It is indeed precisely the biopolitical vocabulary of sex and intimacy, used initially to describe his rule, that likewise describes the regulation of his every physical, sexual, psychological, and biological move after his capture. It is precisely because he is and was *corrupt* that his confession occurs outside of, above, alongside of the law—in an exceptional space where power is manifested not in legal structures, but in the minute control and spectacularization of bare life.

Conclusion

That the press responded with such fascinated horror[128] to the repeated display (in September 1990 and April 1992) of Doe's corpse and to the unauthorized video of Saddam Hussein's hanging (in December 2006) is indicative in a basic way of the continuing positive moral value attached to the "the rule of law" in liberal discourse. That the press simultaneously framed and reframed, produced and reproduced these displays in countless other forms likewise plays up the pornographic, biopolitical, and indeed totalitarian potential of this same rule of law. By the end of their time in power, Samuel Doe and Saddam Hussein existed only in exceptional space, they operated only as half-fictional, half-real stars on the local and international stage, and they were politically meaningful only as their dead bodies began to decay. Indeed, as time passed and various newspapers printed obituaries and retrospectives of the two, the display of their bodies and their corpses became key elements in the narrative and in the construction of each as a corrupt leader. Illegitimate by background, temperament, education, style, and physiognomy, Samuel Doe and Saddam Hussein asked for everything they got, including and especially their well-framed deaths.

In general, therefore, turning Doe, Saddam Hussein, and Abdülhamid II into celebrities, emphasizing the bodily, corporeal and fleshy aspects of their rule, was a necessary precursor to their positioning as, quite literally, poster boys for the corrupt leader. They were illegitimate precisely *because* their politics was biological, but it was likewise only the biopolitical nature of their rule that rendered it relevant to liberal legality. It was not, in other words, just that each had some political tarnish on his claim to rule—that Saddam Hussein and Samuel Doe were of "tribal" extraction, whereas Abdülhamid II came to power in the wake of his brother's deposal. It was that these various political questions could be turned into biological ones—that "tribal" was an excellent cipher for "lawless," and thus a solid foundation on which to construct the biological and erotic edifice of the corruption narrative. The emphasis on intimacy, infancy, the monstrous and the diseased, thus became integral to turning these leaders into stars.

Moreover, *as* stars, they transcended national and regional boundaries, serving—in their very degradation from political leader to corrupt leader—a greater rhetorical purpose than they ever had before. The collective that they created, the imagined community of newspaper readers and pornography consumers,[129] was quite emphatically an international one—one that, despite "cultural difference," recognized the basic narrative plot: the leader was first made human and then increasingly made sex, flesh, and blood. He was caught, humiliated, *de*humanized, and then repositioned within the second part of the narrative—the confession. In the confession, he was stripped, exposed, and celebrated—a central player in the discourse of the rule of law.

The stories of Abdülhamid II and Saddam Hussein are thus simply concrete examples of a more pervasive and abstract narrative. The eroticized vocabulary in which corruption is analyzed turned both into celebrities and stars. In the case of Abdülhamid II, it was between 1876 and 1908 that the newspaper-reading population became his intimate friend—his fears, sexual preferences, illnesses, passions, rages, and weaknesses all displayed for popular consumption prior to his eventual deposition and interrogation by the Young Turks. In the case of Saddam Hussein, it was between 1990 and 2006 that this same process occurred—that learning about the private life of the corrupt leader became a cozy installation in the morning ritual of millions of consumers. His violence, family problems, fashion sensibilities, and secret self-esteem issues were all dissected, discussed, and analyzed for over a decade before he, too, finally succumbed to the confessional apparatus and was exposed to public view. Although separated by a century, in other words, the narrative structures of these two stories—like that of Samuel Doe—are essentially interchangeable. Again, however, in pornography it is not the plot that matters; it is the repetition, the sensation, and the thrill.

3

Condemning the Corrupt System

Thus far I have looked at the implicit rather than explicit ways in which narratives of corruption have served to carve out exceptional space. What I would like to do in this chapter is to engage more directly with these processes—to examine exactly and in detail the analyses and condemnations of corruption that have placed states, regions, and even continents into the realm of the legal exception. In particular I will be interested in the self-consciously liberal literature that mingles and merges condemnations of corrupt systems with condemnations of totalitarian systems—that gradually displaces lawless corrupt space onto lawless totalitarian space. At the same time, however, I will suggest throughout this chapter that although in many ways these analyses play up the separate nature of areas under the (liberal) rule of law, in many other ways they have led to a situation in which the difference between lawful violence and lawless violence—between, say, taxation and torture—is not in any way an obvious one. Just as the first chapter of this book addressed the simultaneity of the well-regulated body politic and the body politic out of control, therefore, and the second chapter highlighted the overlap between pornographic testimony and legal testimony, this final chapter will consider the possibility that the corrupt/totalitarian violence described by anticorruption advocates is very much a product of—indeed a reproduction of—its noncorrupt/liberal counterpart.

With that in mind, I would like to contextualize this chapter within a short discussion of the paradoxes at the heart of the (potentially or implicitly) corrupt/totalitarian system described by the Marquis de Sade. In his *Erotism*, Bataille addresses these paradoxes at length, noting in particular that what begins in Sade's work as "an attitude of utter irresponsibility . . .

ends with one of stringent self control"[1]—that in Sade's universe, violent chaos, deliberate lawlessness, and calculated irrationality arrive in the end at order (if not peace), rules (if not laws), and relentless logic (if not rationality). Sade's republic, in other words, is a republic that would be quite familiar to the anticorruption advocates I mentioned earlier, and whose work I will address in detail next—those analysts who have attempted to link corruption on the one hand to totalitarianism on the other. As a corrupt system, the sadistic state is out of control, unbounded by law, and irrational. As a totalitarian system, it likewise exerts excessive control, regulates areas of life that are supposed to remain untouched by politics, and rationalizes the minutiae of sexual or biological identity. These two systems of political control seem in every way unrelated to one another—*but*, if Sade and the corruption analysts are to be believed, they in fact meet at a number of key points. It is the purpose of this chapter to address these points of intersection.

The following pages will therefore examine the linkages, sometimes overt and sometimes implicit, sometimes mundane and sometimes fantastic, between narratives of corruption and narratives of totalitarianism. The corrupt system as a system that dehumanizes, that in its very weakness and parochialism is capable of brutalizing and destroying an individual's humanity is a theme that runs throughout the anticorruption literature. But it is not *just* the dehumanizing nature of corruption that horrifies its concerned spectators. After all "good" bureaucracy also dehumanizes—and indeed civic uniformity at the expense of idiosyncratic individualism is quite explicitly the ideal. What I will try to demonstrate in this chapter is thus that the apparent difference between corrupt and noncorrupt, bad and good, bureaucratic systems as they are described in the anticorruption literature is not that one system brutalizes whereas the other does not. Rather, I will suggest that the former engage in "corrupt/totalitarian" forms of dehumanization, whereas the latter engage in "legal/liberal" forms. What is at issue, therefore, is not that there is a constant process of ordering, inclusion, and exclusion—this obviously occurs in both. It is instead that the rationale—rational or not—behind this process is terrifyingly different.

At the same time, however, as I previously noted, this rhetorical difference between the corrupt/totalitarian and the legal/liberal does not necessarily stand up to close examination. If anything, indeed, it suggests areas of overlap and highlights the uncomfortably close relationship between the apparent rule of law and the apparent state of exception. To the extent that each space is bounded in a biopolitical vocabulary, each necessarily assumes the other. Although I will situate this chapter within a discussion of totalitarian space, therefore, and will devote time to addressing the literature that positions corrupt systems within this space, I will be equally dedicated to the suggestion that this space is in fact universal—and that the rule of law is, in itself, corrupt.

Biopolitical Space and Totalitarian Space

Bataille is not the only theorist to have noted Sade's relevance to contemporary political structures. Agamben, for example, has also discussed the "modernity" of Sade's work—especially to the extent that it hints at the biopolitical, and thus totalitarian, potential of mass democracy. I would like to begin this chapter outline, therefore, by turning to Agamben's analysis of sadism, biopolitics, and totalitarianism. "Sade's modernity," he argues,

> does not consist in his having foreseen the unpolitical primacy of sexuality in our unpolitical age. On the contrary, Sade is as contemporary as he is because of his incomparable presentation of the absolutely political (that is, "biopolitical") meaning of sexuality and physiological life itself. Like the concentration camps of our century, the totalitarian character of the organization of life in Silling's castle—with its meticulous regulations that do not spare any aspect of physiological life (not even the digestive function, which is obsessively codified and publicized)—has its root in the fact that what is proposed here for the first time is a normal and collective (and hence political) organization of human life founded solely on bare life.[2]

Agamben focuses more on the "stringent self-control" of Sade's universe than he does on the "utter irresponsibility" that underlies much of Bataille's work, but he is making a similar point about the relationship between sadism and contemporary politics. Sade's state is well ordered, well regulated, and wildly violent. It is "totalitarian," however, not because of this order, regulation and violence. It is totalitarian because these structures target the bodily, the biological, and the physiological—because it is founded on sex "rather" than on law.

In this way, Sade's state is not greatly removed from the postcolony as it is described, for instance, by Mbembe. According to Mbembe, "the postcolony is characterized by a distinctive style of political improvisation, by a tendency to excess and lack of proportion," but it is "also made up of a series of corporate institutions and a political machine that, once in place, constitutes a distinctive regime of violence."[3] The excessive, the obscene, and the vulgar indeed have a conspicuous purpose in the postcolony, "the production of vulgarity . . . a deliberately cynical operation . . . political in the sense intended by S. Wilentz when he argues that every polity is governed by 'master fictions' little by little accepted into the domain of the indisputable."[4] Like Sade's republic or Silling's castle, in other words, the postcolony here is simultaneously disordered but overregulated, nonsensical but relentlessly logical, and above all sexual—but sexual for purely political reasons.

I bring up these various spaces—the camp, Silling's castle, Sade's republic, the postcolony—because I want to engage explicitly with their "totalitarian" (and thus "corrupt") nature. Each of these spaces is characterized by a bureaucracy, by well-ordered political structures, and by a distinctly logical regime of violence. But each is also cut off from the rational, the liberal, and the rule of law. The difference between the two ought to be insurmountable. In fact, however, the only apparent difference—the thing that renders the totalitarian and corrupt completely distinct from the liberal and the rational—is that the former is a biopolitical system and the latter a "purely" political one. Indeed, what becomes clear in reading anticorruption literature is not that violence in corrupt systems is somehow more extreme than violence in their noncorrupt counterparts—it is simply that the violence in the former is biological "rather" than legal. Inclusion or exclusion in the former is governed by flesh or sex—nepotism or bribery, say—and therefore collectives are formed according to biology instead of law, blood instead of political identity. Unlike noncorrupt, liberal systems that brutalize and dehumanize via containment in a passport photo or a marriage license, corrupt, totalitarian systems situate the political within what Bataille has called the "obscenity" of the naked, undifferentiated body.[5]

Again, however, although most anticorruption literature rests squarely on the assumption that these dichotomies—biology versus law, blood versus politics, totalitarian/corrupt versus liberal—are valid ones, I want to suggest in this chapter that these easy distinctions are not as clear as they might be. Each section of this chapter will thus address first the rhetorical overlap between corruption and totalitarianism—and the way in which this overlap has served to carve out and differentiate exceptional space. Each section will also, however, question the apparent distinctions between biopolitical structures resting on blood or sex and political structures resting on law or civic identity—between exceptional space and space operating within the rule of law.

In the first section, therefore, I will discuss an influential interpretation of the collision of corruption and totalitarianism in Sade's political theory—Pier Pasolini's film *Salo*. In this film, I will argue, Pasolini not only portrays one logical conclusion to the biopolitical focus on bare life, but also emphasizes the uneasy and close relationship between corrupt, totalitarian, and lawless space cut off from the rest of the world (the villa), and the noncorrupt, liberal, lawful structures within which it must operate. The second section, "Bandits and Bureaucrats," will sketch a number of different types of "real" spaces that are in one way or another tied back to Pasolini's villa (or Silling's castle). After first discussing the conflation of the bandit and the bureaucrat in the anticorruption literature and the way in which this rhetorical device serves to define these spaces, I will then address various manifestations of it in the colonial and neocolonial imagination. These spaces, I will argue, are defined above all as spaces in which collectives are based on blood, sex, or biology "rather" than law—and in which, therefore, any political behavior is necessarily corrupt and/or totalitarian.

The next section will go into detail about one particularly hyperbolic manifestation of the corrupt and therefore totalitarian state—the twentieth- and twenty-first-century "torture nation." The torture nation is exceptional, biopolitical space brought to its logical conclusion, a space in which all collective, political activity is emphatically bodily and biological, where corruption and totalitarianism are in fact interchangeable. It is defined indeed as a "torture nation" not because torture necessarily happens within its borders, but because anything that happens within its borders is necessarily "torture"—necessarily an illegitimate disordering and destabilizing of bodily or biological boundaries. Like Pasolini's villa, however, the torture nation is also linked inextricably to liberal structures, produced by and productive of the noncorrupt rule of law.

The final two sections of the chapter will look in more detail at the precise ways in which collective affiliations are formed—and in which bureaucratic processes occur—within this exceptional space. In the first of these, "Bribery, Nepotism, and Decay," I will suggest that the bodily or biological nature of corrupt political affiliation produces an emphatically *not* metaphorical manifestation of the body politic gone out of control. Drawing on two centuries of literature condemning the corrupt bureaucracy, I will show that anticorruption advocates see a direct linkage between political corruption on the one hand, and actual (rather than metaphorical) racial miscegenation, incest, and totalitarian control on the other. The final section of the chapter will take this interpretation of the corrupt/totalitarian bureaucracy one step further. Returning to my analysis of the torture nation, I will suggest in this section that to the extent that noncorrupt/liberal bureaucracy dehumanizes via law whereas corrupt/totalitarian bureaucracy dehumanizes via blood or biology, any political activity in the latter necessarily codes as "torture." At the same time, however, to the extent that exceptional space gradually becomes universal, torture likewise becomes a key element in all forms of political affiliation. The chapter thus concludes by gesturing toward the uncomfortable parallels between the corrupt/totalitarian destruction of citizens in Iraq's Abu Ghraib prison and the noncorrupt/liberal creation of citizens in the new Iraqi constitution.

Salo: The 120 Days of Sodom

One of the most straightforward linkages between corruption and totalitarianism, biology and structured irrationality occurs in Pier Pasolini's film *Salo*.[6] Repeatedly described as an "indictment of fascist corruption"[7]—without any attempt to deal with the apparent contradiction in associating (overcontrolled) fascism with (out of control) corruption—it portrays all of the "irresponsibility" and "stringent self-control" of Sade's universe. Set during the Second World War in a villa situated in the fascist stronghold, Salo, the film makes clear the aesthetic, if not necessarily political, connections between a state that attempts to rule every minute detail of the citizen's life and a state that will interact with these same citizens only at the level of biology, physicality, and sexuality. Inclusion within and exclusion from the system make sense, but only if we accept the primacy of blood rather than citizenship.

Likewise, the fixation on rules, ceremony, and fairness that we see in the film is a perfectly reasonable bureaucratic fixation, but only if we accept that the equality promised by these structures is a biological and sexual equality in which no one is exempt from torture or humiliation. The prostitute/narrators confess their stories voluntarily, for example, but the humiliating violence of these confessions is made clear, and indeed mirrored, by the involuntary spasms of the victims in the last scene. Throughout the film, the constant message is that a corrupt space is a totalitarian space, that a totalitarian space is in turn a lawless space, and that in lawless spaces anything (physical) can happen. But, at the same time, this "anything" is ordered, and in its order it is not greatly removed from the protected and protective realm of law—where ostensibly (if not actually) one's biology is left alone.

One of the more insistent impressions produced by *Salo*, for example, is that there is a direct link between political corruption and incest—a cinematic convention that is certainly not unique to *Salo*, with Roman Polanski's *Chinatown* the other obvious example. After first "marrying" one another's daughters,[8] the four fascist bosses—the duke, the president, the bishop, and the banker—also solicit stories of young, filial girls masturbating various father figures from the narrator/prostitutes, and encourage their victim/participants to call them "daddy."[9] From the very beginning, that is, the abstract political, legal, religious, and economic power embodied by the four bosses is tied, incestuously, to flesh and sex. From the very beginning, it is made clear that entry into their regimented and rule-oriented system is predicated on biology and sexuality, and in fact on an especially deviant and excessively intimate biology and sexuality.

The victim/participants are included or excluded on the basis and perfection of their naked bodies, and to the extent that they rise or fall in the hierarchy, it is their flesh rather than any abstract identity that secures them a position in the system. Indeed, the offering up of flesh or fluid as a bribe is a recurrent theme, and although she may be doing it involuntarily, it is the girl who cannot stop crying—echoing the melodramatic or pornographic heroine described by Williams—who finds herself the most caught up in the quasi-state apparatus. It is, in other words, precisely the inefficiency of the corrupt system—accessed by virtue of the apparently disorganized biological (nepotism) or the apparently unproductive material (bribery)—that allows for an efficient totalitarian system, so effective in its control over the individual that nothing remains unregulated.

Indeed, the corrupt system as a totalitarian system has, if anything, *more* rules and *more* regulations than the noncorrupt, law-based system. Existing as it does in a lawless space, it is, if anything, more fascinated with detail, with clarity, and with fairness than a system situated in a lawful space. Upon their arrival at the villa, for instance, the victim/participants are made to understand the "new laws"—a situation that is disturbing, however, only because (1) the new laws define the villa as a space that is separate from, and outside of the protective gaze of, the old (presumably rational) laws, (2) the new laws regulate inappropriate (private) biological and sexual things rather than appropriate public civic things, and (3) in their regulation of the private, the new laws are an apparent aberration from accepted moral standards. The new legislation is problematic, in other words, solely because it creates a separate space in which individuals are defined and administered biologically—aside from that, it is identical to legislation in a noncorrupt space.

And indeed, this similarity between inappropriate, sadistic rules and appropriate, humanitarian rules is highlighted a number of times in the film. In her narration of her first sexual experience, for instance, the first narrator/prostitute is admonished to "omit no detail" about the size of her partner's penis and the nature of his ejaculation. She must do so, however, purely "for clarity's sake." Likewise, when the four bosses choose "the most perfect ass" from among the victim/participants, they insist on covering the latter's faces so that "not knowing which is whose, we'll be impartial in judging.... we will not judge based on a previous preference." In the midst of their discussion, one of the four similarly states that his preference is "only an opinion. I submit to the majority." Again, the disturbing aspect of these passages is that the vocabulary of bureaucratic impartiality, judicial clarity, and democratic process is mobilized on behalf of the sexual, the biological, and the physical.[10] But it is not just a question of vocabulary—the prostitute's narration *does* in fact become more clear, and the decision with regard to the victim/participants' asses *is* in fact impartial. The only difference between the humanitarian and the sadistic, between the rational and the corrupt, is therefore, once more, that the former exists in an apparent world of (public) law, whereas the latter exists in an apparent world of (private) flesh.

But Pasolini was not an anticorruption advocate, and his point was certainly not that the corrupt and the noncorrupt, the totalitarian and the nontotalitarian were discrete categories. Indeed, the categories overlap in a number of areas, especially in the more legalistic scenes—in the repeated marriage ceremonies, for instance. Before even getting to the villa, the bosses marry one another's daughters. Once at the villa, there is first a "normal" marriage ceremony between a young girl and a young boy—after which the bosses regulate and participate in the consummation. Following this original ceremony, one of the boys is dressed in a wedding dress and, along with his new husband, the bosses, and the other victim/participants, required to eat feces at his wedding feast. And then finally, all four of the bosses cross-dress as bourgeois women and marry four of the boys who are dressed in masculine clothing.

The point of subverting and mocking the marriage ceremony is not simply that doing so undermines bourgeois moral values. It also highlights the fact that in overseeing marriage, by turning it into something regulated, taxed, and registered, the *non*corrupt or *non*totalitarian bureaucratic apparatus is also defining citizens biologically and sexually—that the line between regulating the ceremony and regulating the feast or the consummation is not as clear as it might be. Another way of conceiving of the overlap between the lawless and the lawful space in the marriage ceremony is to return to Bataille, who argues, for instance, that transgression "persists at the very basis of marriage," that the marriage ceremony is in fact no different from the blood sacrifice: "laws that allow an infringement and consider it legal are paradoxical. Hence, just as killing is simultaneously forbidden and performed in sacrificial ritual, so the initial sexual act constituting marriage is a permitted violation."[11]

The dichotomy between the corrupt system and the noncorrupt system, wherein the former is biological, sexual, and private, whereas the latter is civic and public, wherein the former operates within a lawful, abstract space and the latter in a lawless, fleshy, sexual, and concrete space, that is, *breaks down* as soon as a marriage ceremony is performed. The repeated marriage ceremonies in *Salo* therefore make far more sense as indictments of nonfascist noncorruption than necessarily "fascist corruption." The unfortunates who get taken to the villa end badly because the simultaneously totalitarian and corrupt fascist regime creates a situation in which they become bodies, defined and regulated as bodies, and nothing else.[12] The eventual message, however, is that the line between the abstract, rational, and noncorrupt and the fleshy, irrational, and corrupt is not an obvious one—that to the extent that all modern bureaucracy is about dehumanization, it does not make a great deal of difference whether this occurs in a passport photo or in a torture chamber.

As I will suggest below, it is this fear of (and desire for) an overlap between the corrupt and the noncorrupt system that drives the anticorruption literature of people and organizations less sophisticated than Pasolini. Narratives of the corrupt system take it as a fundamental given that the corrupt space is diametrically opposed to the noncorrupt space (even as the former is often placed—if sealed off—within the boundaries of the latter, as prison, camp, or colony). They take it as a given that the biological and sexual are diametrically opposed to the legal, and that as soon as the former is ascendant in defining the citizen, the latter is subverted, satirized, or simply disappears. Nonetheless, even as this dichotomy is created and defended by anticorruption advocates, the porous boundaries between the corrupt and the noncorrupt, between appropriate and inappropriate dehumanization are played up. As lawless space is created, it is also consumed—allowing for a private penetration of the public that is far more effective than anything wrought by a bribe-taking bureaucrat.

Bandits and Bureaucrats

It is a commonplace in both late nineteenth- and late twentieth-century corruption narratives to define the corrupt bureaucrat as a "bandit" or a "brigand." That banditry in particular should be seen as synonymous to bribe taking, nepotism, or preferment—activities that at first glance seem far removed from the world of brigandage—should not, however, be surprising. It is, after all, only activities like banditry or brigandage that evoke the aura not just of law-breaking, but of a complete existence outside of the law. Bandits are not just criminals; they are quite literally outlaws, and it is indeed precisely because of the "outlaw" (rather than "criminal") status of the bandit that late nineteenth- and late twentieth-century colonial regimes became obsessed with the activity.[13] These regimes were engaged in a constant battle with "illegitimate" and usually "corrupt" forms of alternative sovereignty, and the exceptional rhetoric of the bandit served them far more effectively than less exceptional talk of law-breaking criminals—allowing them to define entire populations collectively as bandits or brigands and deal with them accordingly. I want to suggest that this focus on the outlaw in colonial rhetoric has been key to formulations that portray the corrupt system—and especially the corrupt colonized system—as a system composed of brigands in place of civil servants.

In the colonial imagination, both bandits and corrupt bureaucrats created or were thought to create a political space in which alternative affiliations could be formed—and in particular in which biological affiliations could be formed at the expense of civic and legal ones. Corruption narratives quickly picked up on this relationship and, as a result, the fluidity between bureaucrat and bandit became a key defining characteristic of the corrupt system or corrupt state. At the same time, however, the arena occupied by the corrupt bandit/bureaucrat became increasingly circumscribed over the years—eventually represented not just by the colony, but by the interior of a transport truck, train, or jet. Like Pasolini's villa, in other words, violently lawless space gradually became an area that existed *within* noncorrupt structures while nonetheless also sealed off from them. By the late twentieth and early twenty-first centuries, indeed, we arrive at a situation in which corruption is said to lead directly to crimes like "people smuggling" or torture, and in which responsibility for these crimes is placed squarely on the shoulders of, first, the bandit, and second, the corrupt bureaucrat. The corrupt state—the area represented by, say, "Egypt"—thus became inextricably linked to the interior of the bandit's freight container full of "smuggled" immigrants—and by the time the corruption eruption occurred, its lethally claustrophobic nature became clear: once sealed up in the colony or the freight car, there was no more escape.

But this is a late twentieth-century manifestation of the corruption narrative. One hundred years before, it operated with less inexorable certainty. Between 1904 and 1908, for example, Rais Uli, the Moroccan "bandit chief," captured the imagination of the North American and Western European newspaper reading public. "Picturesque" and "intelligent," Rais Uli represented, far more than the Orientalized Moroccan sultan, both North African governance and its corrupt nature. As Rais Uli's story unfolded over these four years, the message that was in fact repeatedly relayed was that there was no actual difference between Moroccan bandit and Moroccan civil servant—that the not quite sovereign status of Morocco had produced an ineradicable tension between legal affiliation and biological affiliation.

Rais Uli's story (or at least his celebrity) began when he captured a U.S. citizen whom he then held hostage until various demands were met. In addition to a ransom, Rais Uli asked for the withdrawal of Moroccan forces from his district, legal immunity for himself and his followers, and U.S. and British recognition of the validity of these stipulations. The response on the part of the U.S. government was to send its navy to the coast of Tangiers to "rescue the captives and to bring the outlaw to book for his crimes." The *New York Times* article that discussed the incident on May 29, 1904, argued that "to grant [the stipulations] would be equivalent to forcing the Sultan of Morocco to abdicate in favor of a brigand so far as a considerable part of Moorish territory was concerned."[14] The next week, a shorter article ran, in which the sultan's foreign minister "appeal[ed] to the tribes to capture the bandit Raisuli (sic), stating that this alone can save Morocco from invasion."[15] Eventually, however, neither Rais Uli's capture, nor U.S. military violence was necessary—Perdicaris, the hostage/citizen was released, and gave his own version of the story in a final *New York Times* article entitled "Perdicaris's Story of Wild Trip with Bandit: Captives Clubbed with Rifles and Menaced with Knives: Calls Raisuli a Gentleman: Says Kidnapping Was Chiefly to Secure Release of His Tribesmen—Betrayed by Treachery of a Tangiers Official."[16]

In early 1907, Rais Uli once again made the papers in an article intriguingly entitled "Capture of Europeans Ordered by Rais Uli: He Was Disgusted Because His Men Got Only Spaniards."[17] A few months later, in July 1907, he was a bit more successful and made off with (the British) Sir Harry Maclean, an advisor to the Moroccan government. In addition to a ransom, Rais Uli demanded his own *re*appointment as governor of Tangiers, his appointment as commandant of police, and the recall of the current Moroccan minister of war.[18] This time around, the media response was less outraged, and indeed a *New York Times* editorial ran ten days later arguing that

> the Brigand is really one of the strongest administrators and far seeing diplomats that Morocco ever had; and it is little wonder that so able and intelligent a man as Perdicaris himself should recommend that his captor be put officially in charge of all Northern Morocco, to restore order among the fierce tribes and keep the caravan roads free from bandits.[19]

Throughout August, the newspaper ran repeated articles about Maclean's "safety," and the fact that Rais Uli was after only "justice," until Maclean was finally released.[20] Rais Uli's story nonetheless ended on a tragic note. In an article in February 1908, we finally learn that "Rais Uli, the Bandit,

Reported Poisoned: Moorish Captor of Perdicaris and Sir Harry Maclean Again Declared to be Dead: Won International Fame: No Longer Bandit but Provincial Governor."[21]

The relentless progression of these stories makes clear the overlap between Moroccan bureaucrat and Moroccan bandit in the mind of "the newspaper reading public." Although Rais Uli's initial appearance was met with disapproval, it was only his designation as an "outlaw" who needed to be "brought to the book," his entrance onto the scene as a tribal threat to legitimate Moroccan sovereignty, that made possible the eventual portrayal of Morocco as a corrupt space when he was finally appointed governor. The abstract sovereignty of the Moroccan sultan is nothing compared to the personal loyalty that the tribes apparently feel toward Rais Uli—a fact indeed reinforced by the statement of the Moroccan foreign minister—and the implication of the articles is that this is as it should be.[22]

In the end, indeed, it is Perdicaris who has the last word on the subject, and who irrevocably defines Morocco as corrupt (and biologically determined) rather than noncorrupt (and legally determined). Although his trip was "wild," although Rais Uli is a "bandit," and although there was much physical clubbing and menacing with knives, Perdicaris insists that the brigand is also a "gentleman," who was merely responding to the "treachery of a Tangiers official." By making this move, Perdicaris implies that in the Moroccan context, the official and the bandit are synonymous—in fact, if anything, the sly corruption of the former is even less legitimate than the wild, impetuous violence of the latter. Likewise, just as the governors of Tangiers and Fez were linked *personally* rather than *legally* to Rais Uli by their apparent dislike of him,[23] it is the personal and tribal/biological loyalty that Rais Uli feels for his fellow tribesman that is key (and is "good") in this story, and not any official or legal loyalty that he might feel for the state and its officials. Morocco is then, according to Perdicaris, an explicitly lawless space, where loyalties are defined biologically, and where indeed anything can happen.

The interlude with the disappointing Spaniards, for instance, could not have happened without the original narrative of Morocco as a corrupt arena, where Rais Uli represented the appropriately inappropriate "bandit rule" that such spaces engender. It was only within the context of this narrative, indeed, that kidnapped (white) Europeans and Americans could effectively reinforce the dichotomy between a racially/biologically determined lawfulness[24] and an equally racially/biologically determined lawlessness.[25] The fluidity between Moroccan bandit and Moroccan bureaucrat could occur, that is, only against the backdrop of a "captured" European who, against all odds, related better with the former than with the latter. Capturing Spaniards made things too complex. Spaniards first of all were not white enough, and, moreover, they were defined more often than not—especially by the end of the nineteenth century—as little less corrupt than the populations they had formerly governed.[26] In order for the dichotomy to remain effective, therefore, Rais Uli had to be "disgusted" with the Spaniards.

With Sir Harry Maclean, things were back on track. White, calm, and civilized, Sir Harry represented law and rationality more effectively even than Perdicaris. It was with the capture of Maclean, therefore, that "bandit rule" was advocated even more explicitly than before as the only appropriate rule for Morocco—Rais Uli was needed to restore "order" (but not law) among the "fierce tribes" that he knew intimately (but not lawfully) so well. Morocco was, again, a lawless space anyway, a space in which order rather than law would reign and where biology rather than citizenship would determine loyalty. There was, however, a price to pay for operating within such a space and according to such rules. In the end, Rais Uli was poisoned—unnaturally eliminated in the same way that any other body within that space might have been eliminated. Moreover, the ironic tragedy of the story—that he was "no longer" a bandit and instead a provincial governor—was not and could not even be truly ironic. In Morocco, the two roles were one, and upon his appointment as bureaucrat Rais Uli had become more than ever a bandit—it was therefore only fitting that he should die like a bandit by violence.

The corrupt and lawless space with its conflation of bandits with bureaucrats on the one hand, and biology with law on the other, did not have to exist in an overseas colony, however. In the United States, for example, the rhetorical construction of "Chinatown" from the late nineteenth century onward produced a corrupt space that was physically and territorially, as well as politically and militarily, within a noncorrupt, legally defined political structure. The most obvious artistic representation of this construction is, again, the film *Chinatown*—a story of civic corruption in Los Angeles that ends (tragically) in Chinatown for no obvious reason other than the "fact" that one can get away with murder (and incest) there. But this spectacle of corruption in the not-quite American Chinatowns of the United States is certainly not something that existed only in the imagination of Hollywood producers. Newspaper reports of Chinese gangs, gambling, and massage parlors—along with their unfortunate relationship with corrupt urban police forces—play up with nearly as much fervor the overlap between bandit and bureaucrat and the tension between biology and citizenship that plague the corrupt system.

What is perhaps most fascinating about reporting on and within Chinatowns is the extent to which the vocabulary of the 1890s is nearly identical to the vocabulary of the 1990s. In the 1890s, for example, there was a great deal of discussion of illegal Chinese gambling houses that, first, prevented Chinese immigrants from satisfactorily aligning themselves with an abstract civic national identity and, second, infected local (white) police forces who succumbed to the (Asian) temptation to take bribes. As one *New York Times* article noted,

> there are twenty Chinese gambling houses in the district and it is charged that the police received over one hundred dollars a week to protect them. . . . [T]he Reverend Dr. Paddock, pastor of St. Andrew's Protestant Episcopal Church, who, with other pious men and women, has laboured hard for the education and Christianization of the Chinamen, said today that their greatest obstacle has been the Chinese gambling houses, which the reverend doctor says have been protected by the police for money. It is believed that this is the beginning of the exposure of a vast system of blackmail and extortion by the police.[27]

It is gambling, in other words—a problematic material vice—that prevents the Chinese from giving up their equally problematic biological racial affiliations and joining the lawful Christian and American collective. Moreover, the (corrupt) ease and laziness associated with gambling and extortion are set up in rhetorical opposition in this passage to the (noncorrupt) "labor" that the Reverend Dr. Paddock has exerted in trying to educate the Chinese. The situation is one in which the "vast system of blackmail and extortion" produced by the police overlaps with "Chinatown" writ large, as both are highlighted against the backdrop of appropriate Christian and American labor. Chinatown is in this way defined as corrupt simply because corruption is anything that happens in Chinatown. It is a lawless space, and the police—by entering it—have become lawless as well.

In the 1990s, gambling was still the crime most often associated with the gangs who "terrorized Chinatown." And, just as before, gambling came to represent not just a material vice, but also the far more sinister threat and draw of Chinatown as a separate, corrupt arena—Pasolini's villa—within the larger noncorrupt state structure. In Chinatown of the 1990s as well, flesh and money rather than law determined loyalties. In Chinatown of the 1990s, as well, the activities of humanitarians out to open up the corrupt space were obstructed by forces beyond their control. As one "expert" on Chinese gangs noted, for instance, "there is too strong a demand for gang services—like protecting illegal gambling places, massage parlors, collecting loans, settling disputes among individuals and fraternal organizations and smuggling immigrants." Money, flesh, and fraternity, in other words, defined interactions and loyalties in Chinatown, services associated with them were in high demand, and it was gangs rather than civil servants who necessarily could provide these services.

The gangs themselves, however, like the bandits of old, were not just criminal but barely human—"wolf packs" as the district attorney designated them.[28] And, just as in the nineteenth century, the Revered Dr. Paddock despaired of turning gambling Chinamen into properly educated Christian Americans, by the end of the twentieth century, it was still the bandit gangs who prevented Chinese assimilation, turning Chinese Americans not just into permanent immigrants, but not quite human "aliens." Indeed, by "smuggling" unwitting Chinese into the United States, the bandit gangs produced a situation in which, even when their victim/collaborators were let out of the claustrophobic freight containers, they were forced to remain hiding in the equally claustrophobic Chinatown—a space defined essentially as its own container, caught forever in "the grip of violence and lawlessness." Just as in the 1890s, therefore, in the late twentieth century as well even "lawful" things became corrupt in Chinatown—a place that spawned businessmen such as "Moi bon Shek, who prosecutors said was audacious enough to set up and operate an illegal gambling business inside the state's Offtrack Betting Corporation office in Chinatown."[29]

Whereas Chinatown remained an enclosed corrupt space, and Morocco a corrupt space in the open air of the Atlas mountains, South America and the Caribbean operated in the late nineteenth and twentieth centuries essentially as both. With a dizzying speed, the bandit/bureaucrat who defined the corrupt system was narrated first as a leader, then as a prisoner, then as a jailor, then as a burglar, and then back to a leader again. The area and system that he ruled, subverted, imprisoned, and violated switched with equal rapidity from a tiny jail cell to an open continent, from the enclosed and constrained to the irresponsibly free. Once again, however, the defining characteristic of the continent of South America as a huge, corrupt system was that individuals caught up within it affiliated via flesh and property rather than via legal norms—and that this process of affiliation was a spectacular thing.

Early twentieth-century Venezuela, for instance, especially under the rule of Cipriano Castro, "the cattle bandit of the Andes," received a great deal of attention from a watching liberal public. Castro's successful bid for the Venezuelan presidency in particular was described, above all, as the revenge of a tax-dodging cattle thief caught by the law who thereupon vowed to take the law into his own hands:

> Castro is nothing if not picturesque, and of course he gave the affair [his revolution] a political coloring. He said he was not fighting for his stolen cows (of course the stealing he referred to was the operation the tax collectors classified as confiscation) but for a principle, and his neighbors flocked to his standard. . . . [W]ithin two weeks they were in possession of the state capital.

What is "picturesque" in this passage, in other words, is that Castro the cattle bandit, like Rais Uli, the gentleman bandit, should claim any abstract political or legal motivation at all. He became president because his banditry was being curtailed by the lawful government, and the only possible response was for him to turn the entire state into a lawless arena. The issue of "taxes," for example, occurs repeatedly in discussions of Castro's rule. Over and over, with various different formulas, we are told that whereas Castro evaded legitimate tax collection, the taxes that his own government collected were nothing more than "plunder." Indeed, he ran his state "according to the brigand code by which he shaped his life, [and] fed his followers liberally with the spoils of the enemy." Likewise, the relations that he had with the "respectable classes among his fellow countrymen" were nothing more nor less than "those which the jailor has with his prisoners and the burglar with those whom he robs," whereas "the savage Andinos, of whom his armies are almost exclusively composed, adore their repulsive robber chief . . . [because he] is exceedingly generous with his brigand followers." The result, in the end, was a situation in which

> in his treatment of the people of the capital and the commercial cities of the Orientals, or eastern province men Castro was a law unto himself. No rights were respected and the constitutional safeguards everywhere were thrown aside. But to his own people, the hardy mountaineers of the Yachira and Grujillo provinces, which lie to the south and west of Maracaibo on the Columbian frontier, he was a generous patron.[30]

Castro and his (tribal) followers, that is, flew out of the mountains and instituted in Venezuela a corrupt system—a system indeed explicitly regulated according to "the brigand code," where honor and loyalty had nothing to do with law and everything to do with intimate personal relations. In fact it was only with those *excluded* from his system—the people of the capital, the eastern province, and the Orientals—that Castro apparently spoke in the language of law, interacting with them first as "enemy," next as "jailor," eventually as "robber," and then finally as "law unto himself." Like the four fascist bosses of Pasolini's villa, he first suspended the old law with its "constitutional safeguards," he then redefined in an irrational, personal manner the friend/enemy distinction—turning the respectable fellow countryman into "enemy" and the savage into "friend"—and then finally replaced law and civic responsibility with order, plunder, and blood. The structures, however, remained in place. The bureaucracy continued to operate—it simply operated materially rather than legally. Taxes were collected—but they were redefined as plunder. Even the courts operated—staffed, however, not by "specialists" but by "barbers" and "mule drivers."[31] Castro thus turned Venezuela into both an overregulated "prison," where the individual's every move was watched, and an underregulated free-for-all, where norms were denied or turned carnivalesque and it was the individual's idiosyncratic flesh and money before anything else that placed him within the hierarchy.

This portrayal of South American and Caribbean space as corrupt space, in which bandits become bureaucrats and bureaucrats behave as bandits did not change much over the next one hundred years. If anything, it became even more explicit, with the "guerrilla leader" replacing the "cattle thief," and the "prison gang" replacing the "bandit operation." In an article in July 1992, entitled "Kidnapping and 'Taxes' Transform Guerilla Inc.," for example, we learn that

> with the collapse of the Soviet Union and the near bankruptcy of Cuba, South America's orphaned guerilla groups survive by honing their skills at local fund raising.... [T]he guerillas lose their ideological coloring and become a bureaucracy.... [T]hey take on a corporate structure and have to finance it.... [T]oday, to keep their fighters fed, clothed, and armed, the groups extort "war taxes" from rural businesses and provide armed guards for cocaine laboratories and plots of opium poppies.... [T]o prevent double billing by common criminals, Peru's guerilla extortionists have printed receipts, which they call "war bonds."[32]

In Puerto Rico, things are nearly identical, except that there they happen in the enclosed space of the (actual rather than metaphorical) prison. We are told that Puerto Rican prison gangs are like prison gangs everywhere, except—being Caribbean—they have formed nonprofit organizations in addition to extortion rings and drug-selling schemes. These nonprofit organizations "illegally" apply for government grants to run prison programs and have become so successful that "the gang functions like a 'shadow governing body,' enforcing its own rules and discipline, deciding which inmates to 'expel' from the general population and which to have reassigned to protective custody or other institutions, and controlling inmate privileges."[33]

Just as before, it is tax collection and fund raising in particular that mark these groups not just as criminal but as outlaw, not just as immoral but as corrupt. By taking on the role of bureaucrat and civil servant, indeed by applying for grants and providing services, these late twentieth-century bandits are playing up even more than Castro did the extent to which "law" is a mockery in South America and the Caribbean, and likewise the extent to which the corrupt space forces a personal rather than a legal relationship between friend and enemy, between excluded and included. The Puerto Rican prison gang decides who may and may not be a part of the general population, and this decision is made according to irrational notions of "gang loyalty" rather than to the presumably rational criteria produced by the "real" prison administrators. Moreover, the fact that this inclusion and exclusion occur in the constrained, and sealed-off space of the prison further highlights the claustrophobic nature of corrupt space. Whether included or excluded, the individual still cannot escape and remains at the mercy of the lawless bandit/bureaucrats.

Likewise, just as occurred with Castro, the movement from bandit to bureaucrat back to bandit denies either group any sort of "real" political affiliation. The guerrilla leaders, like Castro before, have no "ideological coloring." As bureaucrat/brigands, they have only loyalty and disloyalty, inclusion or exclusion, where neither is defined politically or legally, but instead in direct opposition to appropriate and "real" legal or corporate structures. Whether contained within an entire continent or within a prison cell, whether defined by its wild abandon or its "stringent self control," that is, South American corruption, too, brings together brigandage and extortion, robbery and bribery, murder and nepotism. The bandit/bureaucrats of South America, like those of Morocco and Chinatown, produce lawless spaces and corrupt systems, in which affiliation is determined by blood, flesh, and property rather than by law, citizenship, and specialization. The result is a simultaneously overregulated and underregulated space, in which "anything" can happen and responsibility disappears, but in which, simultaneously, noncorrupt bureaucratic structures appear largely functional.

The Ottoman Empire, run by a celebrated and celebrity corrupt leader, was obviously a space equally well defined by a dehumanizing corrupt system. In the Ottoman Empire, too, the line between bureaucrat and bandit was fine to nonexistent. Likewise, collective affiliation was determined not legally but materially, and the state was in turn reconstructed as a lawless space. I would like to focus in this section on two examples of this process before turning to its rearticulation in late twentieth-century

Turkey. In these examples, the Ottoman Empire is narrated, first, as a state run by and for brigands and, second, as a space in which the lawful are forced either to participate in inappropriate sadomasochistic relationships or to redefine themselves according to the "new" laws (or order). In 1883, for example, the *New York Times* ran a letter entitled, "Hadji Ali and his Bandits," in which we learn that

> at the time of the Russo-Turkish war, in response to an appeal from the Padishah, [Hadji Ali] recruited at his own expense several hundreds of Zeibees and scoundrels of the worst class, whom he led to Bulgaria where, with the help of the Circassians, they committed the atrocities which made his name infamous and horrified all Europe. This you know, but you may not have heard that on his return to Syria this brigand chief received from his sovereign the order of the Medjdie and the title of Pasha for eminent services rendered to his country. . . . [H]e exercises in this region almost absolute power, and during the last eight years the governors-general of Smyrna have had several times to implore his aid in the suppression of the brigands which desolate our provinces.[34]

Hadji Ali, in other words, is the product of a corrupt system and the producer of a lawless space—the bandit turns bureaucrat following an appeal from the political leader, and indeed, much like Rais Uli, he eventually receives a commendation from the government. Moreover, like Castro, Hadji Ali makes use of his illegitimate legitimacy to set up a new friend/enemy relationship, in which (nonwhite) "scoundrels of the worst class" are set loose on (white) "law abiding citizens." The replacement of rational law with irrational order, the conflation of bandit with bureaucrat thus produces the inevitable result: the legal governors of Smyrna have no power and must implore the aid of the illegal bandit.

Discussions of corrupt Ottoman systems do not just focus on individual bandits, however—more often than not it is simply the system itself, old and new, that is and will always be outside of legal norms. In an early twentieth-century newspaper article on corruption and violence in Armenian and Kurdish Anatolia, for instance, we learn that—as was the case, again, with Castro—it was inappropriate attitudes toward taxes and taxation especially that led in the end to death and destruction in that area. Upon conducting an investigation of tax collection in its eastern Anatolian provinces, the article notes, the Ottoman government apparently learned that it was not receiving its "proper share" of the money. The government found this unacceptable—not, however, because a functional state collects taxes from all of its citizens, but because "the idea of an untaxed Christian community in Turkish territory was abhorrent to Muhammedan sentiment and logic."[35] The government therefore sent new officials to collect the taxes, but "the Kurds got there first, and 8,000 Armenians are said to have perished. . . . [T]he Turkish officials, deprived of their taxes, found it easier to complete the work of destruction and death than to return to Constantinople empty handed."[36]

What is remarkable about this narrative is, again, the extent to which it implies that *no* system of taxation can be anything but corrupt—and eventually violent—in the Ottoman state structure.[37] It is not simply that the Ottoman bureaucrats turned bandit because doing so was easier than returning without anything. Nor is it that prior to the arrival of the officials, Kurdish bandits had been playing the role of tax-collecting bureaucrat quite comfortably for a number of years. It is that the abstract notion of "taxes" in the Ottoman state is inconceivable. Taxes for the Ottomans—like for the Venezuelans under Castro—have nothing to do with state function, with legal norms, or with rationality. They have to do with something called "Muhammedan sentiment and logic," clearly irrational, and clearly outside of the law. They have to do with an inappropriate friend/enemy dichotomy, in which friends are defined not by citizenship but by blood. Any attempt to collect taxes on the part of the Ottoman government is therefore by definition corrupt. Like the Puerto Rican prison gang, it is the very fact that money should accrue to an Ottoman structure at all that is unacceptable. Similarly, like the Chinatowns in the United States, the Ottoman Empire is defined as corrupt not because bandits operate as bureaucrats within it, but because any official upon entering Ottoman space necessarily *becomes* a bandit. It is not that the space is distinguished by the behavior that occurs within it—it is that the behavior that occurs within it is and becomes tainted.

The Portable Torture Nation

Whereas prison cells in Puerto Rico, continents like South America or Africa, urban areas like Chinatown, and colonized or quasi-colonized states like Morocco and the Ottoman Empire all to a greater or lesser degree represent corrupt and lawless space, it is only the more abstract "torture nation"—developed rhetorically in the late nineteenth century, but mobilized most effectively in the late twentieth—that brings the corruption narrative to its logical conclusion. The torture nation is almost without exception a colonial or neocolonial political structure in which the things that "we" do not do (even if we want to) are allowed and indeed encouraged. The torture nation is a creation of the imperial relationship—in fact more often than not it exists both outside and inside the vaguely defined imperial political boundaries—but it represents the continuing failure of the imperial civilizing mission. Like all corrupt places, it is defined *eo ipso* as corrupt. It is not that the torture nation is so called because torture happens there. It is that torture happens, corruption happens, lawlessness happens because it is a torture nation and therefore anything or anyone who enters it necessarily becomes uncivilized.

The importance of the space and its enclosed, claustrophobic, and often mobile nature is indeed repeatedly emphasized in discussions of the phenomenon. Like the train that goes to the concentration camp, for example, the jet that goes to the torture nation is the subject of much literary and media attention. It is evocative, fascinating, and largely—like the train—seen as an extension of the nation itself, an enclosed, lawless space traveling through or existing within other ostensibly open, lawful spaces. It is the apparent alterity that produces the frisson, and the apparent power of the place—where one step over a quite physical line or through a quite physical door eliminates the safeguard of law and citizenship and places "us" into Pasolini's villa.

The torture nation, its appendages, and what it does to civilized people who enter it are again, however, not just products of the late twentieth century. At the turn of the nineteenth century, the U.S. government produced one of many prototypes for the contemporary torture nation when it embarked on the liberation/colonization of the Philippines. The primary stumbling block to this program in the eyes of U.S. policy makers was the persistence of the Filipino "bandits" who opposed the American occupation and engaged in all sorts of inappropriate and illegitimate violence against their bewildered liberators. Eventually, in January 1901, General Arthur MacArthur gave an interview to the *New York Times*, entitled "Filipino Bandits' Methods: Gen. MacArthur's Remarks on Their Inhuman Ways—Several to be Hanged," explaining the situation to the American public:

> in one case the accused [Filipino] belonged to an organized band which, under the name of "Guardia de Honor," had for its declared object the murder of peaceful and unoffending victims, if found necessary to gratify either a desire for revenge or a feeling of envy against the rich. "These inhuman methods," says Gen. MacArthur "remove all the participants whether chief, or willing followers of the bands, from the pale of the law and place them among that class of cowardly and secret assassins which all civilized men the world over hold to be enemies of mankind" . . . . [R]ecently two Americans were taken

into the camp as prisoners and, for no other reason that that "they were enemies," they were ordered to instant death.[38]

In this way MacArthur and the *New York Times* successfully, if gradually, begin defining the Philippines as a torture nation. There is first and most important the (vaguely convoluted) appropriation of a legitimate, civilized friend/enemy distinction and the delegitimization of the bandits' similar distinction. The bandits' "declared" enemies are, on the one hand, "peaceful and unoffending victims" and, on the other, "Americans." Their friends are "cowardly and secret assassins," criminal "chiefs" or weak-willed "followers." This is clearly an irrational and illegal distinction. It is not that the bandits' enemies have any kind of political or legal identity—"occupiers" or "soldiers," for example—they are simply outside of the gang and therefore a fair target.

The second part of the process is a bit more difficult (if an excellent example of the strange logic, noted by Carl Schmitt, that occurs when imperial expansion is based on a humanitarian rhetoric).[39] MacArthur and the *New York Times* proceed to displace "law" onto "humanity." The bandits are described as beyond "the pale of the law," outlaw in other words, and *therefore* "enemies of mankind," "inhuman," or, for that matter, not human. The implication is that it is solely by being defined legally and politically that an individual can be deemed "human." If an individual is not defined in this way, if he or she affiliates "tribally," biologically, or simply in an "uncivilized" manner, that person is open to any and every kind of tribal, biological, or uncivilized violence. He or she exists, that is, in lawless space where anything can happen.

This distinction works well for the imposition of colonial control— the Filipinos are not human, therefore they can be hanged with impunity. Indeed, it is hardly different from any other colonial structure, in which a temporary emergency can last for seventy years, as in the case of British-occupied Egypt, and an entire population can be collectively criminalized and dealt with accordingly.[40] The problem, however, occurred when the logical conclusion to this creation of the colonized space was reached. By spring and summer of 1902, for instance, the U.S. public was shocked and outraged to discover that "we" were "as bad" as the inhuman Filipino bandits—that U.S. soldiers had "disgraced the uniform they continue to wear" by engaging in the same violent practices that the Filipinos themselves had, inflicting torture, and in particular the "water cure," on helpless victims.[41] Finally, a senate commission looked into the allegations of torture and attempted to reach a conclusion about the corruption of American soldiers on duty in the Philippines. One soldier went before the commission and stated in great detail exactly what had happened, describing the infliction of the cure upon a dozen natives at the town of Leon, Province of Panay. He said that they were captured and tortured in order to secure information of the murder of Private O'Herne of Company I, who had not only been killed, but roasted and otherwise tortured before death ensued. . . . [H]allock added that he had witnessed the torture but had not participated in it, and that while it was in progress Capt. Gregg was at company headquarters less than 100 yards distant. "Did Capt. Gregg known (sic) of the torture?" senator Rawlins asked. "All the command knew it, and I don't see how he could have helped knowing it." "What was the effect of the punishment?" "The stomach would swell up and in some cases I witnessed blood come from the mouth" . . . . [A]ll the details [of O'Herne's death] had the witness said, been gathered from the confessions of the men to whom they had given the cure.[42]

The "information" that was gathered from the interrogation and torture of the Filipinos was simply further detail about the torture of a soldier already known to be dead. What was sought was nothing more than an extensive narrative, the point being a production and reproduction of lawless violence. This production and reproduction, moreover, eventually came before the senate, and then the U.S. public—who, of course, had the right and duty to know. Both the torture of the Filipinos and the corruption of the U.S. soldiers thus became simultaneous consumer objects and objects of liberal humanitarian outrage. But the extra charge was situated in the fact that the Philippines now existed both inside and outside of familiar political boundaries. The soldiers were corrupted by entering the torture nation, but the torture nation existed, like the various identical Chinatowns, *within* American space. And indeed, it was this dangerous overlap that led inevitably to the proliferation of copycat, postmodern variations on "Filipino torture," producing headlines of the "Two Robbers Torture Deaf-Mute in Flat: Bind and Gag Helpless Man and Then Give Him the 'Water Cure' Because He Didn't Speak," sort.[43] What began with inhuman Filipinos eventually infected and tainted U.S. soldiers as well, and then finally seeped into the domestic space of the homeland, too.

Although lawless violence of this sort was always in danger of spilling over and corrupting the civilized, however, I want to emphasize that this corruption was not the same as the corruption that existed in the uncivilized colony. There were flare-ups at the metropole, individuals might be tainted, and terrorism might occur—indeed, these things added an extra thrill to the stories of corruption and violence that came back "home." But these flare-ups merely accentuated the protecting nature of the domestic, and the security of the homeland. In the civilized nation, *an* individual might become corrupted. In a torture nation, *any* individual who entered became potentially if not actually so, and the key role played by basic, geographical space was emphasized over and over. If we compare two passages on torture and violence from the late nineteenth and early twentieth century, for example, this dichotomy becomes clear. In the first, on Spanish occupied Cuba, we are told that

> the afternoon papers today sent a thrill through the city with a report that a torture and execution chamber had been found at the residence of the Spanish Military Governor, adjoining the palace. . . . [T]he reported "torture chamber" is a room about eight feet square, just off the dining room. As a matter of fact, it was probably used as a pantry. In the wall there is a dirty iron bar, evidently used to hang meat on, and a piece of discolored rope is suspended on it. It is inconceivable that Gen. Parrado practiced torture next to his dining room.[44]

In the second, on torture in the Ottoman Empire under Abdülhamid II, we learn

> what has added to the horror with which the story has been followed, added to it more than all else, is the fact that these terrible deeds were committed in the palace, in the private park of the Sultan, and that, invisible to all, concealed behind a curtain, his Majesty himself sometimes assisted in the dreadful scenes of cruelty that took place there. . . . "[T]he Garden of Suffering" is what the Turks call this torture chamber in the Sultan's park.[45]

The Spanish, if quickly slipping, remained within the realm of the civilized world. Although the report of the torture chamber in the governor's house—Spain within Cuba—was "thrilling," therefore, it was also "inconceivable." And it was inconceivable solely because there is domestic space and nondomestic space, the dining room (and adjoining rooms) are part of the former, and torture simply cannot happen there. If torture must (unfortunately) happen, it will happen in an appropriate area, set aside for that purpose, and not part of the domestic realm.

When we get to the quasi-colonized torture nation embodied by the Ottoman Empire, however, this eminently logical argument falls apart. In the torture nation, torture can and does happen anywhere. Indeed, what makes Ottoman governance and the Ottoman state so horrific is precisely the abandonment of the spatial rules that divide the "conceivable" from the "inconceivable." The sultan enjoys his torture in a private, domestic spot. Ottoman torture occurs precisely where the Spanish governor's torture simply *could not*. And it is this corruption of *even* domestic space—this saturation of, if not the lawful, then the private, with the unlawful and the public—that remained a defining characteristic of the corrupt system.

By the end of the twentieth and the beginning of the twenty-first century, therefore, the narrative of the torture nation as a space that, first, corrupts rather than having been corrupted and, second, is contained within—but apart from—the civilized state had a long history upon which to rely. But it also became far more emphatic and developed. Indeed, following the torture of Iraqi citizens in the Abu Ghraib prison, the revelation of that torture, and the commodification of that revelation, the narrative took on a truly aggressive dimension. Liberal humanitarian outrage combined with the liberal humanitarian right and duty to know, see, and consume to produce a situation in which the discussion and construction of the corrupt, lawless space became a pastime and necessity in "civilized nations" everywhere. It was this elaboration that turned Abu Ghraib from a pure carnival[46] to a carnival with a message: that we (politically) are lucky to be (physically and biologically) where we are.

Abu Ghraib worked as a motif only because Iraq was, is, and always will be a torture nation. The discussion of other torture nations and their place in the larger U.S. imperial framework in the months that followed simply reinforced this division of space. In these articles, for example, the torture nation is usually described as a country "where concern for human rights and the rule of law don't pose obstacles to torturing prisoners," "countries where torture is practiced," or sometimes simply as "outlaw regimes," where "foreign torturers" have free rein. We then get a list of various torture nations that might be defined in such a way. More often than not, however—and this is worth emphasizing—this list preceded by "like" or "such as." That is, torture nations are countries *like* or *such as* "Egypt, Syria, Saudi Arabia, Jordan, and Pakistan." The torture nation, in other words, remains largely an abstract concept. Egypt et al. are simply *examples* of the more fundamental, theoretical outlaw space. It is, again, not that torture happens in Egypt and therefore Egypt is a torture nation. It is that the abstract notion of the torture nation manifests itself concretely in places "like" Egypt. Indeed, the obvious unstated point in all of these articles is that torture (i.e., Filipino water cure) happens everywhere. The question is where it is normal (i.e., something that everyone does or potentially will do upon entering the space) and where it is aberrant or exceptional (i.e., something that an individual might do despite the space).

The answer to this question is obvious. Upon defining the torture nation or the outlaw regime, and expounding on the dangers of getting too close to these regimes, the lesson to be learned is that the line between corrupt and noncorrupt, between legal and biological, is nonetheless ineradicable even as we occasionally step over it. We learn, for instance, that "the C.I.A. has sent prisoners to countries where they were tortured for months and then either disappeared or were released because they knew nothing. The guilty ones can never be brought to justice—not after they have been illegally imprisoned and even tortured." Likewise, although it is understandable that the line might be crossed, that one might take information from the "oppressive governments of Central Asia and the Middle East," given that "Islamism remains a psychopathic and totalitarian creed," "the reasons why first England and then the civilised world rejected torture were practical as well as moral. Most people break under torture."[47]

In other words, it is precisely the horror with which we respond to the close relationship between the "civilized world" and "outlaw regimes" that defines us as untouchable, protected, and safe in our homeland. Islamism is psychopathic and totalitarian. It is, in other words, not an ideology of law, but an ideology of disordered order. Although we might deplore the treatment that Islamists receive at the hands of (Muslim) Central Asian and Middle Eastern torture nations, this is solely because the line between us and them, between law and biology, continues to exist and is even reinforced. The clear message is that they—even as victims—do not deplore it. In the same way that a specific torture nation is simply the concrete manifestation of an abstract concept, therefore, the tortured likewise becomes a concrete manifestation of a related concept—the physical manifestation of "victim" rather than the physical manifestation of "outlaw regime." And just as "even" an American soldier will become tainted on entering the corrupt space, the Islamist, the victim, carries the torture nation with him "even" into the civilized world. We of the civilized world might enter the carnivalesque atmosphere of the torture nation and lose ourselves, in other words, but we can always go home, where law reigns supreme. Indeed, the guilty U.S. torturer is eventually tried in a rational, legal setting. The guilty "Islamist" tortured, however, "can never be brought to justice." He carries the corrupt space with him, and can serve no purpose other than as biological backdrop to the legal performance of civilized nations.

This stark dichotomy between corrupt and noncorrupt space reaches its most effective formulation in the discussions of the airplanes that ferry the victims from detention center to torture nation and (sometimes) back again. Like the immigrant smuggling freight container displaced onto Chinatown displaced onto China, the jet represents an enclosed, emphatically lawless space that exists equally emphatically within the civilized sphere. The jet is, indeed, fetishized. It is described in intimate, exact detail—its make, its model number, its history, its paint job, and especially its tantalizingly close if nonetheless out-of-reach nature being relayed in countless media reports. Even as the plane is portrayed as (suspiciously) sealed up and sealed off, however, the message that all of the media representations of it repeat is that contamination is still (thrillingly) possible. One *Boston Globe* report, for example, argues that the "secretive Massachusetts-registered company" that owned the plane transferred its "registration to [an] Oregon company . . . the same day the *Globe* published details of the plane's flights transferring prisoners to countries that use brutal interrogation techniques." It then quotes one activist, saying that "if torture has a Massachusetts connection, Massachusetts citizens must go [protest]."[48]

This take on the torture jet is nearly identical to the take we see simultaneously in local Scottish newspapers. After describing the plane in fascinated detail, these articles argue that Scotland should not allow itself to be "used as a re-fuelling base for a jet used by American intelligence agencies to fly terrorist suspects to countries that torture prisoners."[49] The list of other places that the plane has visited—Islamabad, Karachi, Riyadh, Baghdad, Tashkent, Azerbaijan, Morocco, Kuwait, Jordan, Frankfurt, Larnaca, Indonesia, Egypt, and Washington, DC—indeed implies nothing if not the possibility of infection—the entry of the uncivilized world into the civilized. In both Boston and Glasgow, that is, local populations brushed up against the mobile, corrupt torture nation. Both Boston and Glasgow—spaces that epitomize the lawful and the civilized—thus served as a context in which the brutally physical nature of the torture nation as well as its strange ability to expand and contract itself could be understood. One step through the door of the jet and the universe changes. One step over a very physical line and law is suddenly eliminated and replaced with order, violence, and flesh. The torture nation, like Pasolini's villa, is thus eminently accessible even as it is sealed off—mobile, infected, and on its way elsewhere.

Bribery, Nepotism, and Decay

This section concerns bribery and nepotism—two issues that seem relatively straightforward but that, like other aspects of the corruption narrative, become unexpectedly complex on further examination. Both bribery and nepotism involve, first of all, the breaking down of legal norms or rational order and the building up of material norms or irrational order. When a bureaucrat takes a bribe, he is allowing the briber to enter a system on a material rather than on a civic basis. The relationship between bureaucrat and citizen thus becomes not just inappropriately, but materially intimate. Likewise, when a bureaucrat appoints his, say, nephew to an administrative post, the nephew has also entered the system on a biological rather than a civic basis. The result in the corruption discourse is clear—an incestuous mess of mixed blood and inverted biological hierarchies.

In general, in other words, entry into the corrupt system via bribery and nepotism does not simply undermine the effective functioning of an abstract legal or bureaucratic system. It produces an entirely alternate set of relationships based on money and blood that lead inexorably to precisely the sort of intimacy that it is the duty of the modern state to prevent. Discussions of the corrupt bureaucratic system thus return repeatedly to themes that seem to have little to do with bribery and nepotism per se. Incest, miscegenation, and the inappropriate disposal of corpses, for example, receive a great deal of attention in these narratives—implying and sometimes stating outright that the logical conclusion to a system accessed via flesh and money rather than via citizenship and specialization is, for example, the reanimation of corpses and contamination of blood. These discussions then jump immediately back to the political, however, linking in turn the rotting corpse and the miscegenated monster with the disordered order of the totalitarian state. The result is thus not simply an evocative metaphor—Bataille's "dead man . . . part and parcel of his own disorder"[50] serving as a symbol of the rotting state. In these narratives, the relationship is instead concrete—bribery and nepotism lead to *actual* incest, miscegenation, and bodily disorder; these activities in turn lead to the *actual* creation of totalitarian structures.

One of the more overt arenas in which this strangely appealing sequence—bribery to sex, sex to death, and death to totalitarianism—plays out is in discussions of late nineteenth- and late twentieth-century Russia and Italy. Russia and Italy, like Spain, represent points of anxiety in narratives of both corruption and civilization. The line between corrupt and noncorrupt is supposed to be clear—indeed explicitly black and white. Russia and Italy, however, slip back and forth over this line, sometimes colonizing and civilizing, sometimes in need of colonization and civilization themselves. Rais Uli, no doubt, would have been just as disgusted, for example, had his men brought him Russians or Italians as he was with the Spanish he did inadvertently take. When they *are* corrupt, therefore, Russia and Italy are extraordinarily so, but when they are not, they are completely "clean."

In 1889, for example, George Kennan wrote an article for *Century Illustrated Magazine* on "The Russian Police" broadly defined. The principal purpose of the article was to explain their corruption—in particular why and in what way it developed, grew, and played out. After first noting, therefore, that the police (and the bureaucracy in general) were underpaid, and that "honest and capable men" could not work for such salaries,[51] Kennan goes on to discuss a number of specific examples of extortion, bribery, and nepotism. Two of these examples stand out. In the first, a rural police officer uses an unidentified dead body to extort money from a number of peasants who, if they do not pay, will be required to care for the body until the arrival of the surgeon. Kennan tells us that in order to work this scheme, the police officer, upon appropriating the corpse, ordered that it be moved to a nearby village where he knew there was no morgue. When he reached the village, he then had the body

> taken to the house of one of the most prosperous peasant farmers in the place, whose daughter, he had heard, was about to be married. The ghastly burden was borne on an extemporized litter of pine boughs to the well-to-do peasant's door and deposited on the ground in the full sight of the windows, while the police officer went in and announced to the horror stricken peasant proprietor that, as there was no dead-house in the village, he should have to put the body in the peasant's house until the district surgeon should come to make the post mortem examination [the peasant then bribed him to take it away].... [I] heard of one instance where the same body was used to "work" two or three villages in succession.[52]

In the second example, an official tells the peasants of his village that he has received orders that they be instructed in "the laws the Empire." He then forces them to abandon their agricultural work at the height of the wheat harvest, gathers them together in his office, and proceeds to "open [a] big quarto [and] read unintelligible laws to these unhappy peasants all the afternoon." By early that evening, Kennan notes, the peasants had "sent a deputation to [the official] to ask how much he would take to let them off from any more laws. He agreed to graduate them all with the degree of LL.D. for 20 kopeks a piece."[53]

Both of these anecdotes are simultaneously (and no doubt deliberately) farcical and morbid. The first, in fact, follows with remarkable accuracy the plot line of R. L. Stevenson's *The Wrong Box*, which also appeared in early 1889. In this novel, an unclaimed dead body changes hands and is "worked" a number of times until it is finally taken away (still unburied) in a cart. As one scholar has noted, the dead body's movements throughout the story are both "erratic" and "erotic," indicative of a "physical intimacy between men who seek to dissociate themselves from the contaminating effects of the corpse either by burying it, passing it on to another unsuspecting recipient, or treating it as a joke . . . [b]y the novel's end, all of the characters are implicated in, and contaminated by, the transgressive desire of/for the deceased body"[54] The fact that Kennan's rearticulation of this anxiety and desire occurs both as a means of bolstering the corruption narrative and against the backdrop of a marriage ceremony simply reinforces the extent to which bribery and extortion had taken on complex and multifaceted meanings by the late nineteenth century. The abuse of the corpse—its wanderings and workings—would not have been possible if the corrupt structure were not in place, if the officer did not think he could make money from both helpless peasants and the helpless dead body. It is bribery, in other words, that made the corpse's travels possible.

As the corpse made its journey, however, it also signified the extent to which a corrupt political system can contaminate *every* aspect of the individual's biological and sexual life. When it makes its appearance at the bride's house, for example, it emphasizes both the (legal) transgression of the marriage ceremony noted by Bataille and also the (illegal) transgression of male intimacy previously noted. Bribery makes not just the abuse of corpses possible, in other words, but also the (legal and illegal) abuse of living bodies. Likewise, as the corpse is taken from house to house and village to village, it gradually implicates each and every peasant in this corrupt—and now sexualized—relationship. The disorder that is created by the continued nonburial of the corpse, therefore, is the erotic disorder described by Bataille, a disorder held up in distinct opposition to appropriate, noncorrupt, legal order.[55] Indeed, by the time we get to the peasants prevented from harvesting their wheat, it is the law itself that has become a source of oppression, not, however, because of its meaning—the text is explicitly "unintelligible"—but simply because of its physical presence in big quartos that bodily restrain the peasants from their work. The laws here thus also leave the realm of the abstract and themselves become part of the physicality of the corrupt, material, and biological system. The peasants then earn their "degrees" by entering into this system, by paying their bribe and going back to the fields.

But Kennan's purpose in telling us these stories, farcical as they are, is to expose the more sinister nature of Russian political corruption. Indeed, he both begins and ends his piece by reminding us that

> there is probably no country in the world where the police power occupies a wider field, plays a more important part, or touches the private personal life of the citizen at more points

than it does in Russia. In a country like England or the United States, when the people are the governing power, the functions of the police are simple and clearly defined.[56]

While we in the noncorrupt world administer our governments so that they do not administer us, in other words, the Russian peasant is "used to oppression, he is used to extortion"[57] and the two are inextricably linked. The totalitarian (or in this case prototototalitarian) nature of Russian society is in this way portrayed a direct result of the (comical, morbid, sexual) disorder produced by the corrupt system. Bribery leads to abuse of corpses, which leads in turn to the oppressive, lawless, overregulation of the private. When entry into the system is material rather than legal, physical rather than abstract, the eventual result is clear—once again, a bodily, bloody upset of established biological norms.

It was similarly clear in Italy. In a *New York Times* article from 1898, for example, the inevitable progression is narrated in an almost identical manner. Particularly concerned with the "rose-colored" visions of the Italian political system produced in newspapers like the *London Times*, the author of the article is out to show that Italy is riddled with corruption and "draining the blood of the Italian people." After first discussing a questionable construction deal struck between the government and an unsavory firm, the article continues that "the government majority are as much mercenaries as the negro battalions of Baratieri." In addition to removing antiquities from "the womb of the earth" and selling them abroad to pay for "the African insanity" [i.e., colonial expansion into Africa], for example, the government also maintains its "inquisitorial" practice of tax collection, this time "to feed the African madness." In the end, the system leads to nothing but "the cruelest oppression, the most arbitrary arrests, the grossest abuse of power by civil or military underlings, [and] the greatest iniquity of impure tribunals."[58]

The Italian bureaucrats, then, are much like Cipriano Castro, a man who is "without education, conscience, or scruples [which] brings him in closest sympathy with a great number of his fellow countrymen of mixed blood and utterly lawless antecedents."[59] Their followers are like his followers and indeed the Venezuelan republicans who "married Indian women, as did undoubtedly the emigrant ancestors of both Castro and Gomez, but they kept their blood absolutely free from the African admixtures which cannot be said of all who remained behind on the littoral and accepted the republican regime."[60] Italian bureaucrats and civil servants are, in other words, corrupt not just politically but racially as well. The repeated return to blood (to its draining and mixing), to race (the government majority takes bribes just as the "negro battalions of Baratieri" apparently do), to sterility (the womb of the earth is ripped open and made empty), and to racialized (African) insanity makes clear the price of entry into the biologically determined corrupt system. Taking bribes turns people "negro," the corrupt republicans of both Italy and Venezuela become African, and being "utterly lawless" is the same as being "of mixed blood." In the same way that entry into Russia's corrupt system led to the disordered abuse of corpses, that is, entry into Italy's and Venezuela's corrupt system leads likewise to miscegenation and sterility. Both types of disorder, however, also lead in turn to an oppressive, arbitrary, impure and *overcontrolled* system. Even as regulations are overturned and arbitrary physical affiliation replaces rational civic affiliation, other, more stringent, regulations are simultaneously produced.

And indeed, one hundred years later, the same themes were playing out. In Russia, for example, it was still the low salaries that encouraged corrupt behavior among bureaucrats, and it was still the dishonest, the "greedy," and the "oppressive" who became civil servants. Officials undertook surprise inspections of small businesses, and then demanded "fines" that had nothing to do with "any statutory penalties."[61] They "suffocated" and "strangled" reform, and received "their jobs through networks of friends and [kept] them on the basis of personal loyalty rather than competence."[62] In Italy, politicians were still "selling influence and taking graft to fund their parties and line their pockets."[63] The resulting disorder, however, had little to do with business and bureaucracy, and far more to do with flesh and sex. As a means of entering the corrupt system, for instance, citizens were encouraged to "fake handicaps" or claim to be "chronically ill or disabled" in order to take jobs. In the Italian universities,

> one professor was given tenure after he was dead. Medical students in Genoa were allowed to pass an obstetrics exam by performing a uterine operation—on a male cadaver ... [and] descriptions of the university scandal [were] virtually interchangeable with depictions of how the Mafia operates, minus the dead bodies.[64]

Clearly, however, descriptions of the corrupt university system involved just as many dead bodies as descriptions of Mafia misbehavior. Just as before, material and biological entry into the corrupt system—the giving and taking of bribes, the making use of blood ties or personal connections—led straight to the abuse of corpses and to the disordering of blood and sexuality. It was not just an unqualified professor who was granted tenure—it was a *dead* professor. Likewise, the male cadaver that was ripped open in Genoa served no apparent purpose other than to maintain corrupt relations and contaminate those involved in them. The parallelism between the confused gender of the cadaver and the confused physicality of the healthy/ill job candidates is indeed identical to the confused race of the Italian and Venezuelan republicans, to their mixed-up, drained, and lawless blood. In both the late nineteenth and the late twentieth century, in other words, political and financial corruption, bribery and nepotism, led in the end to sexual, biological, and material disorder. As a direct and concrete result of an individual's entry into the corrupt system, corpses were abused, gender was crossed, blood was mixed, and physical "ability" turned farcical. Again, this was no metaphor or analogy. It was actual. And the end point in the twentieth century was the same: the growth of disturbingly totalitarian structures, in which even apparent disorder was turned to effective, lawless order.

Far more so than Russia and Italy, however, China and the Ottoman Empire were described in the late nineteenth century as states supported by and supportive of corrupt bureaucratic systems. The *only* way to enter and to operate Chinese and Ottoman bureaucracies or judicial structures was via bribery or nepotism, with their *only* access material and biological. Both states thus became rhetorical flashpoints of material and biological mixing and disorder. Bodies, blood, flesh, and sex were mixed, bended, blended, and abused, leading in the end to an irrational, if nonetheless relentlessly ordered, political, biological, and sexual system. And again, this progression was not simply an abstract one. In China and the Ottoman Empire, too, bribery and nepotism led to *actual* biological disorder that led in turn to *actual* overregulated order.

More often than not, Chinese and Ottoman bribery and nepotism were explicitly linked in corruption narratives to the dehumanization of the populations residing within Chinese and Ottoman borders. In 1892, for example, a *New York Times* article on "How China Is Governed" returned repeatedly to the linkage between China's corrupt system, on the one hand, and the Chinese citizen's physically dehumanizing entry into it, on the other. Covering many and varied aspects of state power, it referred most frequently to the justice system, which it described as fascinatingly and enthrallingly corrupt. Trials in China, it noted,

> are always public and are usually attended by great crowds of people, as are torture chambers, but so awful are the cruelties practiced that but few persons ever care to witness them. The Judge conducting the trial sits behind a large table covered with a red cloth. The prisoner is made to kneel in front of the table and perform the tow-tow (sic) as a mark of respect to the court, by whom he is presumed guilty until proved innocent—

a not difficult undertaking, provided he has enough money to bribe the mandarins or Judges. . . . [I]n all Chinese courts of law the extent to which bribery and corruption is carried is simply astounding. The verdict of the court is generally at the disposal of those who first interview the mandarins and Judges and offer them the largest sum of money. The notoriously bad character of the courts is known all over China, but so prevalent is vice and corruption in Chinese official circles that no reforms can be hoped for.[65]

The most obvious point to note here is that trials in China are identical to torture chambers—both public, both attended by great crowds, and both awful and cruel. The jump, therefore, between the physical entry into the system and physical disorder is a negligible one. To the extent that torture is an abuse or disordering of the body, so, too, is the corrupt Chinese trial. The bureaucrat or judge is accessed before hand materially (via bribery) and during the trial physically (via "tow-towing.") Law and rationality are absent from the relationship, and instead, affiliation is purely physical, often painful, and always sullied by the watching crowd.[66]

The result of this physical as opposed to legal intimacy is, likewise, as it was in Russia and Italy, more often than not the abuse and reanimation of corpses, the contamination of pure blood, and the disordering of sexual and biological structures. In two articles from 1889, for example, the first in *Forum* and the second in *The Eclectic Magazine of Foreign Literature*, we are told that "the Chinese lesson" is that "it is meritorious for a man to squander his entire patrimony in the funeral obsequies of his father," even though "the memory of the dead is more highly honored by using his legacy in the advancement of truth than by using it to load his grave with funeral baked meats." Moreover, "love of clan comes before love of country," in China, even though "nepotism is political incest, and . . . it will breed the progeny of incest."[67]

The second article begins by informing us that "the corruption of the unspeakable Turk is as purity itself when compared with the unbridled rapacity and elastic 'squeezing' capacity of the provincial officials of China, from silver buttoned mandarin to coral-crested viceroy." This argument continues, however, with the seeming nonsequitur:

China, be it known, is one vast charnel house. The dead are for the most part buried, not, as with us, in ground set apart for that purpose (though one frequently lights upon cemeteries duly chosen with regard to their "lucky" positions), but they are simply laid down anywhere and everywhere. . . .

[T]he Chinaman, as is well known, maintains a sacred reverence for the spot where his relatives, and especially his ancestors, have been buried . . . there is no denying the fact. But there is also no denying that the reverence of the average Celestial for the graves of his ancestors is only second to his reverence for the almighty dollar. This has been proved times without number in the neighborhood of the treaty ports, where the foreigner has erected his own "uncanny" abodes, which frequently interfered with the "feng-shui" of places of burial or, as was often the case, necessitated the removal of the burial mounds of coffins; but a few dollars to the representative of the family almost invariably smoothed the difficulty.[68]

In both articles, in other words, we encounter a number of seemingly unconnected rhetorical leaps: from nepotism to incest to funeral meats to bribery to the random but obsessive disposal of corpses. In them, nepotism leads directly to incest or sterility, and corruption produces not just the haphazard laying down of dead bodies, but also (upon payment of U.S. dollars) their disinterment and reburial elsewhere. The original corruption of the country, where love of clan comes before citizenship, thus turns it necessarily into one vast "charnel house"—dead bodies everywhere with no sense of order. More important, however, the "average" Chinese citizen's disregard for his "own" customs—the fact that local reverence can be bought with foreign currency—likewise turns the space not just into a charnel house, but into a nightmarish land of open graves, where rotting bodies are ripped from the ground in exchange for a few dollars illicitly slipped to "the representative of the family."[69]

Again, however, this reanimation and abuse of dead bodies along with the incestuous disordering of sexual/political structures had its parallels in contemporary accounts of (political) corruption in the late nineteenth-century Ottoman Empire. The "unspeakable Turk" may have been pure compared to the "squeezing Celestial"—even as Ottoman administrators had a tendency to rely on "scientifically Chinese"[70] methods of enforcing state power—but compared to the white European, he was as impure and African as the Italian was. The mixing up of blood, race, and role, the production of miscegenated monsters that resulted from entry into the corrupt system, is indeed made most overt in stories of "Englishmen" taking on Oriental roles. Although the white Northern European's penchant for cultural cross-dressing was more "voluntary" than (presumably) the degeneration of his not quite white Mediterranean counterpart, and although the cross-dressing did nothing if not play up the difference and purity of the "original,"[71] I want to suggest that it nonetheless produced a disordering of the racial hierarchy that was in turn directly linked to a corrupt state structure. In the same way that the male cadaver crossed gender on its entry into the corrupt system, in other words, it was bribery and nepotism that, however briefly, turned the play-acting Englishman into a miscegenated monster.

An 1890 article entitled "The Experiences of the Multazim," for example, narrates this progression in detail. In it, Hasketh Smith, "the only Englishman, at any rate of the present generation or century, who has undertaken the office," discusses his tenure as a *multazim*, or tax farmer, in Ottoman Syria. He begins with a general description of the "unjust rapacity" of the Ottoman system, where "justice and fair dealing have no place," and where every "officer in the country, from the highest government magnate down to the lowest menial . . . is not impervious to a bribe."[72] He then moves on to his own position within this structure. He tells us that

> after due consideration, I determined to comply with [the peasants'] request [that I be multazim]. There were several reasons which induced me to do so, the chief of which was, that I felt that an opportunity was thus offered of teaching both our own villagers, and others as well, that honesty was really the best policy.[73]

This hands-on approach to the civilizing mission was not as easy as it first appeared, however. The Ottoman government, for example, did not allow foreigners access to *iltizams* (tax farms), and so Smith had a "native" buy one in his own name and then combine their legal identities. Moreover, halfway through the season, the villagers became involved in a lawsuit that quickly escalated and required the *multazim*'s attention. Smith met with the judge and asked that the case be withdrawn, but the (strangely forthright) judge responded with "that is all very well, but where is my *bakshish*. Unless you give me a substantial bribe, I shall not allow the case to be withdrawn." The bribe "was soon forthcoming," but the judge still insisted on trying the case which, in the end, he nonetheless decided (after much perjury) in favor of the villagers. "And the whole party returned to the village, triumphantly rejoicing over the success of their proceedings."[74]

Although Smith manages by the end of the season not to "rape" the villagers as other *multazims* do, in other words, his entry into the corrupt system nevertheless concludes with a clear—if nonetheless farcical—disordering of biological and political structures. It is not simply that he mixes his legal identity with that of the "natives"; he sullies his social identity, too, buying tax farms and bribing judges just as the Syrians do. The cross-dressing may have been a voluntary, posed sort of play acting, but the message remained intact: material entry into the corrupt system results directly in the blending, contaminating, and confusion of blood. This in turn leads to the infliction of inappropriate forms of state violence on the private lives of the citizens, and Smith's "own" villagers thus remain "bound hand and foot in the clutches of the accursed moneylender . . . crying out for bread."[75]

Dehumanizing Bureaucracies

The purpose of this final subsection is to take these stories one step further, and to situate the corruption narrative within a broader discussion of bureaucracies and the way in which they dehumanize. It is a truism at this point that the purpose of modern, functional, bureaucratic structures is to replace the idiosyncratic "human" with some variation on the (nonhuman or suprahuman) uniform and political.[76] At the same time, however, the line between functional and dysfunction bureaucratic processes—between noncorrupt structures that dehumanize through, say, the issuance of identity cards, and corrupt structures that dehumanize through more physical or biological means—is not as clear as it might be. Indeed, although one of the most frequently cited perversions of functional, noncorrupt bureaucracies is the dysfunctional, corrupt use of "systematic" torture—the demolition of humanity or idiosyncratic identity via the painful disordering of the flesh or psyche—the definition of "torture" itself has been expanded and resituated to such an extent in these narratives that it has become essentially synonymous with "corruption."

In the same way that the chaotic blending and mixing of blood, race, sex, and death gradually have come to signify the corrupt system writ large, in other words, "torture" in the corrupt system has likewise come to mean *any* form of "biological" dehumanization. To the extent that bureaucratic processes—especially in the colonial context—might lead to an apparent change of race, sex, or even species, therefore, these processes have necessarily coded as both corrupt and torture. A corrupt bureaucratic system has thus become identical to a system of torture—productive of a space in which biological lines are crossed, recrossed, or erased, and in which the "voluntary" verbal confession gives way to the brutal physicality of the biological shudder.

In both late nineteenth-century Morocco and late nineteenth-century China, for example, one of the more common themes of the corruption narrative is the unfortunate convict or prisoner, bound, exhibited, and often tortured before the idle gaze of the crowd. This theme is one that, of course, situates China and Morocco in a basic Orientalist way in the uncivilized European past. But I want to suggest that the purpose of these discussions was not *simply* to emphasize the extent to which Morocco, China, and other such nations were backward—the extent to which they had not progressed from the early modern spectacle that was physical punishment to the modern secret that was disciplinary punishment.[77] Nor was their purpose simply to play up the contaminating nature of the irrational backward penal system of the European past and the non-European present. Rather, I will argue, narratives of public punishment in the corrupt states of the late nineteenth and early twentieth century focused just as much on the (biological) disorder produced by such punishment. It was not so much the horror,[78] in other words, that was at issue in these narratives. Almost more so, it was the confusion that this horror provoked. The humanitarian shame of the tortured body on display was certainly part of the discussion, but this humanitarianism was underscored by the sneaking notion that the (nonwhite) body racked with pain and exhibited to the crowd had ceased to be human—if it ever was to begin with. Torture and spectacle in the dehumanizing corrupt system thus became—like bribery and nepotism—a story as much about biological boundaries crossed and species mixed as a story of liberal progress or the lack thereof.

In Morocco, for example, the sultan was occasionally more successful with bandits than he had been with the elusive Rais Uli. A less fortunate "specimen," El Roghi, ended up under the sultan's control, for instance, and the tale was narrated as follows:

> Bu Hamara,[79] otherwise known as El Roghi, the rebellious subject of the Sultan of Morocco, who was captured recently and brought into Fez in an iron cage, is still exposed to the gaze of the passing crowds in his open cell. He shows his scorn and disdain. When several Europeans approached him to take photographs of his cage, El Roghi shook his fist at them and shouted words of insult.[80]

Like Saddam Hussein, El Roghi is denied here the capacity of producing articulate speech. He sits in his iron cage, shows his scorn and disdain, shakes his fist, and shouts words of insult—although what those words might be we do not know. He behaves like a zoological specimen while European tourists—thrilled by the proximity of the danger but protected by the bars of the cage—take pictures of him as a bit of local color.[81] What is made clear in this passage, therefore, is first, that corrupt Moroccan justice produces not the dehumanization of the incarcerated modern prisoner described by Foucault, but a physical and biological extraction of the prisoner's humanity. The Moroccan system thus turns its victims literally, rather than figuratively, into animals. The public nature of this dehumanization, the relationship between the brutal and brutalized prisoner and the passing crowds (at least those crowds not protected by outside/inside tourist status) in turn contaminates everyone involved not just with the taint of backwardness,[82] but with a latent bestiality.

If we shift focus to China, we find a similar narrative being produced. An article from 1894, for instance, states that "at the treaty ports even offenders are often placed in cages, through the tops of which their heads protrude, with support of the feet only strong enough to prevent instantaneous dislocation of the neck. The victims must die of starvation and of exhaustion and the mob must jeer."[83] Here the relationship between the dehumanized offender and the dehumanized mob is made explicit. The "victim" must die of starvation because he is physically immobile and has no choice. The mob, however, is equally without choice—it is not just that it does jeer, but that it *must* jeer. The dehumanization of the prisoner,[84] his public exhibition like an animal in a zoo, in this way spreads throughout the entire system, producing shock waves of biological and physical disorder, emphasizing and reemphasizing the species slippage produced by the corrupt system on prisoner, judge, and watching crowd.[85]

It is not just corrupt *punishment* that allows for this blending of biological identity, however. In the corrupt system, judicial procedure and testimony are equally brutal. The running theme of the "extorted" confession, for example, plays up explicitly the intimate relationship between corruption and an individual's disordered physical identity. The confession "extorted" under pain and duress (as opposed to the confession "freely given" in a noncorrupt system) is a confession at once about flesh and identity. It is a commonplace that such a confession is rarely "true"—but abstract (legal) "truth" is not at issue.[86] Rather, within the late nineteenth-century narrative, true and not-true come together in the extorted confession to produce the animal/human, female/male, impure/pure logic of corruption. Judicial torture and the extorted confession are thus, again, productive not so much of horror as they are of confusion. The humanity and identity extracted are extracted just as they would be in a noncorrupt system, but they are then reconfigured into monstrous, unnatural, bare and physical, rather than legal, truth.

In Morocco, for example, the sultan "first personally question[s]" suspects, and then has the hands and feet of the men and the teeth of the women removed by a public executioner.[87] In discussions of China, judicial torture became one of the defining characteristics of the state, appearing and reappearing with increasing frequency in intimate "exposés" of Chinese governance. In one article, the corrupt nature of the court indeed eventually gives way to unrestrained brutality, where "if answers are not given willingly or are not what the Judge wishes them to be, then torture is resorted to." There follows an exhaustive list of the various "systems of torture" in use in Chinese courts, with a particular emphasis on the various body parts that are the focus of these systems, including the shoulder blades, the cheeks, the teeth, the mouth, the ankles, the arms, the breast, the hollow of the back of the knee, the legs, and the naked neck. We also learn that "torture systems are not confined to the prisoners alone, but are almost as often applied, at the discretion of the Judges and Mandarins, to the witnesses who may be called in to give evidence at the trial." In the end, the article notes, the trial becomes almost carnivalesque, a situation in which "it is very often a difficult if not impossible matter for a visitor to a Chinese court to tell which is the prisoner and which the witnesses; all seem equally guilty, if we are to judge by the torture applied to all alike."[88]

In the first passage, therefore, even as there is gender division in deciding which body parts to remove, the brutal focus on the prisoners' bodies *as* bodies removes any "true" sexual distinction. The result is a disorder of flesh and sex that would not have been possible in an abstract, legal system—a system that, "paradoxically," with its focus on equal citizenship would have maintained a proper gender divide. Similarly, in the second passage, the progression from corrupt system to bodily disorder is explicit. The court first extorts money from the defendant and then extorts a confession. The confession of the defendant, however, is patently not "true," given that he simply says what the judge wishes him to say. But as this untruth becomes truth, and as the trial progresses, the logical conclusion to the corrupt system is made apparent. Even as the body parts are described in detail—it is not just the knee but the "hollow of the back of the knee," not just the back but the "shoulder blades," not just the neck but the "naked neck"—they begin to run together. The result is a physical disorder not dissimilar from the disorder of Moroccan sexuality described before. The cheeks, the teeth, the mouth, the ankles, and so on all come together to form one lump of disorganized flesh, indicative solely *of* flesh and solely of physical identity.[89] The result is inevitable: it is impossible for the (legally defined, uncorrupted, Western) visitor to tell prisoner from witness. Legal roles and political hierarchies break down—in the same way that the corrupt system disorders gender and bodily framework, so, too, does it disorder the political and judicial system writ large.

But this relationship between torture in the corrupt system and the blending and mixing of things that ought to remain apart and distinct becomes far more clear when (white) Europeans and North Americans get caught up in it. In such cases, first of all, "torture" takes on a relatively broad meaning, such that any activity on the part of the corrupt penal system (like that of the corrupt system of taxation earlier) is necessarily irrational, violent, and brutal. Second, the most common effect as well as side effect[90] of the torture—indeed the torture in and of itself—is the brutal "miscegenation"[91] of the "victim." Torture in the corrupt system, in other words, sometimes deliberately produced, sometimes inadvertently produced, and sometimes in and of itself, *was defined as* the blurring of racial boundaries and the mixing of pure blood. The corrupt system, therefore, dehumanized and tortured white men quite precisely by turning them into—and extorting confessions from them that they in fact were—interchangeable with nonwhite, feminine savages.

In 1903, for example, the *London Times* ran an article entitled "Moroccan Brigands Torture Journalist." The article described the harrowing experiences of Mr. Harris,[92] the journalist, who was simultaneously captured, tortured, and saved by Rais Uli. The "torture" bit of the story, however, although quite detailed, leaves something to be desired. It notes, first of all, that Mr. Harris was "taken to a room in Rais Uli's house, where the first object he saw was a headless corpse extended in the middle of the floor. The corpse was shortly afterward taken away for burial and the floor washed, but bloody finger marks on the walls were allowed to remain." Second,

> the only time the correspondent was allowed to leave quarters for more than a few minutes was when he was taken to see the corpse of a cavalry soldier whose body had been horribly mutilated. Mr. Harris was informed with grim humor that he would look like that in a few days. After nine days at Zinat, Mr. Harris' friends of the Anjera tribe surrounded Raisuli's village and demanded that Harris be handed over to them. . . . [H]e was treated as one of the Anjera tribe, wore their dress, shaved his head, and conformed to all of their customs.[93]

A decade earlier, in China, two American citizens, Mr. Parkes and Mr. Loch, were similarly mistreated "under torture"—an experience that involved, first, soldiers "brandish[ing] swords over their heads," second, being put "in a cramped attitude into carts, that jolted over stones," and, third, being "separated, heavily pinioned, and put with native prisoners." The article concludes that "the only excuse which could ever be found for the indifference of the Chinese to the sufferings of others was expressed by Topffer in his memorable phrase, 'Chinamen are not people like us.'"[94] Finally, in the midst of all of this, in the Ottoman Empire, the deplorable state of (white)

Christians and their torture at the hands of (nonwhite) Muslims is described in a similar manner. After first noting that "the fact that a man is a human being seems to have no place in the criminal code of the land,"[95] the article presents a communication "from a man who has been living in that hell-hole for over a month and is no more worthy of such treatment than thousands of readers of this letter." The letter begins,

> our condition in prison passes description. Only he who sees can understand it. Most of the occupants of every room are Christians, but many are Moslems. Life would be a shade more tolerable if the subject race were not compelled thus to associate with the dominant race, whose temper, tastes and habits are so different. . . . [O]ut of this throng of prisoners more than a hundred are in daily suffering from the gnawings of hunger and from nakedness, but there is no one to pity. Many praying men are tempted to cease praying, many are tempted to change over to the Moslem faith. In truth all of us are dumb: what to say we know not.[96]

In Morocco, China, and the Ottoman Empire, in other words, the corrupt system and its concomitant torture both *were* and *resulted in* racial disorder. Mr. Harris is inducted into and tainted by the corrupt system by witnessing the dismembered corpse. He is then told that he and a second, equally disordered corpse are one. But then he finally gets off with relative ease (Rais Uli being a gentleman) by shaving his head and becoming one with the Moroccans instead. Mr. Parkes and Mr. Loch are less lucky—the natural collectivity of the two as white men is destroyed when they are separated. Worse, they are then physically restrained and—with an irrational and sadistic disregard for proper racial hierarchy and order—forced to become one with the Chinese. And, to emphasize, this in and of itself constitutes "torture." Finally, the Ottoman prison is a hellhole not just because of starvation and cold, but—far more so—because of the forced association between dominant and subject races. The racial mixing indeed serves a purpose identical to more obvious forms of "torture," leading first to the "tempting" realm of dehumanized abandon, and second to a complete loss of coherent narrative and identity ("all of us are dumb")—setting the foundation, like Chinese judicial torture, for the extortion of confessions and the construction of "untrue" identities ("confessions of sedition extorted by torture").[97]

The dehumanizing aspect of racial mixing and disordering is thus made absolutely explicit. The final point of the article on China, for example, that "Chinamen are not people like us," produces a number of overlapping meanings. Are we meant to understand that Chinamen are not people or that Chinamen are not like us? The line between the two is unclear. Undoubtedly, however, the line, such as it was, was meant to be: Chinamen are not like us, and therefore they are not people; at the same time, Chinamen are not people, and therefore obviously they are not like us. That such is the case, however, means that the "torture" of Mr. Parkes and Mr. Loch is far more pernicious than it might originally appear—by turning two white men into momentary Chinamen, the Chinese government was not just violating them racially, it was also making them "not people" and "not like us." Mr. Parkes and Mr. Loch were thus *both* miscegenated *and* placed beyond the pale of humanity (like MacArthur's Filipinos), dehumanized in a far more basic and biological way than could have occurred in any abstract or legal bureaucratic system. Similarly, the entire "communication" of the naked, speechless Christian tempted to change his faith is couched in the notion that "the fact that a man is a human being" does not exist in the Ottoman Empire. Just as in China, in other words, it is precisely the racial and biological overlap that is dehumanizing—torture both is and is productive of a disordering of blood and flesh, a horrifying confusion far more than a confusing horror.

In the late twentieth century, the narrative of the dehumanizing corrupt system—especially to the extent that it condoned "torture" rather than legal methods of extracting humanity—became more elaborate. The Chinese government was still in the habit of extorting confessions,[98] for example, but the totalitarian implications of this practice were made explicit. At the same time, however, even as the line between the corrupt and the noncorrupt system, between the biological and the legal, became rhetorically set, the extent to which noncorrupt dehumanization could slip into corrupt dehumanization also became apparent. Even as the noncorrupt, appropriately legal, liberal bureaucracy went about constructing a uniform political collective, that is, it drew closer to the corrupt, inappropriately biological, totalitarian bureaucracy's process of constructing a uniform physical collective. The mixing up of blood, flesh, and sex in the latter, the blending and confusion that it created, became to a great extent the complement of the abstract order of the former.

Stories of torture in the corrupt system, for example, begin with both the horror of the painfully extorted confession and—more so—the confusion of the "untrue" disordered identity that comes out of it. In late twentieth-century Turkish police stations, for instance, "police used rape to extract . . . false confession[s]." In an article from the *Independent*, we learn that in addition to rape, young women were also beaten, sprayed with freezing water, and suffocated.[99] The primary point of this article, however, was not to list the various ways in which Turkish (and, for the most part, sexualized, female Turkish) bodies were abused in the corrupt bureaucratic system. Instead, it was to play up the strange confusion that resulted from this situation.

The confessions that were extracted from the young women were, for instance, more accurately, "confessions"—not just false, but also mimetic, existing only within quotation marks, incoherently narrated for the sake of pure physicality. More to the point, the title of the article—"Torture Victims Tried for Daring to Speak Out"—plays up the contaminating and contaminated nature of torture writ large in the corrupt system. It indeed becomes clear that it was not just the personal narratives of the tortured women that were confused and mixed, it was the justice system in its entirety and the roles that individuals were supposed to play within it. Just as in late nineteenth-century China, where because of the torture, the outside observer could not differentiate between witness and defendant, in late twentieth-century Turkey, because of the torture, it was the victims who became defendants and the torturers who were victims. The biological confusion of the tortured body was in this way undifferentiated from the psychic confusion of the extorted confession and the judicial confusion of the corrupt bureaucracy—the three interacted to produce a broader narrative of both the nature and effects of corrupt as opposed to noncorrupt bureaucracy.

But corruption and the torture that derived from it did not just create a confused legal establishment. They also disordered, for instance, the medical establishment, producing doctors whose contorted approach to their patients'/victims' bodies built something of a bridge between the blending or mixing of blood or flesh and the blending or mixing of identity that came out of the corrupt system. In an article entitled "Outcasts of the Medical World: Doctors Accused of Torture," for instance—an article whose title explicitly placed the "outcast" torturing doctor into the same nonlegal space as the bandit and the corrupt bureaucrat—the *Observer* described the effects of such systems on the role of doctors and the narrative of medical humanism. Focusing in particular on the United States, "Islamic countries," Serbia, and Turkey (and arguing that "any call for sanctions against individual doctors and countries was bound to face charges of cultural imperialism"), the article discussed doctors who saved the lives of condemned criminals in order to execute them hours later, doctors and psychiatrists who ran concentration camps, doctors who advised interrogators on how much pain a prisoner could stand, and doctors who amputated limbs in conformity with criminal sentencing.[100]

Again, the primary point of the article concerned the inverted role of the doctor in the corrupt system (or the "torture nation")[101]—inflicting pain and causing death rather than easing pain and preserving life as the medical establishment ought to do. The confused and conflicted role of the doctor did not just end with the "betrayal" of the Hippocratic oath, however. When doctors attended to the bodies of victims rather than to the bodies of patients,[102] the defining characteristics of their own identity began to blur as well. As the article notes, "in a confession to the *Guardian* this year, [one doctor] accepted responsibility for the atrocities, and said that a 'collective madness' had gripped his community."[103] By both "confessing" and diagnosing, by both accepting responsibility and playing up his own lack of control, the doctor here does not just merge with the torturer but with the victim as well. He is both interrogator (as doctor and torturer) and interrogated (as patient and victim). The narrative of the overcontrolled/out of control corrupt system thus breaks down any obvious lines between and among roles, creating a situation in which a single individual can simultaneously play doctor, patient, torturer, tortured, private individual, and public citizen.

The way in which issues of political affiliation do in the end infiltrate the torture chamber, turning it into a place in which biological dehumanization is intimately connected to legal dehumanization, suggests however the interconnectedness between the corrupt and the noncorrupt bureaucracy. In the same way that the "torture nation" could exist—and indeed move about—within the "civilized nation," the physical dehumanization exacted by the corrupt system could occur even within nations that would likely not make "charges of cultural imperialism" against those who questioned their methods. The most obvious space in which this interconnectedness occurs at the turn of the twenty-first century is in the cell of the "terror suspect"—keeping in mind that the terror suspect always brings the torture nation with him. In an article on May 5, 2004, for example, the *Guardian* received "access" to Mahmoud Abu Rideh, a "terror suspect" held in England's Broadmoor high-security hospital. The article tells us that

> the effects of the legal limbo in which Mahmoud Abu Rideh is trapped are visible on his arms. For 22 months, he has been locked up, without charge or trial, in Broadmoor high security hospital under controversial anti-terror laws. . . . [W]hen he pulls up his shirt sleeves in the visitor room at Broadmoor, he reveals dozens of scars up and down his arms, inflicted using pens, plastic and anything else he can find. Since his detention, he has been repeatedly harming himself, from drinking toilet cleaner to setting himself on fire. "I don't have a criminal record," he told the *Guardian*. "I don't touch kids. I don't take drugs. I don't kill somebody or cut him. This is a hospital for these kinds of people and they put me here with them. Belmarsh

is a prison well known for the worst kinds of criminals and the government put me there. I am living with these kinds of people, what do you expect? Of course I would go mad". . . . [N]ow he harms himself, he says, out of frustration when people are racist or when he goes into a "dark time" experiencing flashbacks of his torture. "I drink shampoo, I drink air freshener, I drink toilet cleaner," he said. "Every week I try something. It's better than being here. The staff don't want me here. They hit me and the patients hit me. What I have been through in this place is worse than when I was detained in Israel when I was tortured. They have destroyed me."[104]

Deliberately or not, the article begins by invoking Franz Kafka's *The Penal Colony*—Abu Rideh's legal identity is physically inscribed on his body. Whereas Kafka was describing an, albeit disturbing, functional, and noncorrupt system, however, the discussion here is of a system in which the very laws are "controversial," and their effects incoherent—a corrupt system within civilized space. It is emphatically *not* Abu Rideh's criminality that is visible on his arms—it is instead the effects of "legal limbo." It is not, in other words, that the dehumanization of the system produces a (just or not) criminal identity—it is that the dehumanization produces an outlaw, a body whose identity is not legally definable.

The result is a strange and incoherent mixture of, and tension between, political and biological existence. The *Guardian*'s "access" to the victim/patient "allows" Abu Rideh to narrate a political and legal identity. The story that he tells, however, is one in which the state's attempt to extort a confession of insanity from him, to mix inappropriately, corruptly, and biologically the sane with the insane, has driven him mad. He is not mad, the *Guardian* tells us, and therefore he has lost his mind. The signifier of the disordered and simultaneously sane and insane victim/patient of the corrupt system is, moreover, an unsettlingly biological one—the (unsuccessful) drinking of shampoo, ingesting of air freshener, and imbibing of toilet cleaner. As the corrupt system tortures and extracts Abu Rideh's physical humanity, in other words, forcing psychobiological mixing just as the Chinese and Ottomans forced racial mixing, allowing for the chaotic penetration and infection of his body but clamping down with totalitarian thoroughness on his attempts to "take" his own life, the noncorrupt system represented by the *Guardian* produces an alternative. Abu Rideh can also give up his humanity politically and legally. He can narrate a functional identity for the sake of noncorrupt affiliation, in which "they have destroyed me" becomes something to long for rather than something to dread.

A more straightforward (if arguably also more brutal) manifestation of this late twentieth- and early twenty-first-century interconnectedness between corrupt and noncorrupt dehumanization, between the extraction of legal humanity and the extraction of biological humanity, occurred in the U.S. military's occupation and "reconstruction" of Iraq. On the one hand, there was the corrupt—signified most blatantly in the photographs and accounts of torture in Abu Ghraib prison. On the other hand, there was the noncorrupt—usually embodied by the Iraqi elections and more specifically by the writing of a liberal, humanitarian Iraqi constitution. Obviously both moves are colonial or neocolonial ones—it would be difficult for anything happening in occupied Iraq to be anything but. I would also like to argue, however, that Abu Ghraib and the Iraqi constitution are far more closely related than simply in their origin in colonial occupation. The two were part and parcel of an identical process, serving the same purpose, performing for the benefit of both political and consumer culture.

The most notorious photograph that came out of Abu Ghraib, for example, was the "naked pyramid" picture. In this photo, a number of naked (Iraqi) men are stacked on top of one another, a pile of flesh, strangely reminiscent of the "one hundred pieces" torture described with such horror (and confusion) by visitors to nineteenth-century China. The body parts in this photo all blend together, and it indeed becomes difficult to discern which part belongs to which man. Following the global publication of these photographs, the almost immediate response (in addition to humanitarian outcry) was "and this is particularly horrific for *Arab* men because . . . ." The corrupt system's physical dehumanization of the individuals who had entered it, its extraction of their humanity, that is, instantly served likewise as a foundation for the gradual reconstruction, for the extorted confession—verbal or not—of the "Iraqi" read as "Arab," read as (more often than not) "Muslim" man. In the same way that interrogators of "Iraqi"/"Arab"/"Muslim" prisoners chose methods of dehumanization and bodily disorder that simultaneously redefined these prisoners and constructed identities for them (i.e., "Arabs" or "Muslims" are afraid of dogs/naked women/Christian crosses),[105] in other words, the naked pyramid, in the process of removing the slightest physical or biological differentiation among individual bodies, likewise set the groundwork for the creation of an equally uniform political, legal, and "cultural" identity.

It was the existence of the corrupt system, therefore, the delineation of exceptional space, and the physical dehumanization wrought by the torturing interrogator within this space, that made possible the noncorrupt, legally defined, political dehumanization wrought by the humanitarian legal scholar. The coming together of the corrupt and the noncorrupt indeed produced a situation in which the formation of the "new" political identity happened simultaneously with the torturous disordering, blending and mixing of the "old" one. Both were variations on the extorted confession. The secular Ba'thist official is forced by interrogators to kiss a cross, and this is a trauma for him. But it is a trauma only because these same interrogators have previously defined him as one who—despite his secularism, despite the fact that under other circumstances kissing a cross would be meaningless—finds such an act traumatic.

The *actual* physical torture and biological disordering—stripping the official naked, starving him, depriving him of sleep, beating him, and so on prior to asking him to kiss the cross—are thus a necessary prelude to the *possibility* of "cultural torture," to the *possibility* of trammeling a victim's "identity." Kissing the cross in this way *does* become traumatic for the Ba'thist official, and he *does* become a "Muslim"—defined as such by the humanitarian who decries this as a uniquely awful cultural torture and by the legal scholar who creates a liberal state in which such torture cannot happen. His identity coalesces at the exact moment that it is broken apart, no different from that of the tortured white men, placed into a jail cell in the nineteenth century with "natives." The aboveboard, noncorrupt, eminently humanitarian Iraqi constitution—the political and legal construction of the Iraqi citizen and the Iraqi collective—thus *had* to happen alongside the murky, corrupt, sadistic American/Iraqi torture chamber. Defining the Iraqi citizen politically was inextricably linked to defining him biologically and "culturally." The bodily disorder of the naked pyramid, the material, fleshy humanity extracted by the corrupt system indeed produced a uniform, dehumanized Iraqi collective—or, for that matter, "body"—no different from, and arguably no more traumatized than, that created by the public.

Conclusion

I would like to end this chapter by returning to two seemingly unrelated works—*Salo* and the editorials of William Safire. Both Pasolini and Safire, coming from vastly different universes, address the issue of the corrupt system and what it does to "a person." Both make implicit and explicit connections between corruption and totalitarianism, linking the frightening chaos of the former to the equally frightening regulation of the latter. The primary difference between the two—aside, of course, from their choice of narrative style—is that Pasolini implies a disconcerting closeness between the corrupt and the noncorrupt, and, by extension, the totalitarian and the liberal.[106] For Safire, the two spheres are distinct, discrete, and separated by an insurmountable gulf. Even as Safire insists on this distinctness, however, he builds up a strange and effective bridge between the two. In an article entitled "Gravy Trains Don't Run on Time," for instance, this linkage is made explicit.

> the outstretched hand of local politics is no match for the invisible hand of the global market. The dictatorial model, driven by mutual back-scratching of elites rather than a profit motive open to all, rewarded despotism and nepotism at the expense of efficiency and transparency. Now eyes are opening all over the world to the realization that the gravy train does not run on time.[107]

The gravy train does not run on time. Mussolini's trains, however, quite notoriously did, and it is here that Safire's model becomes more complex than it might seem on the surface. The rhetoric is straightforward—regulated markets lead to corruption lead to totalitarianism; private (biological and material) connections cannot compete with public (abstract and legal) ones; the fleshy hand is no match for the invisible one. But the underlying message is more complicated than that. According to the title of the piece and the concluding sentence, it seems that what we are supposed to desire in place of this inappropriate system is "trains running on time"—the well-known shorthand, universal trope, and ineradicable macro for "fascist efficiency."

Even as the corrupt system and the totalitarian system come together in opposition to the noncorrupt and liberal system, that is, in our heart of hearts what we apparently want is the former. And it is here that the role of the bandit bureaucrat, reanimated corpse, miscegenated monster, and sexually confused naked body that populate the corrupt system becomes apparent. These dehumanized "things"[108] are not just symbolic of the horrors that happen in a system built on biology rather than law. They are concrete, they are erotic, and they are desirable even *as* they horrify. They represent and hold out the possibility of an affiliation and dehumanization far more basic than that held out by, say, the *Guardian* to the unfortunate "terror suspect" in legal limbo. Indeed, they embody what the law-based, noncorrupt, not totalitarian nation state is trying and failing to produce—a corrupt/noncorrupt space in which the naked pyramid and the constitution can and do perform the same task.

Conclusion

When the *Daily Mirror* published its unauthorized seminude photographs of the imprisoned Saddam Hussein, human rights advocates were aghast. The line between appropriate and inappropriate, legal and extralegal, punishment had been crossed. The corrupt leader was supposed to be his own victim, not "ours," and anyone imprisoned in a noncorrupt space under the rule of law had certain rights; Saddam Hussein's had been trampled. At the same time, when news emerged that Saddam Hussein was planning on suing the *Mirror*, the absurdity of this shock and horror, as well as the very notion that the imprisoned corrupt leader had rights at all, became clear. Saddam Hussein's lawsuit would have made no more sense than a lawsuit opened up by the pornographic representation of the pop singer or the slashed fictional "real girl." The photographs of Saddam caught off guard in his white briefs—briefs, incidentally, identical to those worn by Samuel Doe in his final moments—were simply the logical conclusion to the narrative of the corrupt leader. There is nothing metaphorical about the stripping of this leader, nothing figurative or abstract about the pornographic nature of his climactic moments. In a straightforward, concrete way, his story is about sex, flesh, and violence. His eventual snuff-film-like end could not have been any different than it was.

I have indeed attempted to emphasize throughout this book the extent to which the corruption narrative—whether it is manifested in the leader, the citizen, or the system—is a narrative of solid, physical, and material intimacy. The opposite of the rule of law and civic rights, a menace to the ideal of universal and abstract equality, stories of political corruption were necessarily stories of the parochially personal. Evocative of the unmentionable, fleshy half of the Cartesian dualism that underscores post-Enlightenment political progress, the corrupt state, corrupt citizen, corrupt leader, and corrupt system had to be defined, contained, constrained, and consumed for the sake of an emergent, legally defined, democratic public.

The first section of this book, in the form of a literature review, therefore discussed the geographical placement of modern corruption into colonized space, and the erotic or pornographic nature of its narration there. By conflating infantile development/sexuality with colonial development/sexuality, the corruption narrative first turned the corrupt state and its citizens into simultaneous victims and perpetrators of inappropriate intimacy. Second, the emphasis on exposing the "dirty" or "rotten" interior of the corrupt state or citizen, as well as the insistence on a purifying or healing confession, placed the anticorruption specialist into a realm not far removed from that of the burlesque show audience. By creating a relationship between the corrupt state and anticorruption agencies that not only mirrored but overlapped with the relationship between confessant and confessor, exhibitionist and audience, the corruption narrative took on the same consumable character as the striptease. Finally, the themes of savagery and feeding that permeate stories, discussions, and analyses of corruption in the nineteenth and twentieth centuries positioned the corrupt leader or corrupt bureaucrat in a special part of the larger imperial imagination. The savage-as-child-as-monster motif that runs throughout colonial literature writ large became more than a motif or a metaphor in the literature—the corrupt bureaucrat an *actual* cannibal, and the corrupt leader an *actual* incestuous rapist.

This literature review set the groundwork for the next two chapters and for a discussion of the political implications of these themes. In the first of these chapters, Abdülhamid II and Saddam Hussein served as case studies in the creation, celebration, and spectacularization of the corrupt leader. Each transcended the typical story of the Oriental despot or Third World gangster and became likewise, or more so, the embodiment of modern corrupt governance. Unlike the noncorrupt leader, whose sovereignty is mediated through law and text, whose presence is abstract and political, the corrupt leader is a feminized celebrity, his rule mediated through physicality and body language, his presence material and biological. The corruption narrative deprived both Abdülhamid II and Saddam Hussein of an articulate voice, emphasized their bodies, their clothing, or their lack thereof, turned them into monsters or masochists, and set the foundation for their eventual confession. This confession, however, like that of the stripper or the porn star, involved not law or language, but physical exposure. It emerged from a space in which every intimate detail of the corrupt leader's biological existence was regulated, packaged, reinterpreted, and turned into spectacle for the watching, law-abiding public.

But the corrupt leader was not the only player in this process. The final section of this book thus addressed the relationship between corruption and regulation on a larger scale. Whereas the corrupt leader became a celebrity or a porn star, exposed and exhibited both within his own (fantasy) world and "our" world of law and rationality, the corrupt system produced a space in which each citizen was similarly regulated and exposed. The narrative of the corrupt system therefore brought together in a paradoxical way the overcontrolled universality of the totalitarian system and the out of control parochialism of the corrupt one. The erotic—or at least sadomasochistic—potential of this relationship became clear in the Pasolini film *Salo*, but it was also reproduced in media reports, academic analyses, and political discussions of the corrupt bureaucracy. The corrupt system created above all else a lawless space, where bureaucrats merged with bandits and civic belonging gave way to blood and biology. The corrupt system was accessed materially and—more to the point—the equalizing dehumanization of the "good" bureaucracy became likewise a material affair. Bribery and nepotism led to torture, and the protective nature of universal constitutionalism took on overtly totalitarian implications.

At the same time, the line between the corrupt and noncorrupt became increasingly fine to nonexistent. And it is here that I would like to return to both Saddam Hussein in his underwear and the pornographic pop star. Another response elicited by the photographs in the *Mirror* is that they are clearly "fake," and that the reaction of both the humanitarians and Saddam Hussein is therefore overblown. If anything, the photographs are pictures of one of Saddam Hussein's body doubles, and consequently meaningless. What the corruption narrative and its false law/biology dichotomy have therefore produced is an inconsistent situation. The reality of biological identity, the materiality of exposed flesh, turns people "fake," deprives them of protection or rights, and subjects them to violence. At the same time, the fiction of legal identity, the intangibility of the passport photo, turns people "real," confers on them rights, and protects them from violence. The biological mass that is Saddam Hussein—his inherently corrupt and corruptible flesh—is thus a fiction, his identity no different from that of the pop singer. Likewise, on a larger scale, the biologically defined living Iraqi prisoner is also a fiction, subject to any and every sort of cartoon violence, while the legally defined dead body of the U.S. soldier is real, protected by the Geneva Conventions, endowed with rights, and sheltered from any and every abuse.

Notes

Introduction

1. See below and Abigail Solomon-Godeau, "The Legs of the Countess," in *Fetishism as a Cultural Discourse*, ed. Emily Apter and William Pietz (Ithaca: Cornell University Press, 1993), 296, 304.

2. "Britney Spears Porn Comix," http://www.celebritygo.net/comics.

3. Coalition Against Trafficking in Women, "The Factbook on Global Sexual Exploitation: India," http://www.catwinternational.org/fb/india.html. This section of the piece is summarizing an investigation conducted by Robert I. Friedman, "India's Shame: Sexual Slavery and Political Corruption Are Leading to an AIDS Catastrophe," *The Nation* April 8, 1996.

4. Karen Halttunen, "Humanitarianism and the Pornography of Pain in Anglo American Culture," *American Historical Review* 100 (2) (1995): 303–334.

5. Cirila P. Limpangog, "Struggling through Corruption: A Gendered Perspective," Tenth International Anti-Corruption Conference, http://www.10iacc.org/content.phtml?documents=111cart=135. Compare to similar scenes in Richard Seaver, ed., *Marquis de Sade: Justine, Philosophy in the Bedroom, and Other Writings* (New York: Grove Press, 1965), 527.

6. Quentin Reed, "Political Corruption, Privatisation and Control in the Czech Republic: A Case Study or Problems in Multiple Transition," Transparency International, www.transparency.org.ru/CENTER/DOC/Book06.doc. Richardson, in other words, rather than Sade. See Samuel Richardson, *Clarissa*, ed. Angus Ross (London: Penguin, 1985).

7. See, among many others, John Githongo, "Corruption as a Problem in the Developing World," Seminar on Corruption and Development Cooperation May 2000, http://www.transparency.org/speeches/githongo.html, who notes, for instance, that corruption creates "an incestuous relationship between business, politics and the bureaucracy."

8. See, for instance, Tunku Abdul Aziz, "ADB-OECD Anti-Corruption Initiative, November 28–30, 2001," http://www.transparency.org/speeches/taa_apac.html.

9. One major anticorruption NGO is called Transparency International.

10. See above, Reed.

11. For instance, SPR, "Somalia: Warlords Have Vested Interest in Perpetuation of Civil War," U4 Anti-Corruption News http://www.u4.no/news/news.cfm?id=107.

12. Demetrios Argyriades, "The International Anti-Corruption Campaigns," in Caiden, 217, notes that "since 1996 a number of agreements, conventions, declarations, and regulations in international aid agencies have focused attention on corruption." He then cites on pp. 217–218 examples such as the 1997 OECD Convention on International Bribery, the December 1996 UN Resolution 51/57 Action Against Corruption, the March 1996 Inter-American Convention Against Corruption, and the February 1997 UN Declaration Against Corruption and Bribery in International Commercial Transactions. See also Robert Williams, "New Concepts for Old," *Third World Quarterly* 20 (3) (1999): 503, who notes that "interest in corruption has grown rapidly in the 1990s. Academic journals, newspapers and magazines are full of articles on corruption. Government departments, international financial institutions and supra national political bodies have all published policy statements emphasizing the significance of corruption."

13. See, among others, Robert Williams, "Introduction," in *Controlling Corruption*, ed. Robert Williams and Alan Doig (MA: Edward Elgar Press, 2000), xii, "The corruption eruption is therefore a global rather than a regional phenomenon."

14. Tracey Jean Boisseau, *White Queen: May French Sheldon and the Imperial Origins of American Feminism* (Bloomington: Indiana University Press, 2004), 15.

15. Emily Apter, "Introduction," in *Fetishism as a Cultural Discourse*, 2.

16. See, for example, Andrei Markovits, "Introduction," in *The Politics of Scandal: Power and Process in Liberal Democracies*, ed.

Andrei Markovits and Mark Silverstein (New York: Holmes and Meier, 1988), 2, 5.

17. Giorgio Agamben, *Homo Sacer: Sovereign Power and Bare Life*, trans. Daniel Heller-Roazen (Stanford: Stanford University Press, 1998) and Giorgio Agamben, *State of Exception*, trans. Kevin Attell (Chicago: University of Chicago Press, 2005), passim. Achille Mbembe, "Necropolitics," trans. Libby Meintjes, *Public Culture* 15 (1) (2003): 22, 30.

18. I am familiar with critiques of the center/periphery paradigm in studies of empire and imperialism (see Michael Hardt and Antonio Negri, *Multitude: War and Democracy in the Age of Empire* [London: Penguin, 2004]). I would suggest, however, that whether or not such a paradigm actually exists, the rhetoric has been important in defining the nineteenth-, twentieth-, and twenty-first-century civilizational hierarchies so central to the contemporary corruption narrative.

19. Michel Foucault, *History of Sexuality*, trans. Robert Hurley (New York: Vintage, 1978), 42.

20. Laura Briggs, *Reproducing Empire: Race, Sex, Science and U.S. Imperialism in Puerto Rico* (Berkeley: University of California Press, 2002), 25.

21. Ann Laura Stoler, *Carnal Knowledge and Imperial Power* (Berkeley: University of California Press, 2002), 57, 63.

22. Ibid., 77.

23. For a further discussion, see Ann Laura Stoler, *Race and the Education of Desire* (Durham: Duke University Press, 1995), 160.

24. As quoted in Robin Theobald, "So What Really Is the Problem about Corruption," *Third World Quarterly* 20 (3) (1999): 491.

25. Williams in *Controlling Corruption*, xiii.

26. "Towards a Grammar of Graft," *The Economist* 183 (June 15, 1957): 958–959. Reprinted in ed. Arnold J. Heidenheimer, *Political Corruption: Readings in Comparative Analysis* (NJ: Transaction Books, 1978), 489.

27. Peter John Perry, *Political Corruption and Political Geography* (Aldershot, England: Ashgate, 1997), 37.

28. For further examples of this twentieth-century geography of corruption, see Gerald E. Caiden, O. P. Dwivedi, Joseph Jabbra, eds., *Where Corruption Lives* (CT: Kumarian Press, 2001): "perhaps things are not as bad in some parts of Asia [as they are in Africa] although some countries on this continent rank among the lowest in governance simply because corruption has always been a way of life." (p. 11) "the general lack of success

in reducing corruption [in the Middle East] has been attributed to 'the overwhelming corrupt culture which permeates all aspects of society.' (Jabbra, 1976, 673)." (p. 29) "In the Indian subcontinent, corruption is a way of life and few public officials can escape it, but endemic corruption is also found in several other countries in Asia" (p. 29). Using a broader approach, ABC-Clio, a database of scholarly publications, returns thousands of results when prompted with the key word "corruption." Nearly 85 percent of these focus on Africa, Asia, South America, and Russia or the Soviet Union. Of those that do discuss corruption in Western Europe, North America, Australia, or New Zealand, nearly half do so historically, positioning it prior to the 1850s. The set contained 1,917 entries.

29. Markovits, vii.

30. See above, "In [Western European] countries, corruption is much the exception. . . . [B]ut in recent years their self image has been besmirched by revelations of scandals in the highest public positions." Caiden, 27.

31. Anna Clark, *Scandal: The Sexual Politics of the British Constitution* (Princeton: Princeton University Press, 2004), 3.

32. Markovits, viii–ix.

33. In which the English press discovered in 1961 that Christine Keeler was the mistress of both Jack Profumo, the Minister of War, and Eugene Ivanov, a Russian naval attaché. Robin Gaster, "Sex, Spies, and Scandal: The Profumo Affair and British Politics," in *The Politics of Scandal*, 63.

34. In which the U.S. press discovered that Richard Nixon, the president, had been connected with a burglary of the headquarters of the Democratic National Committee and had then attempted to block FBI attempts to investigate it. Markovits, "Watergate and the American Political System," in *The Politics of Scandal*, 19.

35. In which the French secret service blew up the *Rainbow Warrior*, a ship owned by Greenpeace and about to protest French nuclear testing outside of New Zealand. Stephen E. Bornstein, "The Greenpeace Affair and French Politics," in *The Politics of Scandal*, 96.

36. Jean-François Bayart, Stephen Ellis, and Béatrice Hibou, *The Criminalization of the State in Africa* (Bloomington: Indiana University Press, 1999), xiii.

37. Douglas Andrew Yates, "France's Elf Scandals," in *Where Corruption Lives*, 69.

38. Yates, 78.

39. Bayart, xv.

40. A search on the Lexis-Nexis database of newspaper articles, limited to the years 2001–2005 and to the terms "state prison" and "abuse," for example, produces 484 hits. A one-year search on the same database using the terms "Abu Ghraib" and "abuse" times out at over 1,000 hits.

41. Among a number of other articles, for example, consider the following progression: On May 1, 2004, the *Washington Post* ran an article in which President Bush is quoted saying, "this treatment does not reflect the nature of the American People. That's not the way we do things in America." Dana Milbank, "U.S. Tries to Calm Furor Caused by Photos," *Washington Post* (May 1, 2004): A1. On May 7, 2004, the *New York Times* ran two articles. In the first, Prime Minister Blair is quoted saying, "we went to Iraq to stop that kind of thing, not to do it ourselves." Alan Cowell, "Bush's Words Do Little to Ease Horror at Prison Deeds," *New York Times* (May 7, 2004): A1. In the second, Mrs. England, the mother of one of the more prominent perpetrators of the abuse, is described as "worried that the war, Iraq, and Abu Ghraib have changed her daughter forever." James Dao, "From Picture of Pride to Symbol of Abuse," *New York Times* (May 7, 2004): A3. For a further elaboration of the implications of these notions, see chapter three.

42. Robin Gaster, "Sex, Spies, and Scandal: The Profumo Affair and British Politics," in *The Politics of Scandal*, 63.

43. Press release, Transparency International Corruption Perceptions Index, 2003.

44. There has been a great deal of scholarship on the role of spectacle in the construction of colonial relationships. Among others, see Timothy Mitchell, *Colonising Egypt* (New York: Cambridge University Press, 1991). For one of many late nineteenth-century examples of the phenomenon, see the discussion of the Ottoman delegates to the Chicago Exposition in Cl. Huart, "L'Ancien régime dans l'Empire Ottoman," *Revue du Monde Musulman* 7 (3) (March 1900): 285. For the extent to which the creation of spectacle was a mutual endeavor, and to which the Ottoman population, for example, was very aware of it, see the political cartoons in Turgut Çekiver, *İbret Albümü, 1908* (Istanbul: Kültür İşleri Dairesi Başkanlığı Yayınları, 1991), 29. For the extent to which these cartoons were intended for an international audience, see, for example, Çekiver, 31, 32, 86, 93, and K. J. Basmadjian, "La Révolution en Turquie," *Revue du Monde Musulman* 5 (8) (August 1908): 726–729, in which they reappeared. For more on Ottoman political cartoons of this era, see Palmira Brummet, "Dogs, Women, Cholera and Other Menaces in the Streets: Cartoon Satire in the Ottoman Revolutionary Press," *International Journal of Middle East Studies* 27 (4) (November 1995): 433–460.

45. Press release, Transparency International Corruption Perceptions Index, 2003. This obviously gets at issues of where "Europe" begins and ends as well.

46. See also the TI Executive Summary, *Global Corruption Report 2004*, which argues more explicitly that "the larger the oil sector relative to a country's economy, the greater the potential for political corruption," 3.

47. "Levels of corruption are worryingly high in European countries such as Greece and Italy, and in potentially rich oil-rich countries such as Nigeria, Angola, Azerbaijan, Indonesia, Kazakhstan, Libya, Venezuela and Iraq." Ibid.

48. Ibid.

49. Richard D. White, Jr. "Corruption in the United States," in *Where Corruption Lives*, 42.

50. Victor T. Levine, "Controlling Corruption: A Review Essay," *Corruption and Reform* 5 (1990): 157.

51. Agamben refers to the space delimited by the legal and political state of exception as a zone of indistinction: "the decisive fact is that, together with the process by which the exception everywhere becomes the rule, the realm of bare life—which is originally situated at the margins of the political order—gradually begins to coincide with the political realm, and exclusion and inclusion, outside and inside, *bios* and *zoē*, right and fact, enter into a zone of irreducible indistinction. At once excluding bare life from and capturing it within the political order, the state of exception actually constituted, in its very separateness, the hidden foundation on which the entire political system rested." *Homo Sacer*, 9. In order to engage more broadly with other theorists who have discussed similar themes, I will refer to this space primarily as "exceptional space"—while nonetheless remaining very much aware that its indistinct nature is at the basis of Agamben's analysis.

52. Agamben, *State of Exception*, 59.

53. Agamben, *Homo Sacer*, 135.

54. Mbembe, "Necropolitics," 25.

55. Ibid., 25.

56. Ibid., 23.

57. Veena Das and Arthur Kleinman, "Introduction," in *Violence and Subjectivity*, ed. Das, Kleinman, Ramphele, and Reynolds (Berkeley: University of California Press), 1.

58. See, for example, Agamben, *Homo Sacer*, 61 and Achille Mbembe, *On the Postcolony* (Berkeley: University of California Press, 2001): 189.

59. Georges Bataille, *Erotism: Death and Sensuality*, trans. Mary Dalwood (San Francisco: City Lights Books, 1986), 17–18.

60. Agamben makes a similar point in his discussion of modern and contemporary sadism, *Homo Sacer*, 135.

61. Solomon-Godeau, 296, 304.

62. Linda Williams, "Power, Pleasure, and Perversion: Sadomasochistic Film Pornography," *Representations* 27 (1989), 41.

63. Ibid.

64. Linda Williams, "Film Bodies: Gender, Genre, and Excess," *Film Quarterly* 44 (1991), 4.

65. Ibid.

66. Williams, "Power," 37–65, and Williams, "Film Bodies," 2–13.

Chapter 1. Political Corruption as Sexual Deviance

1. For an excellent discussion of both of these metaphors, see Sarah Hanley, "Social Sites of Political Practice in France: Lawsuits, Civil Rights, and the Separation of Powers in Domestic and State Government, *The American Historical Review* 102 (1) (February 1992): 27–52. See also Alan Hyde, *Bodies of Law* (Princeton: Princeton University Press, 1997): 190–191.

2. Madelyn Gutwirth, "Sacred Father, Profane Sons: Lynn Hunt's French Revolution," *French Historical Studies* 19 (2) (Autumn 1995): 270.

3. Jean Stengers and Anne Van Neck, *Masturbation: The History of a Great Terror*, trans. Kathryn A. Hoffman (New York: Palgrave, 2001), 83–84.

4. Gutwirth, 270.

5. Inderpal Grewal, *Home and Harem: Nation, Gender, Empire, and the Cultures of Travel* (Durham: Duke University Press, 1996), 50.

6. Stengers and Van Neck, 61, 63–64.

7. Ibid., 63.

8. Tissot as quoted in Stengers and Van Neck, 65–66.

9. Ibid., 57.

10. Robert Payne, *The Corrupt Society: From Ancient Greece to Present Day America* (New York: Praeger Publishers, 1975), vii–5. Compare Ghilan, "La Décomposition du corps social en Perse," *Revue du Monde Musulman* 4 (January 1908): 85–96.

11. See above, Solomon-Godeau, 296, 304.

12. Linda Williams, in her discussion of sadomasochistic film pornography comes to a similar conclusion when she notes that "like pornography, the slasher film pries open the fleshy secrets of normally hidden things. . . . in the genre's obsession with maiming and dismemberment we see 'in extraordinary detail' the 'opened body.'" Williams, "Power," 40.

13. As Kantorowicz states at the end of the book, "the theory of the 'King's two Bodies' in all its complexity and sometimes scurrilous consistency was practically absent from the Continent." Ernst H. Kantorowicz, *The King's Two Bodies: A Study in Medieval Political Theology* (Princeton: Princeton University Press, 1957), 447.

14. Agamben questions Kantorowicz's focus on Christianity per se. *Homo Sacer*, 101.

15. Ibid., 91.

16. Kantorowicz, 206.

17. Ibid., 381.

18. Ibid., 212.

19. Ibid., 218.

20. Ibid., 9.

21. Ibid., 394.

22. Ibid., 381.

23. Ibid., 149.

24. Ibid., 143–144.

25. Agamben, *Homo Sacer*, 94.

26. Ibid., 101.

27. Ibid., 92.

28. Carl Schmitt, *Political Theology*, trans. George Schwab (Chicago: University of Chicago Press, 1985), 36.

29. Schmitt expands on this tension between legality and legitimacy in his book by the same name.

30. Foucault, *History of Sexuality*, 148.

31. Ibid., 42, 109–110, 129.

32. Ibid., 110–111.

33. Frederick Whiting, "The Strange Particularity of the Lover's Presence: Pedophilia, Pornography and the Anatomy of Monstrosity in *Lolita*," *American Literature* 70 (4) (December 1998): 834, 856.

34. Stoler, *Race*, 141

35. For a more concrete, contemporary discussion of this narrative of infantile sexuality, see the proceedings of an 1864 debate on child masturbation held at the Surgical Society in Paris. *Bulletin de la Société de Chirurgie de Paris pendant l'année 1864* 2 (5) (1865): 10–15. As quoted in Stengers and Van Neck, 111–112.

36. Thomas E. Will, "Political Corruption: How Best Oppose?" *The Arena* 10 (6) (November 1894): 845.

37. "Responsibility for Political Corruption," *Century Illustrated Magazine* 44 (3) (July 1892): 473.

38. As Stoler and a number of others have argued, colonies served more often than not as the "laboratories of modernity," in which "those most treasured icons of modern western culture—liberalism, nationalism, state welfare, citizenship, culture, and 'Europeanness' itself" were clarified. Stoler, *Carnal Knowledge*, 146–147.

39. For a narrative history of the Boxer Rebellion see, among others, Jonathan Spence, *The Search for Modern China* (New York: W.W. Norton, 1990), 230–235.

40. John Foord, Secretary of the American Asiatic Association, "The Root of the Chinese Trouble," *The North American Review* 171 (76) (September 1900): 401.

41. Ibid.

42. See, for example, Theobald, 492.

43. E. Barnes, "Natural and National Unions: Incest and Sympathy in the Early Republic," *Incest and the Literary Imagination*, ed. E. Barnes (Gainesville: University Press of Florida, 2002): 138.

44. See, for instance, the state–family analogy elaborated in Pierre Leroy-Beaulieu, "Le problême Chine," *Revue des Deux Mondes* 54 (January 1899): 44.

45. Githongo.

46. P. Riley, "The Political Economy of Anti-Corruption Strategies in Africa," in *Controlling Corruption*,105.

47. See also the elaboration on the notion that "women are both more vulnerable to the impact of corruption and less able to challenge the corrupt" in "U4 Anti Corruption Website, Frequently Asked Questions," http://www.u4.no/document/faqs1.cfm.

48. Mary Robinson, "Ethical Governance and Globalization—10 Years of Fighting Corruption," http://www.transparency.org/speeches/robinson (Freie Universitat, Berlin 19 June 2003).

49. Ibid.

50. Robinson, "Ethical Governance."

51. Ibid.

52. Ibid.

53. Ibid.

54. Peter Eigen, "Security and Opportunity through Law and Justice, July 2001," http://www.transparency.org/speeches/pe_stpetersburg.html.

55. Githongo.

56. Peter Eigen, "The Central role of Civil Society in Combating Corruption in the Era of Globalization," ress.html. (Transparency for Growth Conference, May 1999).

57. Miguel Schloss, "Combating Corruption for Development," http://www.transparency.org/speeches/ms_brazeil_ethos.html (Conferencia de Responsibilidad Social Empresarial en las Americas, June 1999).

58. Peter Langseth, "The Role of a National Integrity System in Fighting Corruption," in *Controlling Corruption*, 53, 60.

59. Herbert Welsh, "Campaign Committees: Publicity as a Cure for Corruption," *Forum* (September 1892): 26.

60. Githongo.

61. Robinson.

62. Eigen.

63. Githongo.

64. See also "the private sector, too, shares responsibility by using bribery in its interactions with officials; the public at large is part of the problem, willing to pay bribes or acquiescing in conduct it should not accept. The ethics of the public service reflect in large measure those of society as a whole. So that this is not a struggle of "us" against "them": rather it is a struggle of all of us together to build stronger ethics among society at large." Peter Eigen, "Closing the Corruption Casino," http://www.transparency.org/speeches/pe_gf2_address.html (Global Forum II, May 2001).

65. Michael H. Wiehen, "Transparency in Government Procurement and the Fight against Cross Border Corruption," http:// (EC Meeting on Transparency in Government Procurement, 16 May 2003).

66. Jeremy Tambling, *Confession: Sexuality, Sin, the Subject* (Manchester: Manchester University Press, 1990), 101.

67. Ibid., 101.

68. Jon Stratton, *The Desirable Body: Cultural Fetishism and the Erotics of Consumption* (Urbana: University of Illinois Press, 2001), 100.

69. Ibid., 101.

70. Ibid. Similarly, "as Jill Dolan puts it . . . male spectators 'pay to see the image of strippers as commodities; they buy control over the gaze.' In other words, men go to strip shows for the erotic pleasure of controlling women by paying to participate in 'rituals of tipping and looking that embody our culture's patriarchal commodification and objectification of females.'" Katherine Liepe-Levinson, "Striptease: Desire, Mimetic Jeopardy, and Performing Spectators," *TDR* 4 (2) (Summer 1998): 11.

71. Liepe-Levinson, 19.

72. Roberta Sassatelli, "Justice, Television and Delegitimation: On the Cultural Codification of the Italian Political Crisis," *Modern Italy* 3 (1) (1998): 108.

73. Ibid., 110.

74. Ibid.

75. Ibid.

76. Ibid., 114.

77. Payne, 6.

78. Wiehen.

79. Abdul Aziz.

80. See, among others, "for them, the first glimmer of recovery is a signal to return to the good old days of unbridled excesses," Tunku Abdul Aziz, "Has Reform Revived the Miracle? Reforming East Asian Governance: A Business Necessity,10–20 March, 2001," http://www.transparency.org/seeches/taa_chatham.html.

81. Richard D. White, Jr. in *Where Corruption Lives*, 43.

82. Patricia Hill Collins, "A Comparison of Two Works on Black Family Life," *Signs* 14 (4) (Summer 1989): 875.

83. Ibid., 876–877.

84. As Stratton notes, when incest was outlawed in England in 1908, the immediate focus of the legislation was on working class populations. Stratton, 42–43. See also Janice Doane and Devon Hodges, *Telling Incest: Narratives of Dangerous Remembering from Stein to Sapphire* (Ann Arbor: University of Michigan Press, 2001), 31.

85. By the 1990s, for instance, the American incest story was one that was almost always set within a black or a poor, white, and usually

southern (i.e., miscegenated) family. Doane and Hodges, 2. When it was not, it was attacked as inauthentic. Mako Yoshikawa, "The New Face of Incest? Race, Class, and the Controversy over Kathryn Harrison's *The Kiss*," in *Incest and the Literary Imagination*, 360.

86. Doane and Hodges, 31.

87. Abdul-Karim Mustapha, "Absolute Dictator/Absolute Spectator," *TDR* 40 (2) (Summer 1996): 7. It was, he continues, likewise the product of a number of complex relationships among various Nigerian leaders and military regimes, British and U.S. companies, and, especially in the Abacha narrative, the Dutch-owned Shell Oil (ibid., 8). Although Abacha's "corrupt rule" is more often than not epitomized in a single story—Ken Saro-Wiwa's public execution, ostensibly for murder, but more likely for "protesting against Shell Oil Company for dumping waste on [Ogoni] land" (ibid., 7–9)—therefore, Abacha himself was in fact the inheritor of an international and institutional situation that had been developed long before he came to power.

88. Eigen.

89. For variations on this theme, see also Afsaneh Najmabadi, "The Erotic Vatan as Beloved Mother: To Love, to Possess, and To Protect," *Comparative Studies in Society and History* 39 (3) (1997): 442–467; Palmira Brummet, "Dogs, Women, Cholera, and Other Menaces in the Streets: Cartoon Satire in the Ottoman Revolutionary Press, 1908–11," *International Journal of Middle East Studies* 27 (4) (November 1995): 433–460. And many others.

90. I. M. Lewis, "Misunderstanding the Somali Crisis," *Anthropology Today* 9 (4) (August 1993): 1.

91. Ibid.

92. SPR, "Somalia: Warlords Have Vested Interest in Perpetuation of Civil War," U4 Anti-Corruption News http://www.u4.no/news/news.cfm?id=107.

93. For an example of the use of premodern or medieval political designations in describing corrupt leaders, see, "the bosses are no more shamefaced in talking about their grafting exploits than a medieval baron would have been in discussing the produce of his feudal fees and imposts." Heidenheimer, 22.

94. Abdul Aziz, "Has Reform Revived the Miracle?"

95. Rance P. L. Lee, "The Folklore of Corruption in Hong Kong," *Asian Survey* 21 (3) (1981): 357–358. See also "The world's most populous country has slipped into place as the world's second largest economy behind the United States . . . but the cost in corruption has been so high as

to raise serious questions whether the Chinese Communist Party has become kleptomaniac, whether the country's leadership is really serious about tackling corruption and a virulent underground economy, whether age-old corruption practices can be reversed without fundamental changes in Chinese culture." Stephen K. Ma, "The Culture of Corruption in Post-Mao China," in *Where Corruption Lives*, 145. And Leroy-Beaulieu, 52.

96. "The Dry-Rot of States," *Liberty* 10 (20) (1895): 6.

97. Homer Beza Hulbert, "Korea and the Koreans," *Forum* (April, 1889): 222.

98. As both Said and Stoler have noted, "vigor" was a key defining racial characteristic of the European in the colonial context. And "when possible," Stoler continues, "authorities restricted the presence of non productive men and those who might sully the image of a healthy and 'vigorous' race. In Deli, the infirm, the aged, and the insane were quickly sent home." Stoler, *Race*, 35, paraphrasing Said.

99. Caiden, 3, 11.

100. Transparency International, "Global Corruption Report 2004," 2.

101. See also Mbembe's critique of scholarship on "Africa," where he notes that "the continent [Africa], a great, soft fantastic body, is seen as powerless, engaged in rampant self-destruction." *Postcolony*, 8.

102. "Corruption is contagious; it breeds on itself once established it is inhumanly difficult to remove. But unless a nation collectively wants to die, it must, once corruption has settled in it, grapple with the problem or perish." Payne, viii. See also Caiden, 23, 231.

103. For example, "Corruption is a pervasive disease," in Peter Eigen, "The Central Role of Civil Society."

104. United Nations Office on Drugs and Crime, "Why a Global Programme Against Corruption?" www.unodc.org/unodc/en/corruption.html.

105. And causes "leakages" of various kinds. "Transparency International Executive Summary, Global Corruption Report, 2004," 4.

106. Peter Eigen, "WTO Needs to Play a More Active Role in the Fight against Corruption," http://.org/speeches/pe_wto_geneva.html.

107. "[Corruption] hinders the growth of competitiveness, frustrates efforts to alleviate poverty, and makes real economic progress impossible. A self-perpetuating cycle can develop, with a broad expectation of corruption causing an increase in its incidence . . . a "brain drain" often follows." Peter Eigen, "Combating Corruption Around the World," *Journal of Democracy* 7 (1) (1996): 25. As reproduced in *Controlling Corruption*. See also "emerging democracies in particular brave considerable

political risks if corruption is not contained, as the corrupt can greatly weaken the authority and capacity of the fledgling state." Peter Langseth, Rick Stapenhurst, and Jeremy Pope, "The Role of National Integrity System in Fighting Corruption," in *Controlling Corruption*, 53. And, the fact that corruption can contribute to "a further weakening of vital institutions of governance." Githongo, "Corruption as a Problem in the Developing World."

108. Tunku Abdul Aziz, "ABD-OECD Anti-Corruption Initiative."

109. Alan Doig, "Dealing with Corruption: The Next Steps," *Crime, Law and Social Change* 29 (1998): 97.

110. Caiden, 31.

111. Limpangog.

112. Caiden, 30.

113. Githongo. For an early twentieth-century take on this, see Çekiver, 61. In a cartoon entitled "Arap İzzet'in dalaverası," ("Arab Izzet's intrigues"), the head of İzzet Paşa is surrounded by eight tentacles, labeled in French, "École Polytechnique, École de Génie, Étudiant en Theologie, 300,000 lira, Gens de Lettres, Arménien, École de Médecine" ("Polytechnic School, Engineering School, Theology Student, 300,000 lira, Men of Letters, Armenian, Medical School").

114. Foord, 401.

115. Robert C. Brooks, "The Nature of Political Corruption," in *Political Corruption: Readings in Comparative Analysis*, 59.

116. Caiden, "Corruption and Democracy" in *Where Corruption Lives*, 225.

117. Ma, 153, and Foord, 401.

118. See, for example, Caleb Crain, "Lovers of Human Flesh: Homosexuality and Cannibalism in Melville's Novels," *American Literature* 66 (1) (March 1999): 25–53. "In the moral imagination of the nineteenth century, cannibalism was not only very close to homosexuality, it was also close to incest." Crain, 36.

119. As Stratton likewise notes, "in this world dominated by consumption, the desire of appetite and sexual desire meet in cannibalism. . . . [I]n this context, from the late nineteenth century on, the theme of cannibalism has taken on a new cultural salience. Freud's use of it as a metaphor in his discourse of the oral stage can be understood as a late nineteenth and twentieth century male sexual fantasy of adult life." Stratton, 166.

120. For more on inappropriate feeding and political corruption, see Çekiver, 42, 60. The first cartoon, entitled "Kanun-ı Esasi'nin ilanın-

dan evvel fıçılarını doldurup milleti aç bırakan mürtekibler" ("Corrupt officials filling their barrels and starving the nation before the announcement of the Constitution,") shows six bureaucrats sitting in barrels drinking with straws from a trough entitled "Servet-i Osmaniye" ("Ottoman Wealth"). The second is a poem in French entitled "Les Vampires," which discusses the activities of İzzet Paşa especially.

121. Thomas E. Will, "Political Corruption: How Best Oppose?" *The Arena* (10) (6) (1894): 845.

122. Tunku Abdul Aziz, "Has Reform Revived the Miracle?"

123. For more straightforward examples of this conflation of individual and collective in discussions of the diseased and monstrous nature of corruption, see Payne, vii: "to determine whether there exist any medicines to cure the disease [of corruption] in societies and individuals. By corruption I mean the working of those moral and social forces that bring about the decay and ultimately the death of societies and those other forces that arise within individuals and work toward the same end." And Caiden, 19: "The word corruption means something spoiled: something that has been made defective, debased, and tainted; something that has been pushed off course into a worse or inferior form. Whoever corrupts sets out to make something impure and less capable, an adverse departure from an expected course. When applied to human relations, corruption is a bad influence or injection of rottenness or decay."

Chapter 2. Celebrating the Corrupt Leader

1. http://diyboardgames.com/197. See also http://cuepacs.org/analpicturefree.com, which sells the video as well.

2. Stephen Ellis, "Liberia 1989–1994: A Study of Ethnic and Spiritual Violence," *African Affairs* 94 (1995): 169.

3. See Ellis, for example: "even professional soldiers from other countries taking part in peace-keeping duties, who may be assumed to be hardened to acts of violence, recoil before the savagery of the Liberian conflict in which cannibalism, random violence and tortures of every sort imaginable have become commonplace." Ellis, 165.

4. Mark Huband, "Liberian Rebels Replay the Last Hours of President Doe: Mark Huband in Monrovia sees a Gruesome Video of the Former Leader's Torture and Death," *The Guardian* (October 3, 1990).

5. Agamben, *State of Exception*, 59.

6. Agamben, *Homo Sacer*, 135.

7. Catherine Mills, "Linguistic Survival and Ethicality: Biopolitics, Subjectivity, and Testimony in *Remnants of Auschwitz*," in ed. Andrew Norris, *Politics, Metaphysics, and Death: Essays on Giorgio Agamben's Homo Sacer* (Durham: Duke University Press, 2005), 198–202.

8. Williams, "Power," 41.

9. Ibid.

10. Williams, "Film Bodies," 4.

11. Agamben, *Homo Sacer*, 94.

12. Kantorowicz, 431.

13. For more on the inability of the Oriental to represent himself, see Edward Said, *Orientalism* (New York: Vintage, 1978).

14. George Dorys, *The Private Life of the Sultan of Turkey* (New York: D. Appleton and Co., 1901), 86, 142.

15. "Inside Saddam's Court," *New York Times* (October 1, 2000): SM41.

16. "Abdul Described as Abject," *New York Times* (April 28, 1909): 2. "Abdul Reported Dead," *New York Times* (April 28, 1909): 2. "Abdul Not to be Tried," *New York Times* (April 29, 1909): 1. "Abdul Shed Tears as He Lost Throne," *New York Times* (May 2, 1909): C2.

17. William Safire, "Saddam Redux?" *New York Times* (May 2, 1994): A17. Thomas Friedman, "Saddam Does Vegas," *New York Times* (December 19, 1999): WK13. Nicholas Kristof, "If Saddam Were Only Brazilian," *New York Times* (December 17, 2002): A35.

18. "Abdul Hamid Drinking Heavily," *New York Times* (November 30, 1895): 5. "The Sultan Angry," *London Daily Telegraph* (September 19, 1887): 4. "Appeals of Abdul Hamid: He Implores Lord Salisbury to Have Confidence in Him: Promises to Execute Reforms: Gives His Word of Honor," *New York Times* (November 20, 1895): 1. "Abdul Hamid Wants Revenge," *New York Times* (August 30, 1901): 7. "Abdul Hamid Retaliating," *New York Times* (August 31, 1901): 6. "The Infatuation of Abdul Hamid: He Is Said to be Dominated by the Idea of Pan-Islamism," *London Times* (September 5, 1901): 1. "Sultan Abdul Hamid on his Good Behavior," *London Times* (September 18, 1901). "The Sultan Apprehensive," *London Times* (December 17, 1901): 1. "Sultan, in a Panic, Gives Constitution," *New York Times* (July 25, 1908): 1.

19. Leslie Gelb, "Cuddling Saddam," *New York Times* (July 9, 1992): A21. Patrick Tyler, "Who's Acting Tough Now? Why, Saddam Hussein," *New York Times* (October 24, 1991): A4. John Mearsheimer,

"Keeping Saddam Hussein in a Box," *New York Times* (February 2, 2003): 15. Paul Lewis, "Graphic Message from Saddam Hussein: Defiance and Appeals," *New York Times* (July 10, 1993): 2. "Saddam Blasts Bush," *The Frontrunner* (July 1, 2004). William Safire, "Slapping Saddam's Wrist," *New York Times* (June 28, 1993): A17.

20. Williams, "Power," 41.

21. "Abdul Hamid II, Sultan of Turkey," *Current Literature* 19 (January 1, 1896): 1.

22. "People Talked About," *Peterson Magazine* 6 (January 1886): 46.

23. "People Talked About," 47. See also Çekiver, p 48, for a cartoon version of Abdülhamid's Grand Vezir, Küçük Sait Paşa entitled "Meşhür Şapur Çelebi/L'illustre Chapour tchelebi" ("The Famous Şapur Çelebi"—Şapur Çelebi was an Iranian Vezir to whom Sait Paşa had been compared). In this cartoon, Sait Paşa is completely covered in medals and ornamental weapons down to his ankles.

24. Tyler, "Who's Acting Tough Now?"

25. Norma Greenaway, "Murderous Rise to Absolute Rule: Saddam's Path to Power Was Paved by the Blood of Anybody He Saw as a Threat," *Times/Monitor* (March 23, 2003): D6.

26. Dorys, 70.

27. See, for instance, "All his clothes are padded about the neck and shoulder in order to straighten his back and conceal the slight hump with which Allah has afflicted him. . . . [H]is Majesty has very small feet. . . . [the imperial shoes] all have high heels, lined with cork." Ibid., 185–186.

28. "Inside Saddam's Court."

29. Greenaway, D6

30. Dorys, 188–189.

31. "ce prince déshérité, dont la sympathique physionomie, qui contraste absolument avec celle de l'usurpateur." Hidayette, *Abdul Hamid révolutionnaire, ou ce qu'on ne peut pas dire en Turquie* (Zurich: 1896), 28.

32. Dorys, 70–71.

33. Bernard Shaw in Wolf Blitzer, "What Will Happen to Saddam? Interview with Bernard Shaw," *CNN Wolf Blitzer Reports* 17:00. Transcript #121500CN.V67 (December 15, 2003). Byline: Wolf Blitzer, Alphonso Van Marsh, Jane Arraf, Dana Bash, Nic Robertson, Jim Bittermann, Robin Oakley, John Vause, David Ensor.

34. Dorys, 183. See also Hidayette, 202.

35. "Inside Saddam's Court."

36. Ammad Shalabi (sic), Opposition Leader in Charles Gibson, "Unauthorized Saddam," *Primetime Live*. ABC (December 12, 2002). See also, "It's well known he is obsessed with appearance and hygiene and demands the same of high-ranking officials. Because age can be a sign of weakness, he works hard to remain as youthful in appearance as possible. Saddam swims daily, dyes his hair and mustache black, and regularly diets. He has a penchant for fine Cuban cigars, which his friend Fidel Castro regularly sends him." Oprah Winfrey, "What You Should Know About Iraq," *Oprah Winfrey Show* (March 6, 2003), Harpo, Inc. And, interestingly, the following, in which the Orientalist fantasy of the highly sexed Arab, the celebration of the corrupt leader, and the appeal of dictatorial "obsessions with hygiene" all come together in a fascinating amalgam of cleaning ladies as virgins as rape victims as, eventually, towels: "My education in presidential protocol began right away, with the arrival of my 'cleaning ladies'. . . . [I]t was well known, for example, that Saddam was extremely aggressive, culling women from the crowd, coercing them into sex and then discarding them. He used them like towels. . . . [S]addam's favorites by far, I was told, were virgins, probably because of his fear of disease." "Inside Saddam's Court."

37. Arthur Hornblow, in Dorys, vii.

38. Jon Lee Anderson, "Saddam's Ear: An Iraqi Doctor Had a Unique Role in Saddam Hussein's Life," *The New Yorker* (May 5, 2003): 58.

39. Ibid.

40. Dorys, 174–175.

41. "Abdul as Author," *New York Times* (October 18, 1902): BR 8.

42. Ibid.

43. *Oprah Winfrey Show*, March 6, 2003.

44. David Blair, "He Dreamed of Glory but Dealt out Only Despair," *The Daily Telegraph* (March 18, 2003): 2.

45. Peter Beaumont, "Iraq Crisis," *The Observer* (February 23, 2003): 17.

46. See also, "The bungled assassination was later transformed into a heroic saga which became the centrepiece of *The Long Days*, a film of Saddam's life made after he seized power. This epic was edited by Terence Young, who earlier in his career had directed *Dr. No*, *Thunderball*, and *From Russia With Love*. After receiving Young's treatment, the film was cut to a mere six hours and became obligatory viewing in 1980s Iraq." Blair, 2.

47. Patrick Coburn, "Saddam Captured," *The Mirror* (December 15, 2003). See also, "Saddam retreated further and further into a fantasy

world. He wrote two romantic novels, *Zabibah and The King* and *The Fortified Castle*, both inevitable best-sellers. But his isolated refuge was progressively less comfortable, for the unity of his family steadily crumbled." Blair, 2.

48. Compare this also to Dorys, 179–180: "He went through a severe attack only a few months ago, after the sensational flight of his brother in law Damad-Mahmoud Pasha and his two sons, which once more attracted the attention of all Europe to his regime. Mahmoud Pasha's attacks on his Imperial brother-in-law in the European papers, the letters full of cruel truths he wrote to him, sent poor Abdul-Hamid into fits of impotent rage that no sedative could calm."

49. "The Novel would open right after the gulf war with Saddam setting up a series of trading companies. . . . [W]ouldn't that make a great novel—Saddam, the Iranians and a rogue commodities dealer, three of the world's great pariahs and outsiders actually engaged in the ultimate insider-trading deal. . . . [all it needs is a love interest]" Thomas Friedman, "Saddam's Page Turner," *New York Times* (August 18, 1996): E15. "You recall last summer I sent you a proposal for a novel about . . . Saddam Hussein. . . . [W]ell, he's baaaaaaack. Saddam is at it again, and I have a great idea for a sequel novel." Thomas Friedman, "Pulp Fiction," *New York Times* (September 4, 1997): A25.

50. Dorys, 8–9.

51. Ibid., 9.

52. Christopher Hudson, "Saddam the Boy Monster," *Daily Mail* (March 8, 2003): 36. See also, Daniel Goleman, "Experts Differ on Dissecting Leaders' Psyches from Afar," *New York Times* (January 29, 1992): C1.

53. "The Sultan's Letter," *New York Times* (November 21, 1895): 4.

54. "This German support was of great use to the Sultan. It flattered his vanity, and enabled him to feel at ease in his relations with other Powers." R. Hamilton Long, "The Present Government in Turkey—Its Crimes and Remedy," *The Eclectic Magazine of Foreign Literature* 66 (September 1897): 399.

55. "The Sultan's overweening infatuation dates from the Pan-Islamic agitation following the Armenian massacres five years ago. . . . [T]he Sultan is said to be dominated by an absorbing idea of Pan-Islamism." "The Infatuation of Abdul Hamid: He Is Said to be Dominated by the Idea of Pan-Islamism," *London Times* (September 5, 1901): 1. See also, "those best initiated into the mysteries of the Yildiz Kiosk, says the Vienna correspondent of The Times, have for some time represented the

Sultan as being in a state of overweening infatuation, which bodes ill for the tranquility of the Near East. The patronage which Abdul Hamid has received from Germany is said to have contributed more than anything else to turn his head." "Admiral Caillard has Seized Turkish Ports: Sultan May be Obstinate," *London Times* (November 6, 1901): 9.

56. "The Seraphic Soul of Abdul Hamid," *Current Literature* 42 (January, 1907): 36–37.

57. Dorys, 116.

58. Tasma, "Iftar in a Harem," *Arthur's Home Magazine* (September 1891): 728.

59. Beaumont, 17.

60. Youssef M. Ibrahim, "The World: Saddam Hussein, Tactician," *New York Times* (November 1, 1998): section 4, p. 3.

61. Blair, 2.

62. "Abd-ul-Hamid," *New York Times* (October 25, 1885): 11.

63. "Abdul Hamid II, Sultan of Turkey," 1.

64. For more on this, see "Persia's and Turkey's Regicides: Comparison of the Situation by the Young Turkish Party's Organ," *New York Times* (June 7, 1896): 24.

65. Blair, 2.

66. Peter Goodspeed, "From Brutal Despot to Cowering Prisoner," *The National Post* (December 15, 2003): A12.

67. Agamben, *Homo Sacer*, 105.

68. Tasma, 728.

69. Emma Paddock Telford, "Three Sultans," *Godey's Magazine* 134 (800) (February 1897): 122.

70. Dorys, 1–2.

71. We also learn that "Abdul-Hamid came into the world therefore, with the germs of the malady that carried off his father [phthisis] and mother ['pulmonary trouble that left her ravaged and frightfully decomposed'] but so far he has succeeded in resisting them," Dorys, 4.

72. Francis McCullagh, "What Was Found in the Lair of Abdul Hamid: Amazing Discoveries in the Yildiz Kiosk Following the Fall of Turkey's Sultan Reveal a Condition Surpassing Fiction," *New York Times* (June 6, 1909).

73. Dorys, 111.

74. Hudson. For a more medicalized version of this story, see again "a Sunni Muslim, Saddam was born in 1937 in the Tikrit-area village of

al-Ouja to a depressed mother who had unsuccessfully sought to kill herself and her unborn baby. Depending on which account one believes, his father Hussein al-Majid either died before he was born or abandoned his family soon afterwards." Greenaway, D6.

75. See the final section for further discussion of the "bandit" in the corruption narrative.

76. Montgomery. See also Hudson.

77. See, for example, Elaine Sciolino, "Arab of Vast Ambition," *New York Times* (August 5, 1990): 14, and Oprah Winfrey, among others.

78. David Rose, "Baghdad's Cruel Princes," *Vanity Fair* (May 2003): 176.

79. Charles Gibson, "Sons of Saddam: Hunted Down in Iraq," *Primetime Live*, July 22, 2003. ABC News.

80. Jonathan Broder, "Saddam's Bomb," *New York Times* (October 1, 2000): SM38.

81. "Inside Saddam's Court."

82. Mbembe discusses a similar phenomenon in his discussion of political cartoons in African states. "In seizing the power of public imagination," he argues, "the artist amplifies the autocrat's pervasive presence. The autocrat continues, rather, to envelop his subjects, to be so close that he crushes them with his shadow, causing even the activity of creation itself to be deployed beneath his shade. . . . [H]e has his empty spaces, or, to put it differently, his *doubles*. First he is a body. Here he is almost undressed. Wearing only a *cache-sexe*, he is ready for anything, ready to sing and dance . . . [N]ext, the autocrat is a hole, a sort of bottomless, endless, excess with a voraciousness that is quite insatiable." *Postcolony*, 160.

83. As Agamben has suggested, "if it is true that law needs a body in order to be in force, and if one can speak, in this sense, of 'law's desire to have a body,' democracy responds to this desire by compelling law to assume the care of this body. This ambiguous (or polar) character of democracy appears even more clearly in the *habeas corpus* if one considers the fact that the same legal procedure that was originally intended to assure the presence of the accused at the trial and, therefore, to keep the accused from avoiding judgment, turns—in its new and definitive form—into a grounds for the sheriff to detain and exhibit the body of the accused. *Corpus* is a two faced being, the bearer of both subject to sovereign power and of individual liberties." Agamben, *Homo Sacer*, 123–124.

84. R. Hamilton Lang, "The Present Government in Turkey—Its Crimes and Remedy," *Eclectic Magazine of Foreign Literature* (66) (3) (September 1897): 396, 399.

85. See above for a discussion of the contemporary relevance of "The King's Two Bodies."

86. See, for example, Çekiver, 39. The cartoon, entitled "Bir takım hainlerin dünyayı yiyelim diye hücumu," ("Attack on a set of traitors trying to eat the world") in which Abdülhamid's rule is represented as the "set of traitors"—a six-headed dragon bearing the faces of his bureaucrats, Salahi, Fehim Paşa, Kabasakal Çerkes Mehmet Paşa, Süruri, Kayserili Hamdi, and İzzet Paşa.

87. Dorys, 168.

88. See, for example, Kantorowicz's discussion of Richard II, where he argues, "the jurists had claimed that the King's body politic is utterly void of 'natural Defects and Imbecility.' Here, however, 'Imbecility' seems to hold sway. And yet, the very bottom has not been reached. Each scene, progressively, designates a new low. 'King body natural' in the first scene and 'kingly fool' in the second: with these two twin-born beings there is associated, in the half sacramental abdication scene, the twin-born deity as an even lower estate. For the 'Fool' marks the transition from 'King' to 'God,' and nothing could be more miserable, it seems, than a God in the wretchedness of man." Kantorowicz, 34.

89. See, for example, "I suggest that you try to imagine yourself changing from the state you are in to one in which your whole self is completely doubled; you cannot survive this process since the doubles you have turned into are essentially different from you. Each of these doubles is necessarily distinct from you as you are now. To be truly identical with you, one of the doubles would have to be actually continuous with the other, and not distinct from it as it would have become. Imagination boggles at this grotesque idea." Bataille, 14.

90. "Although he rarely appeared in public, by the mid-1990s he had some eight 'doubles' who could impersonate him at public functions; sometimes they appeared at different events simultaneously, causing difficulties for the state-owned media's daily reports on Saddam's itinerary." Coughlin. See also, "as if that's not enough protection, Saddam also employs doubles. . . . [Y]ou start wondering is that Saddam joking about a double or a double joking about Saddam?" Charles Gibson, "Unauthorized Saddam Videos of Hussein" (sic), *Primetime Live* ABC News, December 12, 2002.

91. Gibson, "Sons of Saddam."

92. See, for example, Gilles Deleuze with regard to the simulacrum, "the simulacrum, in rising to the surface, causes the Same and the Like, the model and the copy, to fall under the power of the false (phantasm). It renders the notion of hierarchy impossible in relation to the idea of

order of participation, the fixity of distribution, and the determination of value. It sets up a world of nomadic distributions and consecrated anarchy. Far from being a new foundation, it swallows up all foundations, it assumes a universal collapse, but as a positive and joyous event, as a de-founding." "Plato and the Simulacrum," *October* 27 (1983): 53.

93. Anderson, 58.

94. As Katherine Verdery has argued, "dead bodies have posthumous political life in the service of creating a newly meaningful universe." *The Political Lives of Dead Bodies: Reburial and Postsocialist Change* (New York: Columbia University Press, 1999), 127.

95. See also Thomas W. Laqueur, "this aesthetic enterprise, various forms of which I will consider under the rubric 'the humanitarian narrative,' is characterized in the first place by its reliance on detail as the sign of truth. . . . [U]nprecedented quantities of fact, of minute observations about people who before had been beneath notice became the building blocks of the 'reality effect.'" In Lynn Hunt, ed., *The New Cultural History* (Berkeley: University of California Press, 1989), 177. Although Laqueur is talking about the humanitarian narrative here, the emphasis on detailed descriptions of bodies producing "truth" applies equally well to the modern legal narrative of habeas corpus.

96. "Sultan Murad's Letter: He Writes from Prison to His Brother the Reigning Sultan: On the Recent America (sic) Troubles: Mighty Good Advice from a Man Who Is Alleged to be Insane: He Is Very Progressive in his Views," *New York Times* (September 22, 1895): 9. See also "Four Monarchs in Prison: They are Confined in Magnificent Palaces: Mystery that Prevails in Regard to Them: Otto, Carlotto, Ismail, and Murad," *New York Times* (February 23, 1890): 19. And, "Abdul's Imprisoned Brother," *New York Times* (April 9, 1901): 1.

97. "The Constantinople correspondent of *The Times* says Sultan Abdul Hamid is as usual, painfully apprehensive about his annual visit to Stamboul and mid-Ramadan in order to kiss the prophet's mantle. It is the only day in the year when he will venture out of the Yildiz Kiosk. Many 'preventive arrests' are consequently being made every day." "The Sultan Apprehensive," *London Times* (December 17, 1901): 1.

98. Under this little kiosk, Abdul-Hamid has hollowed out a cave, to which he alone has access, and in which is a safe inclosing his jewels, bonds, and most secret documents. Dorys, 116.

99. Ibid., 201.

100. W. J. Corbet, "Illustrious Lunatics," *The Arena* 21 (5) (May, 1899): 571–580, 579.

101. Ibid., 571.

102. Ibid., 578–580.

103. Coughlin.

104. As Matthew Buckley writes in reference to the nineteenth-century Jack Sheppard crime story, its denouement on stage in which Sheppard is "caught" by a newsboy, and its reception by the mass audience: "From the psychomania of the Newgate scenes, a world generated and governed by his solitary gaze, Sheppard emerges into a world in which his social identity is inescapable, imposed by the gaze of all who recognize in him the figure of his criminal celebrity. The mechanism of that recognition, associated throughout the play with the popular audience, with class resistance and radical political opposition is here unveiled as a machine of surveillance, a nightmarish extension of the gaze of the law" (Buckley, 459). For criminals and the illegitimate, the gaze of the mass audience plays the same role as the law, and thus corrupt leaders, unlike legitimate ones, are afraid to leave their compounds. They refuse to see visitors. They engage in a constant and futile game of distracting the gaze/law from its intended focus and, in the end, with their full confession and exposure, they are placed into a lawless space not of their own, but of the law's own making.

105. Goleman, C1.

106. Greenaway, D6.

107. Wolf Blitzer, "Press Conference Announcing Hussein's Capture," *CNN Breaking News* 07:00. Transcript #121401CN.V00 (December 14, 2003). Byline: Sean Callebs, Dana Bash, Heidi Collins, Barbara Starr, Wolf Blitzer, Nic Robertson, Kenneth Pollack, Aaron Brown, Satinder Bindra.

108. "Abdul Shed Tears as he Lost Throne: First That Ever Wet His Cruel Eyes Says Member of Party That Notified Ruler of Deposition: Abjectly Pleaded for Life: Weeping of Sultan's Young Son Lent Pathos to Scene," *New York Times* (May 2, 1909): C2.

109. Wolf Blitzer, "Saddam Calls First Court Hearing 'Theater by Bush,'" *CNN Live From . . .* 13:00. Transcript #070101CN.V85 (July 1, 2004 Thursday). Byline: Wolf Blitzer, Kyra Phillips, Fredricka Whitfield, Brent Sadler, Dr. Sanjay Gupta.

110. "Abdul Shed Tears as he Lost Throne," C2.

111. Wolf Blitzer, "Special Edition: The Capture of Saddam Hussein," *CNN Late Edition With Wolf Blitzer* 12:00. Transcript #121400CN.V47 (December 14, 2003). Byline: Wolf Blitzer, Nic Robertson, Dana Bash, David Ensor, Christiane Amanpour, Jane Arraf, Barbara Starr, Bob Franken, Ken Pollack.

112. Paula Zahn, "Saddam Hussein Faces Iraqi Justice; Saddam Hussein's Body Language Reveals Secrets; Arab Reaction to Saddam Arraignment Mixed," *Paula Zahn Now* 20:00. Transcript #070100CN.V99 (July 1, 2004). Byline: Paula Zahn, Christiane Amanpour, Brian Todd, Octavia Nasr, Paul Von Fyl.

113. Ibid.

114. Ibid.

115. This becomes particular clear in the choice of celebrity to represent the "fictional" aspect of Saddam Hussein. As Cary Wolf and Jonathan Elmer note with reference to *Silence of the Lambs*, "as a film about law and its (re)enforcement, then, the *Silence of the Lambs* must arrange its meanings so that there can be a 'non-criminal putting to death' of Bill. . . . [I]t is in order to mark such killing as either 'criminal' or 'non-criminal' that the discourse of criminality becomes so crucial." "Subject to Sacrifice: Ideology, Psychoanalysis, and the Discourse of Species in Jonathan Demme's *Silence of the Lambs*," *boundary 2* 22 (3) (Autumn 1995): 146.

116. Dorys, viii.

117. Francis McCullagh, "When Turkey's Sultan Faced His Masters," *New York Times* (January 10, 1909): SM3. "Sultan Faces his People: Drives to Selamlik in Open Victoria While Throngs Line Streets," *New York Times* (April 24, 1909): 2.

118. "Now What for Saddam?" *The Guardian* (December 16, 2003): 2.

119. McCullagh, "When Turkey's Sultan Faced his Masters," SM3.

120. "Sultan's Spy Spent a Week of Terror Here: Zia Bey Told of Murders in Yildiz Kiosk Before Sailing for London: Massacres for Plunder: Confessed His Shame in Turkish Horrors under Old Regime and While Here Trembled at Own Shadow," *New York Times* (September 4, 1908): 8.

121. For example, "Blitzer: Those images of Saddam Hussein, as dramatic as the images of Uday and Qusay his two sons were, this is so much more important." Blitzer, "The Capture of Saddam Hussein."

122. Gibson, "Sons of Saddam: Hunted Down in Iraq."

123. Blitzer, "Press Conference Announcing Hussein's Capture."

124. "Abdul Described as Abject," 2.

125. "Abdul Shed Tears as He Lost Throne," C2.

126. Francis McCullagh, "What Was Found in the Lair of Abdul Hamid: Amazing Discoveries in the Yildiz Kiosk Following the Fall of

Turkey's Sultan Reveal a Condition Surpassing Fiction," *New York Times* (June 6, 1909).

127. Blitzer, "What Will Happen to Saddam?"

128. Mark Huband, "Liberian Rebels Put President Doe's Body on Display" *The Guardian* (September 11, 1990). And "Doe Body Displayed," *The Guardian* (April 22, 1992.)

129. As it is described by Matthew Buckley paraphrasing Benedict Anderson: "As Anderson points out, the constitution of such a community takes place largely 'in silent privacy, in the lair of the skull,' for the sensation of the pictorial and narrative recognition enabled by dramatic realization, like that of reading the newspaper, is an essentially private one, with each participant 'well aware that the ceremony he performs is being replicated simultaneously by thousands (or millions) of others, of whose existence he is confident, yet of whose identity he hasn't the slightest notion.'" Buckley, 452.

Chapter 3. Condemning the Corrupt System

1. Bataille, 174–175.
2. Agamben, *Homo Sacer*, 135.
3. Mbembe, *Postcolony*, 102.
4. Ibid., 118.
5. Bataille, 17.
6. I am indebted to Joseph Pugliese for his presentation at the Cardozo Law School in the fall of 2006 in which he analyzed the relationship between *Salo* and the Abu Ghraib photographs. I am likewise grateful to him for conversations on the subject at that time. For more on this topic, see Joseph Pugliese, "Abu Ghraib and Its Shadow Archives," *Law and Literature* 19 (2) (Summer 2007): 247–276.
7. See, among others: "Given the view of the corrupting power of the institutions, and their erosion of memory and conscience, it is crucial to Pasolini's allegory that De Sade's scenes be identified with a precise, if not singular, institutional context, which society is attempting to repress: Fascism." Thomas E. Peterson, "The Allegory of Repression from Teorema to Salo," *Italica* 73 (2) (1996): 222.
8. Ibid., 220.
9. At one point, for instance, cajoling one of the girls "come little darling to your daddy—he will console you for the loss of your mama."

10. A situation not hugely distinct from the noncorrupt bureaucracy as described by Alfred Weber, in which "personal identity is entirely subsumed in the bureaucratic apparatus through extreme subordination to authority and an almost neurotic obsession with order, utility, and even personal cleanliness," in Richard Heinemann, "Kafka's Oath of Service: 'Der Bau' and the Dialectic of Bureaucratic Mind," *PMLA* 111 (2) (March, 1996): 258.

11. Bataille, 109–110. He adds in a note, "In any case, the *jus primae noctis* which the feudal lord affected as the sovereign power in his own domain was not as has been thought the outrageous privilege of a tyrant who no one dared resist. At least it did not originate in that way."

12. For a further discussion of such space as it is specifically manifested in the concentration camp, see Agamben, *Homo Sacer*, 20.

13. See, for example, Nathan Brown, "Brigands and Statebuilding: The Invention of Banditry in Egypt," *Comparative Studies in Society and History* 32 (1990): 258–281, and Sandria Freitag, "Crime in the Social Order of Colonial North India," *Modern Asian Studies* 25 (1991): 227–261. For an Ottoman take on the connection between bandits and bureaucrats, see *Düstur*, Dersaadet (Istanbul): Matbaa-yı Amire, 1295/1878, 1330/1912, 1333/1915. vol. 3, 19–20, no. 14. 22/12/1328.

14. "American Marines May Invade Morocco: Two Squadrons of Seven Warships Sent to Tangiers—Full Powers to Admirals, Authorized to Send Expedition to Effect Release of Captives of Bandit Raisuli," *New York Times* (May 29, 1904): 1.

15. "Sultan Asks Tribes to Capture Raisuli: Bandit's Demands Unprecedented in Annals of Brigandage," *New York Times* (June 3, 1904): 1.

16. "Perdicaris's Story of Wild Trip with Bandit: Captives Clubbed with Rifles and Menaced with Knives: Calls Raisuli a Gentleman: Says Kidnapping was Chiefly to Secure Release of his Tribesmen—Betrayed by Treachery of a Tangier Official," *New York Times* (June 13, 1904): 2.

17. "Capture of Europeans Ordered by Rais Uli: He Was Disgusted Because His Men Got Only Spaniards," *London Times* (January 9, 1907): 5.

18. "Rais Uli Captures Sir Harry Maclean: Means to Hold Kaid Prisoner until Sultan Grants Demands," *New York Times* (July 4, 1907): 4.

19. "Capture of Sir Harry Maclean by Rais Uli," *New York Times* (July 14, 1907): SM5.

20. For example, "Sir Harry, Rais Uli declares, is perfectly safe in his hands. He did not capture him for money, but for justice, and this he hopes to

obtain by calling the attention of the British Government to his grievances." "Maclean is Safe, Declares Rais Uli," *New York Times* (August 6, 1907): 5.

21. "Rais Uli, the Bandit, Reported Poisoned: Moorish Captor of Perdicaris and Sir Harry Maclean again Declared to be Dead: Won International Fame: No Longer Bandit but Provincial Governor," *New York Times* (February 13, 1908): 4. For more on Harry Maclean's capture, see L. Martin, "Relation éxacte de la capture de Sir Harry Maclean: Dans la montagne et dans les regions sauvages ce qui lui est arrivé avec Er Reisouli et les gens de la montagne insoumis," *Revue du Monde Musulman* 6 (December 1908): 577–598.

22. On the extent to which "law" in the colonial imagination is something that can exist only in Europe, see Anghie: "It was simply and massively asserted that only the practice of European states was decisive and could create international law. Only European law counted as law. Non-European states were excluded from the realm of law, now identified as being the exclusive preserve of European states, as a result of which they lacked both membership and the ability to assert any rights recognizable as legal." Antony Anghie, "Finding the Peripheries: Sovereignty and Colonialism in Nineteenth-Century International Law," *Harvard International Law Journal* 40 (1999): 24.

23. For example, the ransom money that Rais Uli demanded, he demanded especially from the governors of Tangiers and Fez, "who happen to be [Rais Uli's] bitter enemies." In "American Marines May Invade Morocco."

24. On law, blood, and race, see: "British liberals regarded this breach of a formal treaty [prior to World War I] as a threat to the fundamental system of human relations ordered through the law. In the eyes of the Oxford faculty of Modern History, Britain was at war because 'we are a people in whose blood the cause of law is the vital element.'" Nicoletta F. Gullace, "Sexual Violence and Family Honor: British Propaganda and International Law during the First World War," *The American Historical Review* 102 (3) (June, 1997): 719.

25. As Anghie has argued with regard to the gradual racialization of law, "the naturalist notion that a single, universally applicable law governed a naturally constituted society of nations was completely repudiated by [positivist] jurists of the mid-nineteenth century," in that "the state of nature that naturalists such as Grotius used as a basis for the formulation of rules of international law was unsatisfactory, not only because it was subjective, imprecise, and based on transcendental principles rather than realities of state behavior, but because it failed to make the distinction between civilized and uncivilized. . . . [I]n the naturalist world, law was given; in the positivists

world, law was created by human societies and institutions. Once the connection between 'law' and 'institutions' had been established, it followed from this premise that jurists could focus on the character of institutions, a shift that facilitated the racialization of law by delimiting the notion of law to very specific European institutions." Anghie, "Peripheries," 24–25.

26. Italy and Italians occupied a similarly confused position—that is, were they on the side of the civilized or were they in need of civilization themselves? An article on Italian political corruption in 1898 makes this tension clear by noting that the corrupt nature of Italian politics disqualified Italy from being an effective colonial power. "Secret of Crispi Favor: Africa is the Answer to the Vexing Italo-English Enigma—Aggression, Adventure and Ruin: Most Cruel, Inquisitorial, and Harrowing of all Imposts," *New York Times* (September 21, 1898): 2.

27. "Blackmail by the Police: Protecting Chinese Gambling Houses in Philadelphia," *New York Times* (May 17, 1889): 1.

28. For more on bandits and wolf-men, see Agamben, *Homo Sacer*, 105.

29. George James, "33 Suspected Chinatown Gang Members Are Indicted," *New York Times* (November 22, 1994): B1. See also the discussion of "alien smugglers," torture, extortion, and Chinatown in Selwyn Raab, "64 Indicted as Gangsters in Chinatown: Charges of Racketeering Include Alien Smuggling," *New York Times* (February 24, 1996): 23.

30. Stephen Bonsal, "Venezuela Ruled by a Bandit Army: Savages from the Andes Put in Power by Castro, Too Strong for Gomez—Tax Dodging Led to His Power," *New York Times* (January 4, 1909): 7, and "Cipriano Castro—Cattle Bandit of the Andes: 'Supreme Chief of the High Countries' as He Calls Himself, His Hold on the Government Depends on the Lawless Element." *New York Times* (August 2, 1908): SM7. For an Ottoman comparison, see M. René Pinon, "La Turquie Nouvelle," *Revue des Deux Mondes* 78 (September 1908): 145.

31. Bonsal, "Venezula Ruled by a Bandit Army."

32. James Brookes, "Kidnapping and 'Taxes' Transform Guerilla Inc." *New York Times* (July 24, 1992): D1.

33. Mireya Navarro, "In the Prisons of Puerto Rico, Gangs Have the Upper Hand," *New York Times* (September 10, 1997): A14.

34. "Hadji Ali and His Bandits," *New York Times* (April 27, 1883): 2.

35. "Armenian Wealth Caused Massacres: Turks Found Prosperous People Were Paying Taxes Only to Outlaw Kurdish Tribes: Then Oppression Began: Kurds Retaliated When Their Income Was Cut Off,"

New York Times (April 25, 1909): 3. For a Chinese comparison, see Leroy-Beaulieu, 53.

36. "Armenian Wealth Caused Massacres," 3.

37. For more on the slippages between appropriate and inappropriate taxation, see, among others, Mbembe, who writes that "taxation has provided the ultimate economic foundation of the state, just as the monopoly of legitimate violence was one key to state-building. . . . [I]n the West, for example, taxation has always been more than just a price, even for public services. By paying tax, the individual subject contributes, as an individual, to public expenditure made at common expense. . . . [B]y paying tax and exercising rights over its distribution [citizens] gave legal form to their political capacity and capacities as citizens." *Postcolony*, 89, 94.

38. "Filipino Bandits' Methods: Gen. MacArthur's Remarks on Their Inhuman Ways—Several to be Hanged," *New York Times* (January 14, 1901): 1.

39. "The concept of humanity is an especially useful ideological instrument of imperialist expansion and in its ethical-humanitarian form it is a specific vehicle of economic imperialism. . . . [T]o confiscate the word humanity, to invoke and monopolize such a term probably has certain incalculable effects, such as denying the enemy the quality of being human and declaring him to be an outlaw of humanity; and a war can thereby be driven to the most extreme inhumanity," Carl Schmitt, *The Concept of the Political*, trans. George Schwab (Chicago: University of Chicago Press, 1996), 54. See also Wolfe and Elmer on "noncriminal putting to death": "[*Silence of the Lambs*], like the 'humanism' and 'modernity' critiqued by Derrida, takes for granted the fundamental sacrifice of *non-human* animals." Wolfe and Elmer, 146.

40. See Brown and Freitag.

41. R. Benson, "Comment on the 'Water Cure,'" *New York Times* (July 7, 1902): 6.

42. "The Water Cure Described: Discharged Soldier Tells Senate Committee How and Why the Torture Was Inflicted," *New York Times* (May 4, 1902): 13.

43. "Two Robbers Torture Deaf-Mute in Flat: Bind and Gag Helpless Man and Then Give Him the 'Water Cure' Because He Didn't Speak," *New York Times* (May 4, 1907): 2.

44. "A 'Torture Chamber' in Havana," *New York Times* (January 5, 1889): 7.

45. "The Torture Chamber of the Sultan," *New York Times* (March 28, 1909): SM7.

46. For a more detailed discussion of the carnivalesque nature of torture in Iraq, see John T. Parry, "'Just for Fun': Understanding Torture, Understanding Abu Ghraib," *Journal of National Security Law and Policy* 1 (2005): 279, "The actions of U.S. forces could be carnivalesque—the inversion or parodying of (military) authority and the suspension of official rules, combined with profane physical excess, in all of which the bodies of Iraqi prisoners were mere props."

47. "Torture by Proxy," *New York Times* (March 8, 2005): A22. See also Nick Cohen, "There Is No Case for Torture, Ever: English Law has Long Recognised that Extracting Information by Threats and Brutality Is Barbaric. Moreover, Such Evidence Is Unreliable." *Observer* (October 24, 2004): 31.

48. Farah Stockman, "Jet Linked to Torture Claims Is Sold: Mass. Firm Had Role in Flying Terror Suspects to Egypt," *Boston Globe* (December 9, 2004): B2.

49. Lucy Adams and Ian Bruce, "Stop Torture Jet Flights, Say Politicians: Executive Criticised over Prestwick Halts," *The Herald* (Glasgow) (December 31, 2004): 2. See also "Guantanamo Express: We Cannot Dismiss our Small Role in 'Torture by Proxy,'" *The Herald* (Glasgow) (December 30, 2004): 17.

50. Bataille, 46.

51. George Kennan, "The Russian Police," *Century Illustrated Magazine* 37 (6) (April, 1889): 890.

52. Ibid, 895–896.

53. Ibid., 896.

54. Oliver S. Buckton, "Reanimating Stevenson's Corpus," *Nineteenth Century Literature* 55 (1) (June 2000): 25, 23, 38.

55. Bataille, 18.

56. Kennan, 890.

57. Ibid., 895.

58. "Secret of Crispi Favor: Africa Is the Answer to the Vexing Italo-English Enigma—Aggression, Adventure, and Ruin: Most Cruel, Inquisitorial, and harrowing of All Imposts." *New York Times* (September 21, 1898): 2.

59. "Cipriano Castro—Cattle Bandit of the Andes," SM7.

60. Stephen Bonsal, "Venezuela Ruled by a Bandit Army: Savages from the Andes Put in Power by Castro, Too Strong for Gomez—Tax Dodging Led to His Power," *New York Times* (January 4, 1909): 7.

61. "Hoping Rivals Will be a Bigger Threat than Government: Small Business—Pessimists Say Bureaucrats Have no Interest in a Simpler, Fairer, or Transparent Environment for Entrepreneurs," *The Financial Times* (April 1, 2003): 3.

62. Fred Weir, "Putin's Duel with the Bureaucrats," *Christian Science Monitor* (February 22, 2002): 6.

63. Daniel Williams, "Italian Scandals Spread from Politics to Academia; Investigators Focus on Universities and Public Bureaucracy in Ongoing War on Corruption," *Washington Post* (November 18, 1995): A24.

64. Ibid.

65. "How China Is Governed," *New York Times* (January 26, 1892): 2.

66. The relationship between "justice" and "torture" is made clear in the following passage as well, where peasants become bandits when bureaucrats "turn the screw of extortion": "Very often the revolts break out among the peasants against some particularly obnoxious Mandarin who turns the screw of extortion beyond endurance, or who may perhaps sell justice too barefacedly to the highest bidder. On many other occasions, revolts arise from clan or tribe feuds between marauders occupying lands claimed by immigrants or native banner men." "Safe Only When Isolated: What Railroads and Telegraphs Would Do in China," *New York Times* (March 24, 1892): 9.

67. Hulbert, 222–223. On the same theme see Leroy-Beaulieu, 49, 56.

68. William B. Dunlop, "Railways—Their Future in China," *The Eclectic Magazine of Foreign Literature* 49 (4) (April, 1889): 516–517. See also Leroy-Beaulieu, 58.

69. For a late twentieth-century variation on this theme, see William Safire, "Games Asians Play," *New York Times* (September 20, 1990): A21.

70. See Dorys, 142.

71. On cultural cross-dressing, see Boisseau, 166–167.

72. A Member of Laurence Oliphant's Colony, Hasketh Smith, "The Experiences of a Multazim," *Littel's Living Age* 184 (March 22, 1890): 756, 759. For an Ottoman take on grain, taxes, and corruption, see Ahmed Lütfi, (1851 code), chap. 3, art. 14 and 19 (pp. 169, 171, 173–174).

73. Smith, 759.

74. Ibid., 762.

75. Ibid., 758.

76. Heinemann, 257.

77. On the modernity of disciplinary punishment, see: "punishment, then, will tend to become the most hidden part of the penal process. This has several consequences: it leaves the domain of more or less everyday perception and enters that of abstract consciousness; its effectiveness is seen as resulting from its inevitability, not from its visible intensity; it is the certainty of being punished and not the horrifying spectacle of public punishment that must discourage crime; the exemplary mechanics of punishment changes its mechanisms." Michel Foucault, *Discipline and Punish*, trans. Alan Sheridan (New York: Vintage Books, 1977), 9.

78. Where a "confused horror spread from the scaffold; it enveloped both executioner and condemned . . . often turn[ing] the legal violence of the executioner to shame." Ibid., 9.

79. For a more extended treatment of Bu Hamara, see René Pinon, "Les événemens du Maroc," *Revue des Deux Mondes* 73 (March 1903): 157.

80. "El Roghi Still in Cage: Morocco's Sultan Hopes to Get His Money—Powers to Stop Torture," *New York Times* (August 29, 1909): C3.

81. See also, "Lecter's zoological peculiarity is visually reinforced once again when he is held in what looks like a gorilla cage in the middle of a large exhibition room during his time in Memphis, as if on display to the lucky few who have the privilege of visiting this most terrifying and exotic of zoos." Wolfe and Elmer, 148.

82. The liberal progress theme appears in a number of places in discussions of public torture or public executions—especially when governments that have learned to be civilized slip up and return to the "old" methods: "in the course of a recent trial of government officials charged with betraying the Foreign Office's correspondence touching the Tatsu Maru affair, the Peking authorities resorted to the old method of using torture in order to extract confessions. This is a notable illustration of the extremity to which the Peking Government is sometimes driven." "Torture in Chinese Trial: Peking Officials Use Forbidden Methods," *New York Times* (May 11, 1908): 4.

83. "Chinese Punishment Methods," *New York Times* (November 28, 1894): 5. See also "How China Is Governed," 2.

84. Even if the humanitarian outrage itself defines him as not quite human to begin with: "L'indifférence à la mort sembel être chez eux un caractère presque physique qui provient du peu d'excitabilité de leur système nerveux. A ce dernier sujet, les témoinages sont unanimes: les médecins des hôpitaux européens où sont traités des indigènes, racontent avec stupéfaction comment leurs patiens supportent, sans un cri et sans qu'il soit nécessaire de les anesthésier, les plus douloureuses opérations;

dans l'ordinaire de l'existence, cette absences de nerfs se traduit par la facilité à s'endormir comme à volonté au milieu du bruit et dans une position quelconque, à demuerer dans une immobilité absolue et prolongée, inconnue des Occidentaux, à attendre indéfiniment sans donner jamais signe d'impatience. . . . les tortures varies, les affreux châtimens infligés par les tribunaux en sont un autre, mais ils paraissent assurément moins terribles à supporter aux Célestes qu'ils ne le seraient pour les Européens." ["indifference to death seems to be an almost physical characteristic among them, which shows the minimal excitability of their nervous system. On this last subject, the witnesses are unanimous: doctors at European hospitals where the indigent are treated recount with amazement how their patients, without a single cry and without any anesthetic, tolerate the most painful of operations; ordinarily this absence of nerves is revealed by the ability to sleep in any amount of noise in whatever position, to remain absolutely immobile for prolonged periods, or to wait indefinitely without any sign of impatience, [activities] unknown among Westerners. . . . [T]he various tortures, the dreadful punishments inflicted by the tribunals are another example of this, but they are certainly less difficult to tolerate on the part of the Celestials than the would be on the part of Europeans."] Leroy-Beaulieu, 53–54. For a more recent variation on this approach to pain, humanity, and lack thereof, see the 1969 decision of the European Commission of Human Rights, which observed that "some prisoners may 'tolerate . . . and even take for granted . . . a certain roughness of treatment . . . by both police and military authorities. . . . [S]uch roughness may take the form of slaps and blows of the hand on the head or face.' In these circumstances, the Commission concluded there had been no cruel, inhuman, or degrading treatment within the meaning of the European Convention on Human Rights, because 'the point up to which prisoners *and the public* may accept physical violence as being neither cruel nor excessive, varies between different societies and even between different sections of them.'" As quoted in Parry, 2.

85. For a contemporary Ottoman variation on this, see Çekiver, 40–41, and 59. These cartoons portray corrupt bureaucrats as, variously, scorpions, snakes, donkeys, dogs, and cats.

86. One of the most effective articulations of this point is in Foucault, *Discipline and Punish*, 40–41.

87. "Sultan Tortures Rebels: Hands and Feet of Moroccans Cut Off—Women's Teeth Drawn," *New York Times* (August 25, 1909): 4.

88. "How China Is Governed," 2.

89. This presentation of the disordered Chinese body in the context of the corrupt system is common to photographs of "Chinese torture" from

the period as well. In Bataille's *Tears of Eros*, there is a three-page-long spread of photographs taken in April 1905 detailing the punishment of the *Hundred Pieces*. What is remarkable about the way the photographs are shot is the extent to which *what* exactly is being cut off of the body in the respective pictures is unclear. Bataille, *Tears of Eros*, trans. Peter Conner (San Francisco: City Light Books, 1989), 204–206.

    90. As Foucault notes, "judicial torture functioned in that strange economy in which the ritual that produced the truth went side by side with the ritual that imposed the punishment. The body interrogated in torture constituted the point of application of the punishment and the locus of extortion of the truth. And just as presumption was inseparable an element in the investigation and a fragment of guilt, the regulated pain involved in judicial torture was a means of both punishment and of investigation." *Discipline and Punish*, 42.

    91. I am defining "miscegenation" here broadly—as something "done to" person as well as something "done by" a person or persons. I do so because the concept of transitive miscegenation, as it were, is one that appears with repetitive frequency in the literature.

    92. For more on Mr. Harris, see Pinon, 147.

    93. "Moroccan Brigands Torture Journalist," *London Times* (July 14, 1903): 7.

    94. "Chinese Punishment Methods," *New York Times* (November 28, 1894): 5.

    95. The criminal code in place in the Ottoman Empire at this time was the 1810 French Napoleonic Code.

    96. "Turkey's Terror Record: A Careful List of the Victims Made at Adaiman, Near Aintab: Enforced Telegrams to Sultan: Details of Horrors of Imprisonment at Marash—Confessions of Sedition Extorted by Torture," *New York Times* (February 7, 1896): 5.

    97. For a visual representation of the dehumanizing collectivity of Abdülhamid's prisons (and the relief of throwing them open), see Çekiver, 27: "1324 senesi Temmuzun 16'nçi günü Habishane-i Umuminin kapısı açılıp dışarı çıkan mahbusinin resmidir/La sortie des omnistées de la prison Centrale de Constantinople, le 16/29 Juillet 1908" ("16 July 1324/1908 the official opening of the doors to the General Prison and departure outside of the prisoners/the general departure from the Central Prison of Constantinople, 16/29 July 1906"). The prisoners are represented as a huge, undifferentiated mass, squeezing through the doors and disappearing back into a vanishing point.

    98. "Chinese authorities have demanded that Mr. Fang write an 'admission of guilt,' acknowledging that he helped organize the demonstrations

in Tiananmen Square in May and June last year. American officials said Mr. Fang was unlikely to admit guilt now after having railed against the Chinese Communist Party, complaining of arbitrary dictatorial rule, corruption and nepotism for several decades." Robert Pear, "China Ties New Demand to Dissident's Fate," *New York Times* (April 4, 1990): A12.

99. Justin Huggler, "Turkey: Torture Victims Tried for Daring to Speak Out," *Independent* (January 22, 2001): 14.

100. Nick Cohen, "Outcasts of the Medical World: Doctors Accused of Torture," *Observer* (August 25, 1996): 15.

101. See also, "as a physician at the Human Rights Foundation here, Dr. Onder Ozkalipci tends to the handiwork of sadists. He talks of the most popular methods of torturers as another doctor might talk of the perils of cholesterol." Somini Sengupta, "A Turkish Doctor's Specialty: The Torture Victim," *New York Times* (January 26, 2002).

102. Although see Foucault, *Discipline and Punish*, on the slippage between the "patient" and the "victim" or "accused" in the early modern vocabulary of torture. Foucault, 42.

103. Ibid.

104. Audrey Gillan, "Terror suspect tells of 'torture' that led to death wish: 'Give me an injection and I will be dead': After several months of legal action, the Guardian has won the right to interview foreign nationals being held without charge on suspicion of terrorist involvement: Audrey Gillan goes inside Broadmoor high-security hospital and talks to Mahmoud Abu Rideh about being locked up with no prospect of release and why he has tried to kill himself," *Guardian* (May 5, 2004): 1.

105. For an excellent analytical summary of the growing literature on what "Arabs" or "Muslims" especially "fear," see Parry, 2.

106. In *Homo Sacer*, Agamben notes as well the ease with which parliamentary democracies have turned into totalitarian dictatorships and then turned back again over the twentieth century. Agamben, 122.

107. William Safire, "Gravy Trains Don't Run on Time: Good Riddance, Singapore Model," *New York Times* (January 19, 1998): A17.

108. As Wolfe and Elmer note with reference to cannibalism in *Silence of the Lambs*, "Lecter's relation to language is symptomatic of how 'presymbolic others' embody or 'thingify' the collapse of the distinction between the Symbolic and the Thing, between meaning and enjoyment." Wolfe and Elmer, 163.

Bibliography

Books and Articles

Adams, Lucy. "Guantanamo Express: We Cannot Dismiss Our Small Role in 'Torture by Proxy.'" *The Herald* (Glasgow) (December 30, 2004): 17.

Adams, Lucy, and Ian Bruce. "Stop Torture Jet Flights, Say Politicians: Executive Criticised over Prestwick Halts." *The Herald* (Glasgow) (December 31, 2004): 2.

Agamben, Giorgio. *Homo Sacer: Sovereign Power and Bare Life*. Translated by Daniel Heller-Roazen. Stanford: Stanford University Press, 1998.

Agamben, Giorgio. *State of Exception*. Translated by Kevin Attell. Chicago: University of Chicago Press, 2005.

Ahmed Lütfi. *Mirat-ı Adalet, yahud Tarihçe-i Adliye-yi Devlet-i Aliyye*. Istanbul: Kitapçı Ohannes, 1304/1888.

Anderson, Jon Lee. "Saddam's Ear: An Iraqi Doctor Had a Unique Role in Saddam Hussein's Life." *The New Yorker* (May 5, 2003): 58.

Anghie, Antony. "Finding the Peripheries: Sovereignty and Colonialism in Nineteenth-Century International Law." *Harvard International Law Journal* 40 (1999): 1–80.

Apter, Emily, and William Pietz, eds. *Fetishism as a Cultural Discourse*. Ithaca: Cornell University Press, 1993.

Barnes, Elizabeth, ed. *Incest and the Literary Imagination*. Gainesville: University Press of Florida, 2002.

Basmadjian, K. J. "La Révolution en Turquie." *Revue du Monde Musulman* 5 (8) (August 1908): 718–744.

Bataille, Georges. *Erotism: Death and Sensuality*. Translated by Mary Dalwood. San Francisco: City Lights Books, 1986.

Bataille, Georges. *Tears of Eros*. Translated by Peter Conner. San Francisco: City Light Books, 1989.

Bayart, Jean-François, Stephen Ellis, and Béatrice Hibou. *The Criminalization of the State in Africa*. Bloomington: Indiana University Press, 1999.

Beaumont, Peter. "Iraq Crisis: Countdown to Conflict: Last Days of Saddam." *The Observer* (February 23, 2003): 17.

Benson, R. "Comment on the 'Water Cure.'" *New York Times* (July 7, 1902): 6.

Blair, David. "He Dreamed of Glory but Dealt Out Only Despair." *The Daily Telegraph* (March 18, 2003): 2.

Blitzer, Wolf. "Special Edition: The Capture of Saddam Hussein." *CNN Late Edition With Wolf Blitzer* 12:00.Transcript #121400CN.V47 (December 14, 2003). Byline: Wolf Blitzer, Nic Robertson, Dana Bash, David Ensor, Christiane Amanpour, Jane Arraf, Barbara Starr, Bob Franken, Ken Pollack.

Blitzer, Wolf. "Press Conference Announcing Hussein's Capture." *CNN Breaking News* 07:00.Transcript #121401CN.V00 (December 14, 2003). Byline: Sean Callebs, Dana Bash, Heidi Collins, Barbara Starr, Wolf Blitzer, Nic Robertson, Kenneth Pollack, Aaron Brown, Satinder Bindra.

Blitzer, Wolf. "What Will Happen to Saddam? Interview with Bernard Shaw." *CNN Wolf Blitzer Reports* 17:00. Transcript #121500 CN.V67 (December 15, 2003). Byline: Wolf Blitzer, Alphonso Van Marsh, Jane Arraf, Dana Bash, Nic Robertson, Jim Bittermann, Robin Oakley, John Vause, David Ensor.

Boisseau, Tracey Jean. *White Queen: May French Sheldon and the Imperial Origins of American Feminism*. Bloomington: Indiana University Press, 2004,

Bonsal, Stephen. "Cipriano Castro—Cattle Bandit of the Andes: 'Supreme Chief of the High Countries' as He Calls Himself, His Hold on the Government Depends on the Lawless Element." *New York Times* (August 2, 1908): SM7.

Bonsal, Stephen. "Venezuela Ruled by a Bandit Army: Savages from the Andes Put in Power by Castro, Too Strong for Gomez—Tax Dodging Led to His Power," *New York Times* (January 4, 1909): 7.

Bourdieu, Pierre. "Rethinking the State: Genesis and Structure of the Bureaucratic Field." Translated by Samar Faroge. *Sociological Theory* 12 (1) (1994): 1–18.

Briggs, Laura. *Reproducing Empire: Race, Sex, Science and U.S. Imperialism in Puerto Rico*. Berkeley: University of California Press, 2002.

Broder, Jonathan. "Saddam's Bomb." *New York Times* (October 1, 2000): SM38.

Brookes, James. "Kidnapping and 'Taxes' Transform Guerilla Inc." *New York Times* (July 24, 1992): D1.

Brown, Nathan. "Brigands and Statebuilding: The Invention of Banditry in Egypt." *Comparative Studies in Society and History* 32 (1990): 258–281.

Brummet, Palmira. "Dogs, Women, Cholera and Other Menaces in the Streets: Cartoon Satire in the Ottoman Revolutionary Press." *International Journal of Middle East Studies* 27 (4) (November 1995): 433–460.

Buckley, Matthew. "Sensations of Celebrity: Jack Sheppard and the Mass Audience." *Victorian Studies* 44 (3) (2002): 423–463.

Buckton, Oliver S. "Reanimating Stevenson's Corpus." *Nineteenth Century Literature* 55 (1) (June 2000): 22–58.

Caiden, Gerald E., O. P. Dwivedi, and Joseph Jabbra, eds. *Where Corruption Lives*. Bloomfield, CT: Kumarian Press, 2001.

Çekiver, Turgut. *İbret Albümü, 1908*. Istanbul: Kültür İşleri Dairesi Başkanlığı Yayınları, 1991.

Clark, Anna. *Scandal: The Sexual Politics of the British Constitution*. Princeton: Princeton University Press, 2004.

Clark, Michael, ed. *Corruption: Cases, Consequences, and Control*. London: Frances Pinter, 1983.

Cohen, Nick. "Outcasts of the Medical World: Doctors Accused of Torture," *Observer* (August 25, 1996): 15.

Cohen, Nick. "There is no case for torture, ever." *Observer* (October 24, 2004): 31.

Corbet, W. J. "Illustrious Lunatics." *The Arena* 21 (5) (May, 1899): 571–580.

Coughlin, Con. "The Savage Sunset of Saddam Hussein." *The American Spectator* (January–February, 2003).

Crain, Caleb. "Lovers of Human Flesh: Homosexuality and Cannibalism in Melville's Novels." *American Literature* 66 (1) (March 1999): 25–53.

Das, Veena, Arthur Kleinman, Mamphela Ramphele, and Pamela Reynolds, eds. *Violence and Subjectivity*. Berkeley: University of California Press, 2000.

Deleuze, Gilles. "Plato and the Simulacrum." *October* 27 (1983): 45–56.

DiGiorgio-Miller, Janet. "Sibling Incest: Treatment of the Family and the Offender," *Child Welfare* 77 (3) (1998): 335–346.

Doane, Janice, and Devon Hodges. *Telling Incest: Narratives of Dangerous Remembering from Stein to Sapphire*. Ann Arbor: University of Michigan Press, 2001.

Doig, A. "Good Government and Sustainable Anti-Corruption Strategies: A Role for Independent Anti-Corruption Agencies?" *Public Administration and Development* 15 (1995): 151–165.

Doig, Alan. "Dealing with Corruption: The Next Steps," *Crime, Law and Social Change* 29 (1998): 97–112.

Dorys, George. *The Private Life of the Sultan of Turkey*. New York: D. Appleton and Co., 1901.

Dunlop, William B. "Railways—Their Future in China." *The Eclectic Magazine of Foreign Literature* 49 (4) (April 1889): 516–524.

Dye, Kenneth M., and Rick Stapenhurst. "Pillars of Integrity: The Importance of Supreme Audit Institutions in Curbing Corruption." *EDI/World Bank Institute Working Papers*, (1998): 1–17, 19–21, 23–25.

Eigen, Peter. "Combating Corruption Around the World." *Journal of Democracy* 7 (1) (1996): 25–30.

Ellis, Stephen. "Liberia 1989–1994: A Study of Ethnic and Spiritual Violence." *African Affairs* 94 (1995): 165–197.

Foord, John. "The Root of the Chinese Trouble." *North American Review* 171 (76) (September 1900): 401.

Foucault, Michel. *Discipline and Punish*. Translated by Alan Sheridan. New York: Vintage Books, 1995.

Foucault, Michel. *History of Sexuality*. Translated by Robert Hurley. New York: Vintage Books, 1990.

Freitag, Sandria. "Crime in the Social Order of Colonial North India." *Modern Asian Studies* 25 (1991): 227–261.

Friedman, Robert I. "India's Shame: Sexual Slavery and Political Corruption Are Leading to an AIDS Catastrophe." *The Nation* (April 8, 1996).

Friedman, Thomas. "Saddam Does Vegas." *New York Times* (December 19, 1999): WK13.

Friedman, Thomas. "Saddam's Page Turner." *New York Times* (August 18, 1996): E15.

Gelb, Leslie. "Cuddling Saddam." *New York Times* (July 9, 1992): A21.

Ghilan, "La décomposition du corps social en Perse." *Revue du Monde Musulman* 4 (January 1908): 85–90.

Gibson, Charles. "Unauthorized Saddam." *Primetime Live* (December 12, 2002). ABC News.

Gibson, Charles. "Sons of Saddam: Hunted Down in Iraq." *Primetime Live* (July 22, 2003). ABC News.

Gillan, Audrey. "Terror Suspect Tells of 'Torture' that Led to Death Wish." *The Guardian* (May 5, 2004): 1.

Goleman, Daniel. "Experts Differ on Dissecting Leaders' Psyches from Afar." *New York Times* (January 29, 1992): C1.

Goodspeed, Peter. "From Brutal Despot to Cowering Prisoner." *The National Post* (December 15, 2003): A12.

Greenaway, Norma. "Murderous Rise to Absolute Rule: Saddam's Path to Power Was Paved by the Blood of Anybody He Saw as a Threat." *Times Colonist/Monitor* (March 23, 2003): D6.

Grewal, Inderpal. *Home and Harem: Nation, Gender, Empire, and the Cultures of Travel*. Durham: Duke University Press, 1996. p. 50.

Gullace, Nicoletta F. "Sexual Violence and Family Honor: British Propaganda and International Law during the First World War." *The American Historical Review* 102 (3) (June, 1997): 714–747.

Gutwirth, Madelyn. "Sacred Father, Profane Sons: Lynn Hunt's French Revolution." *French Historical Studies* 19 (2) (Autumn 1995): 261–276.

Halttunen, Karen. "Humanitarianism and the Pornography of Pain in Anglo American Culture." *American Historical Review* 100 (2) (1995): 303–334.

Hanley, Sarah. "Social Sites of Political Practice in France: Lawsuits, Civil Rights, and the Separation of Powers in Domestic and State Government." *The American Historical Review* 102 (1) (February 1992): 27–52.

Hardt, Michael, and Antonio Negri. *Multitude: War and Democracy in the Age of Empire*. London: Penguin, 2004.

Heidenheimer, Arnold J. *Political Corruption: Readings in Comparative Analysis*. New Brunswick, NJ: Transaction Books, 1978.

Heinemann, Richard. "Kafka's Oath of Service: 'Der Bau' and the Dialectic of Bureaucratic Mind." *PMLA* 111 (2) (March 1996): 256–270.

Hidayette. *Abdul Hamid révolutionnaire, ou ce qu'on ne peut pas dire en Turquie*. Zurich: 1896.

Huart, Cl. "L'Ancien régime dans l'Empire Ottoman." *Revue du Monde Musulman* 7 (3) (March 1900): 281–286.

Huband, Mark. "Liberian Rebels Replay the Last Hours of President Doe: Mark Huband in Monrovia Sees a Gruesome Video of the Former Leader's Torture and Death." *The Guardian* (October 3, 1990).

Hudson, Christopher. "Saddam the Boy Monster." *Daily Mail* (March 8, 2003): 36.

Huggler, Justin. "Turkey: Torture Victims Tried for Daring to Speak Out." *Independent* (January 22, 2001): 14.

Hulbert, Homer Beza. "Korea and the Koreans." *Forum* (April 1889): 217–223.

Hunt, Lynn, ed. *The New Cultural History*. Berkeley: University of California Press, 1989.

Hyde, Alan. *Bodies of Law*. Princeton: Princeton University Press, 1997.

Ibrahim, Youssef M. "The World: Saddam Hussein, Tactician." *New York Times* (November 1, 1998): 3.

James, George. "33 Suspected Chinatown Gang Members Are Indicted." *New York Times* (November 22, 1994): B1.

Kantorowicz, Ernst H. *The King's Two Bodies: A Study in Medieval Political Theology*. Princeton: Princeton University Press, 1957.

Kennan, George. "The Russian Police." *Century Illustrated Magazine* 37 (6) (April, 1889): 890–900.

Klitgaard, Robert, "Cleaning up and Invigorating the Civil Service." *Public Administration and Development* 17 (5) (December 1997): 487–509.

Kristof, Nicholas. "Hatreds Steeped in Blood." *New York Times* (March 11, 2003): A25.

Kristof, Nicholas. "If Saddam Were Only Brazilian." *New York Times* (December 17, 2002): A35.

Lee, Rance P. L. "The Folklore of Corruption in Hong Kong." *Asian Survey* 21 (3) (1981): 355–368.

Leroy-Beaulieu, Pierre. "Le problême Chine." *Revue des Deux Mondes* 54 (January 1899): 43–74.

Levine, Victor T. "Controlling Corruption: A Review Essay." *Corruption and Reform* 5 (1990): 153–157.

Lewis, Paul. "Graphic Message from Saddam Hussein: Defiance and Appeals." *New York Times* (July 10, 1993): 2.

Liepe-Levinson, Katherine. "Striptease: Desire, Mimetic Jeopardy, and Performing Spectators." *TDR* 4 (2) (Summer 1998): 9–37.

Long, R. Hamilton. "The Present Government in Turkey—Its Crimes and Remedy." *The Eclectic Magazine of Foreign Literature* 66 (3) (September 1897): 396–405.

Markovits, Andrei, and Mark Silverstein, eds. *The Politics of Scandal: Power and Process in Liberal Democracies*. New York: Holmes and Meier, 1988.

Martin, L. "Relation éxacte de la capture de Sir Harry Maclean." *Revue du Monde Musulman* 6 (December 1908): 577–598.

Mbembe, Achille. "Necropolitics." Translated by Libby Meintjes. *Public Culture* 15 (1) (2003): 11–40.

Mbembe, Achille. *On the Postcolony*. Berkeley: University of California Press, 2001.

McCullagh, Francis. "Sultan Faces His People: Drives to Selamlik in Open Victoria While Throngs Line Streets." *New York Times* (April 24, 1909): 2.

McCullagh, Francis. "What Was Found in the Lair of Abdul Hamid: Amazing Discoveries in the Yildiz Kiosk Following the Fall of Turkey's Sultan Reveal a Condition Surpassing Fiction." *New York Times* (June 6, 1909).

McCullagh, Francis. "When Turkey's Sultan Faced His Masters." *New York Times* (January 10, 1909): SM3.

Mearsheimer, John. "Keeping Saddam Hussein in a Box." *New York Times* (February 2, 2003): 15.

Mills, Catherine. "Linguistic Survival and Ethicality: Biopolitics, Subjectivity, and Testimony in *Remnants of Auschwitz*." In *Politics, Metaphysics, and Death: Essays on Giorgio Agamben's Homo Sacer*, edited by Andrew Norris. Durham: Duke University Press, 2005, 198–222.

Mitchell, Timothy. *Colonising Egypt*. New York: Cambridge University Press, 1991.

Montgomery, Rick. "Saddam Hussein Breaths Fear, Lives in Fear, Deals in Fear." *Knight Ridder/Tribune News Service* (February 23, 2003).

Najmabadi, Afsaneh. "The Erotic Vatan as Beloved Mother: To Love, to Possess, and To Protect." *Comparative Studies in Society and History* 39 (3) (1997): 442–467.

Navarro, Mireya. "In the Prisons of Puerto Rico, Gangs Have the Upper Hand." *New York Times* (September 10, 1997): A14.

Parry, John T. "'Just for Fun': Understanding Torture, Understanding Abu Ghraib." *Journal of National Security Law and Policy* 1 (2005): 253–284.

Payne, Robert. *The Corrupt Society: From Ancient Greece to Present Day America*. New York: Praeger, 1975.

Pear, Robert. "China Ties New Demand to Dissident's Fate." *New York Times* (April 4, 1990): A12.

Perry, Peter John. *Political Corruption and Political Geography*. Aldershot, England: Ashgate, 1997.

Peterson, Thomas E. "The Allegory of Repression from Teorema to Salo." *Italica* 73 (2) (1996): 215–232.

Pinon, M. René. "La Turquie Nouvelle." *Revue des Deux Mondes* 78 (September 1908): 125–159.

Pinon, M. René. "Les événemens du Maroc." *Revue des Deux Mondes* 73 (March 1903): 147–167.

Raab, Selwyn. "64 Indicted as Gangsters in Chinatown: Charges of Racketeering Include Alien Smuggling." *New York Times* (February 24, 1996): 23.

Rose, David. "Baghdad's Cruel Princes." *Vanity Fair* (May 2003): 176.

Safire, William. "Saddam Redux?" *New York Times* (May 2, 1994): A17.

Safire, William. "Games Asians Play." *New York Times* (September 20, 1990): A21.

Safire, William. "Gravy Trains Don't Run on Time: Good Riddance, Singapore Model." *New York Times* (January 19, 1998): A17.

Safire, William. "Slapping Saddam's Wrist." *New York Times* (June 28, 1993): A17.

Said, Edward. *Orientalism*. New York: Vintage, 1978

Sassatelli, Roberta. "Justice, Television and Delegitimation: On the Cultural Codification of the Italian Political Crisis." *Modern Italy* 3 (1) (1998): 108–115.

Schmitt, Carl. *The Concept of the Political*. Translated by George Schwab. Chicago: University of Chicago Press, 1996 (1932).

Schmitt, Carl. *Political Theology*. Translated by George Schwab. Chicago: University of Chicago Press, 1985 (1922).

Sciolino, Elaine. "Arab of Vast Ambition." *New York Times* (August 5, 1990): 14.

Seaver, Richard, ed. *Marquis de Sade: Justine, Philosophy in the Bedroom, and Other Writings*. New York: Grove Press, 1965.

Sengupta, Somini. "A Turkish Doctor's Specialty: The Torture Victim." *New York Times* (January 26, 2002).

Smith, Hasketh. "The Experiences of a Multazim." *Littel's Living Age* 184 (March 22, 1890): 756–763.

Solomon-Godeau, Abigail. "The Legs of the Countess." In *Fetishism as a Cultural Discourse*, edited by Emily Apter and William Pietz. Ithaca: Cornell University Press, 1993, 266–306.

Stengers, Jean, and Anne Van Neck. *Masturbation: The History of a Great Terror*. Translated by Kathryn A. Hoffman. New York: Palgrave, 2001.

Stockman, Farah. "Jet Linked to Torture Claims Is Sold: Mass. Firm had Role in Flying Terror Suspects to Egypt." *Boston Globe* (December 9, 2004): B2.

Stoler, Ann. *Race and the Education of Desire*. Durham: Duke University Press, 1995.

Stratton, Jon. *The Desirable Body: Cultural Fetishism and the Erotics of Consumption*. Urbana: University of Illinois Press, 2001.

Tambling, Jeremy. *Confession: Sexuality, Sin, the Subject*. Manchester: Manchester University Press, 1990.

Tasma. "Iftar in a Harem." *Arthur's Home Magazine* (September 1891): 727–735.

Telford, Emma Paddock. "Three Sultans." *Godey's Magazine* 134 (February 1897): 115–122.

Theobald, Robin. "So What Really Is the Problem about Corruption." *Third World Quarterly* 20 (3) (1999): 491–502.

Turkey. *Düstur*. Dersaadet (Istanbul): Matbaa-yı Amire, 1295/1878, 1330/1912, 1333/1915.

Tyler, Patrick. "Who's Acting Tough Now? Why, Saddam Hussein." *New York Times* (October 24, 1991): A4.

Verdery, Katherine. *The Political Lives of Dead Bodies: Reburial and Postsocialist Change*. New York: Columbia University Press, 1999.

Weir, Fred. "Putin's Duel with the Bureaucrats." *Christian Science Monitor* (February 22, 2002): 6.

Welsh, Herbert. "Campaign Committees: Publicity as a Cure for Corruption." *Forum* (September 1892): 26–38.

Whiting, Frederick. "The Strange Particularity of the Lover's Presence: Pedophilia, Pornography and the Anatomy of Monstrosity in *Lolita*." *American Literature* 70 (4) (December 1998): 833–862.

Will, Thomas E. "Political Corruption: How Best Oppose?" *Arena* 10 (6) (November 1894): 845.

Williams, Daniel. "Italian Scandals Spread from Politics to Academia." *Washington Post* (November 18, 1995): A24.

Williams, Linda. "Power, Pleasure, and Perversion: Sadomasochistic Film Pornography." *Representations* 27 (1989): 37–65.

Williams, Linda. "Film Bodies: Gender, Genre, and Excess." *Film Quarterly* 44 (1991): 2–13.

Williams, Robert, ed. *Controlling Corruption*. Northampton, MA: Edward Elgar Publishing, 2000.

Winfrey, Oprah. "What You Should Know About Iraq." *The Oprah Winfrey Show* (March 6, 2003). ABC.

Wolf, Cary, and Jonathan Elmer. "Subject to Sacrifice: Ideology, Psychoanalysis, and the Discourse of Species in Jonathan Demme's *Silence of the Lambs*." *boundary 2* 22 (3) (Autumn 1995): 141–170.

Zahn, Paula. "Saddam Hussein Faces Iraqi Justice; Saddam Hussein's Body Language Reveals Secrets." *Paula Zahn Now* 20:00. Transcript #070100CN.V99 (July 1, 2004). Byline: Paula Zahn, Christiane Amanpour, Brian Todd, Octavia Nasr, Paul Von Fyl.

Websites

Abdul Aziz, Tunku. "ADB-OECD Anti-Corruption Initiative" (November 28–30, 2001), http://www.transparency.org/speeches/taa_apac.html.

Abdul Aziz, Tunku. "Has Reform Revived the Miracle? Reforming East Asian Governance: A Business Necessity," (March 10–20, 2001), http://www.transparency.org/seeches/taa_chatham.html.

"Britney Spears Porn Comix," http://www.celebritygo.net/comics.

Coalition Against Trafficking in Women, "The Factbook on Global Sexual Exploitation: India," http://www.catwinternational.org/fb/india.html.

Eigen, Peter. "Closing the Corruption Casino," Global Forum II (May 2001), www.transparency.org/speeches/pe_gf2_address.html.

Eigen, Peter. "Security and Opportunity through Law and Justice" (July 2001), www.transparency.org/speeches/pe_stpetersburg.html.

Eigen, Peter. "The Central role of Civil Society in Combating Corruption in the Era of Globalization," Transparency for Growth Conference (May 1999), www.transparency.org/speeches/pe_carter_address.html.

Eigen, Peter. "WTO Needs to Play a More Active Role in the Fight against Corruption," www.transparency.org/speeches/pe_wto_geneva.html.

Githongo, John. "Corruption as a Problem in the Developing World," Seminar on Corruption and Development Cooperation (May 2000), www.transparency.org/speeches/githongo.html.

Limpangog, Cirila P. "Struggling through Corruption: A Gendered Perspective," Tenth International Anti-Corruption Conference, http://www.10iacc.org/content.phtml?documents=111cart=135.

Reed, Quentin. "Political Corruption, Privatisation and Control in the Czech Republic: A Case Study or Problems in Multiple Transition," www.transparency.org.ru/CENTER/DOC/Book 06.doc.

Robinson, Mary. "Ethical Governance and Globalization—10 Years of Fighting Corruption," (Freie Universitat, Berlin June 19, 2003), www.transparency.org/speeches/robinson.

Schloss, Miguel. "Combating Corruption for Development," (Conferencia de Responsibilidad Social Empresarial en las Americas, June 1999), http://www.transparency.org/speeches/ms_brazeil_ethos.html.

SPR, "Somalia: Warlords Have Vested Interest in Perpetuation of Civil War," *U4 Anti-Corruption News*, http://www.u4.no/news/news.cfm?id=107.

United Nations Office on Drugs and Crime, "Why a Global Programme Against Corruption?," www.unodc.org/unodc/en/corruption.html.

Wiehen, Michael H. "Transparency in Government Procurement and the Fight against Cross Border Corruption," EC Meeting on Transparency in Government Procurement (May 16, 2003), http://www.transparency.org/speeches/wiehen.

Anonymous Articles and Essays

"Abdul as Author." *New York Times* (October 18, 1902): BR 8.
"Abdul Described as Abject." *New York Times* (April, 28, 1909): 2.

"Abdul Hamid Drinking Heavily." *New York Times* (November 30, 1895): 5.
"Abdul Hamid II, Sultan of Turkey." *Current Literature* 19 (January 1896): 1.
"Abdul Hamid Retaliating." *New York Times* (August 31, 1901): 6.
"Abdul Hamid Wants Revenge." *New York Times* (August 30, 1901): 7.
"Abdul Not to be Tried." *New York Times* (April 29, 1909): 1.
"Abdul Reported Dead." *New York Times* (April 28, 1909): 2.
"Abdul Shed Tears as He Lost Throne." *New York Times* (May 2, 1909): C2.
"Abdul's Imprisoned Brother." *New York Times* (April 9, 1901): 1.
"Abd-ul-Hamid." *New York Times* (October 25, 1885): 11.
"Admiral Caillard Has Seized Turkish Ports." *London Times* (November 6, 1901): 9.
"American Marines May Invade Morocco." *New York Times* (May 29, 1904): 1.
"Appeals of Abdul Hamid." *New York Times* (November 20, 1895): 1.
"Armenian Wealth Caused Massacres." *New York Times* (April 25, 1909).
"Blackmail by the Police: Protecting Chinese Gambling Houses in Philadelphia." *New York Times* (May 17, 1889): 1.
"Capture of Europeans Ordered by Rais Uli." *London Times* (January 9, 1907): 5.
"Capture of Sir Harry Maclean by Rais Uli." *New York Times* (July 14, 1907): SM5.
"Chinese Punishment Methods." *New York Times* (November 28, 1894): 5.
"Doe Body Displayed." *The Guardian* (April 22, 1992).
"Dry-Rot of States." *Liberty* 10 (20) (1895): 6.
"El Roghi Still in Cage." *New York Times* (August 29, 1909): C3.
"Filipino Bandits' Methods." *New York Times* (January 14, 1901): 1.
"Four Monarchs in Prison: They Are Confined in Magnificent Palaces: Mystery That Prevails in Regard to Them: Otto, Carlotto, Ismail, and Murad." *New York Times* (Feb. 23, 1890): 19.
"Hadji Ali and His Bandits." *New York Times* (April 27, 1883): 2.
"Hoping Rivals Will be a Bigger Threat than Government." *The Financial Times* (April 1, 2003): 3.
"How China Is Governed." *New York Times* (January 26, 1892): 2.

"Infatuation of Abdul Hamid." *London Times* (Sept. 5, 1901): 1
"Inside Saddam's Court." *New York Times* (October 1, 2000): SM41.
"Journaux de Constantinople." *Revue du Monde Musulman* 5 (8) (August 1908): 758–761.
"Liberia's Killing Goes On." *The Economist* (September 15, 1990): 56.
"Maclean Is Safe, Declares Rais Uli." *New York Times* (August 6, 1907): 5.
"Memorandum from Bulgaria to Powers: Government Tells of Turkish Atrocities in Macedonia." *New York Times* (August 17, 1903): 1.
"Monrovia Films a Video Nasty." *Sunday Times* (April 26, 1992).
"Moroccan Brigands Torture Journalist." *London Times* (July 14, 1903): 7.
"Now What for Saddam?" *The Guardian* (December 16, 2003): 2.
"People Talked About." *Peterson Magazine* 6 (January 1986): 45–49.
"Perdicaris's Story of Wild Trip with Bandit." *New York Times* (June 13, 1904): 2.
"Persia's and Turkey's Regicides: Comparison of the Situation by the Young Turkish Party's Organ." *New York Times* (June 7, 1896): 24.
"Rais Uli Captures Sir Harry Maclean." *New York Times* (July 4, 1907): 4.
"Rais Uli, the Bandit, Reported Poisoned." *New York Times* (February 13, 1908): 4.
"Responsibility for Political Corruption." *Century Illustrated Magazine* 44 (3) (July 1892): 473.
"Saddam Blasts Bush." *The Frontrunner* (July 1, 2004).
"Safe Only When Isolated: What Railroads and Telegraphs Would do in China." *New York Times* (March 24, 1892): 9.
"Samuel Doe." *The Times* (September 13, 1990).
"Secret of Crispi Favor." *New York Times* (Sept. 21, 1898): 2.
"Seraphic Soul of Abdul Hamid." *Current Literature* 42 (January 1907): 36–40.
"Sultan Abdul Hamid on his Good Behavior." *London Times* (September 18, 1901).
"Sultan Angry." *London Daily Telegraph* (September 19, 1887): 4.
"Sultan Apprehensive." *London Times* (December 17, 1901): 1.
"Sultan Asks Tribes to Capture Raisuli." *New York Times* (June 3, 1904): 1.
"Sultan Murad's Letter." *New York Times* (September 22, 1895): 9.

"Sultan Tortures Rebels: Hands and Feet of Moroccans Cut Off—Women's Teeth Drawn." *New York Times* (August 25, 1909): 4.

"Sultan, in a Panic, Gives Constitution." *New York Times* (July 25, 1908): 1.

"Sultan's Letter." *New York Times* (November 21, 1895): 4.

"Sultan's Spy Spent a Week of Terror Here." *New York Times* (September 4, 1908): 8.

"To Print the Sultan's Records." *New York Times* (June 5, 1912): 3.

"Torture by Proxy." *New York Times* (March 8, 2005): A22.

"'Torture Chamber' in Havana." *New York Times* (January 5, 1889): 7.

"Torture Chamber of the Sultan." *New York Times* (March 28, 1909): SM7.

"Torture in Chinese Trial: Peking Officials Use Forbidden Methods." *New York Times* (May 11, 1908): 4.

"Towards a Grammar of Graft." *The Economist* 183 (June 15, 1957): 958–959.

"Turkey's Terror Record." *New York Times* (February 7, 1896): 5.

"Two Robbers Torture Deaf-Mute in Flat: Bind and Gag Helpless Man and Then Give Him the 'Water Cure' Because He Didn't Speak." *New York Times* (May 4, 1907): 2.

"Water Cure Described: Discharged Soldier Tells Senate Committee How and Why the Torture Was Inflicted." *New York Times* (May 4, 1902): 13.

Index

Abacha, Sani, 27–29, 36
ABC News, 69–71, 77, 99
Abdülhamid II, xxiii, 40, 43–67, 69, 72–76, 78–84, 86, 88–91, 95–98, 101–104, 128, 156
Abu Ghraib, xxiv, 110, 129, 151. *See also* prisons
Africa, x, xiv–xvii, 15, 18, 26–27, 29–31, 37, 39, 114, 124, 135–136, 139. *See also* Liberia; Nigeria; Somalia
Agamben, Giorgio, x, xviii–xix, 6, 8–9, 40–42, 62, 82, 107
animals, vii, 33, 63, 66, 72–73, 143
appetite, 14, 25, 33, 36, 42, 72–73. *See also* cannibalism; drinking; eating

banditry, 4, 14, 83, 66–67, 82, 109, 113–117, 119–126, 142, 148, 153, 157
Bataille, Georges, xx, xxii, 105, 107–108, 112, 132, 134
biopolitics, xi, xviii–xx, xxiii, 6, 8–9, 40–42, 50, 62, 69, 71, 74, 84, 87, 97, 99–100, 102–103, 106–109
Blitzer, Wolf, 49, 86–87, 90
blood, xxiv, 9, 14, 30, 38, 57, 63–68, 70–76, 79, 104, 108–110, 112, 121–122, 124, 127, 132, 135–139, 141, 145, 147–148, 157

body language, xxi–xxiii, 43, 45–46, 55–56, 87, 89–93, 98, 156
body politic, 4–9, 32, 40, 42, 63, 105, 109
Boxer Rebellion, 13
boxer shorts, 102
bribery, ix, xxiv, 14–17, 19, 22, 108–109, 111, 113, 118, 122, 131–140, 142, 157
Broadmoor Hospital, 149. *See also* prisons
building mania, 47, 59–60, 83
bureaucracy, ix–x, xvi, xxiii–xxiv, 1–2, 19, 26, 29, 31, 33, 43, 46, 50, 54–55, 64, 106, 108–110, 112–114, 116–117, 119, 121–124, 132–133, 135–138, 141, 147–149, 153, 156–157
burglary, 119–120
burial, 133–134, 138–139, 145; and cemeteries, 138; and funeral meat, 138–139
burlesque, 20, 35, 156. *See also* stripping

cadavers, 3, 136–137, 140. *See also* corpses
camps, xviii, 40–41, 86, 107–108, 113, 125–126, 148. *See also* Muselmann

209

cancer, 74–75. *See also* disease; infection
cannibalism, 25, 33–34, 64–66, 72–73, 156. *See also* eating; appetite
Castro, Cipriano, 119–124, 135
celebrity, viii, xxiii, 3, 22, 37, 39–41, 43–47, 49–51, 53, 55, 57, 59, 61–63, 80, 82, 86–87, 89, 93, 95–96, 99, 102–104, 115, 122, 156–157
children, 2, 8–16, 18, 26–27, 35, 38, 42, 53, 55–62, 66–68, 81, 85, 87, 93–94, 98, 56. *See also* infants
China, 12–14, 26, 29–31, 44, 131, 137–139, 141–148, 150–151
Chinatown, 110, 117–119, 122, 124, 127, 131
Chirac, Jacques, xiv
citizenship, xxiii–xxiv, 1–2, 4–5, 8, 12–13, 15–20, 26–27, 29–31, 65–66, 72–74, 77, 80, 95, 102, 110, 112–113, 115, 117, 122–125, 129, 131–132, 134, 136–141, 144–145, 149, 152, 155–157
claustrophobia, 102, 114, 119, 122, 125
clean hands campaign, 22
cleanliness, xii, xv–xvii, 7, 18, 22–24, 49–50, 95, 102, 132. *See also* hygiene
clothing, 20, 42–44, 46–48, 52, 55, 56, 65, 80, 87–88, 90–91, 102, 104, 112, 121, 156–157
CNN, 86–87, 89, 91–93, 99, 102
colonialism, ix, x–xv, xvii–xix, xxii, xxiv–xxv, 3, 11–13, 26–27, 56, 58, 61–62, 66, 109, 113–114, 117, 124–127, 132, 135, 141, 151, 156; and postcolony, x–xv, xxiv–xxv, 107–108. *See also* Mbembe, Achille
confession, xxiii, 4–6, 10, 20–25, 35, 40–42, 47, 51, 55, 77–78, 86–91, 94, 96–100, 102–104, 110, 127, 141, 143–152, 156
consent, 5
constitutions, xxiv, 6–7, 43, 110, 120–121, 151–153
containers, 114, 119, 130; and boxes 45–46
corpses, 4–5, 72–73, 77–78, 97, 99, 103, 132–139, 145–146, 153. *See also* cadavers; necrophilia
courts: and law, 89, 91–93, 96, 121, 137–138, 144 (*see also* judges; trials); and monarchs, 72, 80. *See also* jesters
cousins, 67–68, 70
Corruption Perception Index (CPI), xv–xvii
Craxi, Bettino, 22–23
Cusani, Sergio, 22–23

democracy, ix–x, xiii–xv, xviii, 2, 10, 17, 33–36, 63, 70–74, 107, 112, 156
dentists, 50–51
development, ix, 3, 5, 9–10, 12, 15, 17–18, 20, 24, 32, 35, 42, 55, 156; and states, 5, 9–10, 12, 15, 20, 24, 35, 42, 55
disease, xi–xii, 2–6, 18, 25–26, 31–32, 34, 50, 63–64, 66, 69, 7, 78, 85, 103. *See also* infection
dismemberment, 146
dissection, 4, 41, 46, 90, 104
DNA, 86–87
doctors, 4–5, 35, 50–52, 77, 86, 118, 148–149
Doe, Samuel, xxiii, 37–40, 44–97, 103–104, 155
domestic space, x–xi, 3, 10, 17, 58, 101, 127–129
doubles, xxiii, 12, 62, 68–69, 74–76, 78, 82, 88, 97–98, 100, 121, 157
drinking, 45. *See also* appetite; eating

ears, 39, 50–52, 59, 77
eating, 34, 73, 112. *See also* appetite; cannibalism; drinking
Elf Scandals, xiv
England, xiii, 6, 39, 80, 130, 135, 149
exception (state of), x, xvii–xx, xxii–xxv, 6, 8–9, 12, 16, 40–42, 67, 69, 71, 73, 78, 81, 83, 85, 93, 95, 97, 99, 103, 105–106, 118–110, 114, 124, 129, 151
exhibitionism, 23–25, 35–36, 40, 156
exposure, xi–xii, xiv, 5, 10–11, 16, 20–25, 35, 63–65, 67, 74, 79–80, 83, 86–87, 90–91, 93, 100–104, 118, 134, 142–143, 156–157
extortion, ix, 118, 121–122, 133–135, 143–148, 150–152
eyes, 3, 17, 47, 50, 56, 63, 72–73, 89, 95, 153

facial hair: as beards, 46, 86, 92–94, 97; as moustaches, 47
family, xxiii, 1–3, 5–7, 15–17, 22, 25–26, 28, 36, 57, 67–69, 73, 89, 104, 139
fantasy, vii–viii, 7–8, 10, 15, 42, 52–55, 66, 87, 95–96, 106, 157
fathers, 12–13, 15, 26–27, 29, 64, 66–70, 77, 85, 111, 138
fear, xxiii, 1–3, 5–7, 15–17, 22, 25–26, 28, 36, 57, 67–69, 73, 89, 104, 139
fingers, 34, 49, 51, 59, 90, 94, 145
Foucault, Michel, xi, 9–12, 143
France, xiii–xv, 2–3, 7, 35

Gibson, Charles, 50, 69
Guardian (the newspaper), 37–39, 96, 149–150, 153

habeas corpus, xxiii, 74, 97–100
Hadji Ali, 123
hands, vii, 12, 22, 38–39, 49, 89–90, 141, 143, 153. *See also* clean hands campaign; fingers

Hannibal Lecter, 94–95
health, xiii, 3–4, 7, 17–18, 20, 24, 35, 48, 50, 55, 85, 91, 94, 100, 137
homo sacer, 8, 40, 42. *See also* Agamben, Giorgio
human rights, viii, xv, 40, 96, 129, 155
hygiene, 7, 18, 48, 50. *See also* cleanliness

immigrant smuggling, 114, 118–119, 130
immobility, xxii, 3, 5, 97, 143
impotence, ix, 31–33, 36, 69
incest, ix, 2, 8–9, 15–16, 19–20, 25–27, 30–31, 34, 36, 63–64, 66–67, 69, 71–72, 78, 80, 85, 100, 109–111, 117, 132, 138–139, 156
infants, xxiii, 9, 12–15, 17–18, 20, 36, 53, 57, 59–60, 62, 66, 88, 91, 94, 96, 102, 156; and sexuality, 2–3, 5, 9–11, 16, 19, 35–36, 55, 57. *See also* children
infection, xii, xv–xvi, 31–32, 50, 118, 127, 131, 150. *See also* disease
insanity, 43, 50, 63, 69, 71, 78–85, 135–136, 149–150
internet, vii–viii, 15, 37; and websites, vii–ix, xxi–xxii, 20, 37
interrogation, 4, 21–25, 35, 104, 127, 131, 148–152. *See also* torture
Iraq, xiv–xvi, xxiii–xxiv, 44, 47, 51, 54, 60–61, 66–72, 76, 82–86, 89–94, 96, 99–100, 110, 129, 151–152, 157
Italy, xiv, xvi, xxv, 20, 22–23, 132, 135–139

jester, 75
jet (torture), 114, 125, 131
Johnson, Prince, 37–39, 97, 99
judges, 23, 89, 92–94, 137–138, 140, 143–144. *See also* courts; trials

Kantorowicz, Ernst, 6–9, 42
Keeler, Christine, xiv
kidnapping, 115–116, 121
Kurds, 64, 96, 123–124

Liberia, xxiii, 37–39
Lolita, 10–12

Maclean, Harry, 115–117
madness. *See* insanity
Marie Antoinette, 2, 35
markets, viii, xxiii, 17, 20, 153
marriage, 3, 7, 54, 66, 67–69, 108, 110, 112–113, 133–135
masturbation, 2–4, 10, 36
Mbembe, Achille, x, xviii–xix, 107
melodrama, xxi, 17, 86, 89, 111
miscegenation, 26, 63–64, 66, 71, 78, 109, 132, 136, 139–140, 145, 147, 153
monsters, x, xxiii, 6, 8–9, 25–28, 32–34, 42, 63–65, 67, 69, 71–78, 81–83, 85–88, 97, 99–100, 102–103, 132, 139–140, 143, 153, 156
Morocco, 114–117, 119, 122, 124, 131, 141–146
mothers, 2, 27, 64, 66–68
multazim, 40
Murad V, 43, 78–80
Muselmann, 41, 86, 98
mutants, 66, 69, 72, 85–87

nature, 7, 9, 16, 31, 42, 49, 56, 59, 66–67, 73; and the unnatural, x, xii, 16, 25, 56, 67, 69, 73, 85, 143
necrophilia, 73. *See also* corpses
nepotism, xii, xxiv, 30, 108–109, 111, 113, 122, 131–133, 137–140, 142, 153, 157
New York Times, 44–45, 65, 72, 79, 88, 97, 101, 115, 118, 123, 125–126, 135, 137
Nigeria, xvi, 27, 29–30, 36

oil, xiv–xvi, xxiii
Ottoman Empire, 43, 61, 88, 122–124, 128, 137, 139, 145–147

pain, viii, 14–15, 19, 138, 141–143, 147–148
parents, 56, 58, 61–64, 66
Pasolini, Pier, 56, 58, 61–64, 66. *See also* Salo
peasants, 60, 62, 64, 67, 133–135, 140
Philippines, 29, 125–127, 129, 147
physiognomy, 46, 48–49, 55, 103
police, ix, xiv, 98, 115, 117–118, 133–135, 147
pornography, vii–xi, xvii–xxiii, 1–2, 5–6, 16, 20, 23–25, 35, 37, 39–42, 45–46, 48, 52, 54–55, 62, 71, 73, 82, 85–87, 89–91, 99, 103–104, 105, 111, 155–157
Post, Jerrold, 83–85, 91–93
prisons, xiv, xxiv, 22, 44, 59, 78–79, 81–82, 96, 110, 113, 119–122, 124, 126, 129–131, 137, 141, 143–146, 148, 150–151, 155, 157
private, x–xi, 5, 9–12, 22, 36, 43, 78, 101, 104, 111–113, 128–129, 134–135, 141, 149, 153
Profumo Affair, xiii–xiv
prostitution, viii, 16, 67, 110–112
public, x–xi, xiii–xvi, xxiii, 10–12, 17, 20, 22–23, 25, 30, 32, 36, 39, 51, 53, 68–69, 71, 73–80, 82–83, 85–91, 93–97, 100–102, 104, 111–116, 119, 125–129, 137–138, 142–143, 149, 152–153, 156
Puerto Rico, 121–122, 124

Qusay Hussein, 67–72, 76

race, xi–xiii, xvii, 11, 36, 64, 66, 109, 116, 118, 135–136, 137, 139–140, 141, 145–147, 150

Index

Rainbow Warrior, xiii
Rais Uli, 114–117, 120, 123, 132, 142, 145–146
rape, vii, 52, 70, 72, 87, 140, 147
real girl, xxi, xxiii, 41–42, 52, 54, 71, 73, 82, 85–87, 93–95, 155
Robinson, Mary, 16–17, 19
Rousseau, Jean Jacques, 3–4, 7
rule of law, xiii, xviii, 17, 23, 28, 42, 79, 103–104, 105–109, 129, 155
Russia, 132–138

Saddam Hussein, xxiii, 40, 43–57, 60–63, 65–70, 72–74, 76–78, 82–96, 98–104, 142, 155–157
Sade, Marquis de, 105–108, 110
sadism, 68, 84, 89, 106–107, 111–112, 146, 152
Safire, William, 152–153
Salisbury (Lord), 45, 58, 60
Salo, xxiii, 108, 110, 113, 152, 157. See also Pasolini, Pier
scandal, x, xiii–xvii, 2, 136
Schmitt, Carl, 6, 8–9, 126
secrets, xii, xiv, xvi, xx, 4–5, 10, 20, 24–25, 34, 36, 46–50, 55, 63, 65, 72, 77, 79, 83, 89, 98, 102, 104, 125–126, 131, 142
security, 16–18, 43, 83, 128, 149
sedition, 146
self-control, 21–22, 24, 106–107, 110, 122
self-hatred, 26–27, 31
self-regarding behavior, 20, 36
slavery, vii, 16, 33
snuff films, xxiii, 35, 37, 43, 45, 86, 155
soft states, 32
soldiers, xiv, 102, 126–127, 130, 145, 157
Somalia, xiv, 27–30, 36
sovereignty, xviii, xxv, 6–9, 42, 59, 63–64, 69, 75, 78–79, 114, 116, 123, 156

Spain, 115–117, 128–129, 132
spectacle, viii, x, xv, xxiii, 2–3, 5, 12, 17, 19–22, 24–25, 35, 58, 61, 68, 71–72, 77, 82, 86, 97–98, 101, 103, 117, 119, 142, 156
Stalin, Joseph, 47
sterility, 31–33, 69, 135–136, 139
Stoler, Ann, xi, 11
stripping, vii, xx, 5, 20–25, 27, 34–35, 47, 50, 55, 90–91, 104, 152, 155–156. See also burlesque; confession

taxation, 45, 105, 112, 119–124, 135, 140, 145
tears, 44–45, 88–89
tentacles, 33
testimony, xx, xxii–xxiii, 39–42, 83, 86, 94, 105, 143. See also witnessing
therapy, 24–25, 81
Tissot, Samuel–Auguste, 3–5, 7
torture, vii, ix, xiv–xv, xxiii–xxiv, 37–39, 44, 70–71, 97, 105, 109–110, 113–114, 124–131, 137–138, 141–152, 157; and torture nation, xxiv, 109, 124–131, 148–149
totalitarianism, xxiii–xxiv, 47, 88, 95, 98, 103–105, 113, 130, 132, 135, 137, 147, 150, 152–153, 157
tourism, 142–143
Transparency International, ix, xv–xvii, xxii, 6, 20, 32
trials, 2, 22–23, 35, 89, 96, 99, 137–138, 144, 149. See also courts; judges
tribes, 103, 115–117, 120, 126, 145

Uday Hussein, 67–72, 76–77, 98
uncles, 60, 68–69

United States, xiii–xiv, xvi–xvii, 10, 12–13, 15, 25–26, 35, 44, 86, 90, 99, 115, 117, 119, 124–127, 129–130, 135

Venezuela, 119–121, 124, 135–137
victims, xxiii, 10–19, 22, 25, 31, 35, 39, 56–57, 61, 69, 77, 110–112, 119, 125–126, 130, 143, 145, 148–150, 152, 155–156
violence, viii, x–xvi, xviii–xix, xxi, 4, 13, 27–31, 33, 35–37, 39–42, 47, 52–54, 56, 58, 64–67, 69–72, 76–79, 81, 85, 88, 90, 97, 104–108, 110, 114–117, 119, 123–128, 131, 141, 145, 155, 157

water cure, 126–129
Watergate, xiii
Williams, Linda, xxi–xxiii, 41, 45, 55, 89, 111
witnessing, 12, 40–41, 44, 49, 99, 127, 137, 144, 146, 148. *See also* testimony

Zahn, Paula, 92–96